NORTHRIDGE HIGH
FOOTBALL CAMP

NORTHRIDGE HIGH
FOOTBALL CAMP

a novel by

S. JOSEPH KROL

THE GAY MEN'S PRESS
LONDON

First published 1996 by GMP Publishers Ltd,
P O Box 247, London N6 4BW, England
World copyright © 1996 S. Joseph Krol

British Library Cataloguing in Publication Data
Krol, S. Joseph
  Northridge High Football Camp
  1.English fiction - 20th century
  I. Title
  823.9'14 [F]

ISBN 0 85449 225 9

Distributed in North America by
Inbook, Login Publishers Consortium,
1436 West Randolph Street, Chicago, IL 60607

Distributed in Australia by Bulldog Books,
P O Box 155, Broadway, NSW 2007

Printed and bound in the EU by Nørhaven A/S, Viborg, Denmark

With special thanks to:

Matthew Estes, for his sharp eyes, patient ear,
and loving friendship;
David Fernbach, for understanding my characters so well;
Dr Leigh Smith, for showing me the path to sanity;
Diane Reagan, for encouraging a seventh-grader to keep writing;
and of course,
Anna Noyes, for making so many things possible.

This book is dedicated to:
C. T.

with gratitude for
friendship, tech support
and guy talk

1

Vinnie dropped his helmet loudly onto the floor and slammed his locker shut. He paused and closed his eyes tightly, trying to force the throb in his head away. Goddamn headaches, he always got these goddamn headaches before a practice. It was anticipation of the brutal attack he would take on the field—the fun and games of being a tackle.

He didn't mind the beating, in fact he thrived on it, but it usually took a few minutes to adjust to the hits and pounding before he could bring up enough anger and power in himself to blindly go full force into the game. Then and only then, with all his muscle and size, could he lose his thoughts and let pure physical force run him. No headaches then. In fact, a sneer of passion would cross his lips as he plowed into the defensive tackles, bodies falling under his immense weight.

Vinnie took in his surroundings in the locker room as he slowly re-opened his eyes. Northridge High looked like every other athletic facility he had known. In all his other schools, including those that he had visited to play games against, the locker rooms all seemed pretty run-of-the-mill. He had no reason to believe that Northridge would be any different.

Rows of steel grey lockers lined the cool, dank locker room. Even now, in early August as the try-outs were first underway, the same old feeling existed here in the football locker area. Actually, Vinnie had been a bit surprised when he first visited Northridge and discovered that the football team had their own locker room. *Pretty fuckin' impressive*, he had thought to himself. Northridge was proud of its team, and the townsfolk had decided that their football squad was going to have the best they could offer. In all Vinnie's other high schools, the squad was never valued enough to be given their own locker room. Good. Don't have to share with any of the other faggot sports teams. This wouldn't be a hangout for the loser soccer fags or softball fairies. No, this would be exclusive. Football only! The biggest and the best.

The early morning silence brought good feelings back to Vinnie. The summer wasn't even over, but it had been too long already. Each summer for the past three years, Vinnie lived for the try-outs, the football camp, and the start of the season. School sucked, but football was everything. And Vinnie was football. All he could think about from sunrise to sundown was football. He practiced it, he read about it, he watched it... and he dreamed about it. Now here he was in his senior year, at a new school, and with the potential for showing this town what he was made of—Vinnie was pleased.

He picked up his helmet and walked on over to the sink area. He ran cold water into the sink, reached down with one hand and cupped a palm full of water. Looking up at his reflection in the mirror, he forcefully doused his face and plastered the short black hair down his forehead with the pressing of his hand. He squinted his eyes to form the cold, forced stare he often gave his opponent on the field. He watched his changing expression for a moment; the calculated change into the feared football entity—the large, cruel hulk that took all opponents as victims with his intimidation. After staring at this image for a few seconds, Vinnie cracked a smile, then a laugh. At seventeen, he had the world by the balls.

Here he was, the first morning of the try-outs, and he was here only as a formality. Vinnie had been approached within a couple of days of his arrival in Northridge. The school principal, head football coach and this year's team captains all came in a gesture of welcome to Vinnie's house. They had heard of his outstanding reputation in previous schools, and pretty much told him and his parents that they wanted him; playing unseen.

Vinnie stood six foot two and weighed a solid and bulking 230 pounds. His jet black hair was cut short, cropped Marine-style, his flashy white grin alternating in an unconscious sneer. His eyes tightened into a piercing glare whenever mention was made of anything he slightly disagreed with. Yes, they were offering him guaranteed starts every game. They had heard all about him, and now they offered this without even seeing him actually play. All they needed to see was this massive Italian hitting machine in person, to know that what they had all heard was true: he was the best. He even could intimidate the school officials, when he got that sneer on his puss. Yes, sir... he had the world by the balls!

Vinnie looked down from the mirror and ambled away from the sink area. His walk was somewhat constrained by the padding under his football pants and the large set of shoulder pads resting atop his torso. He liked this walk though. He sometimes thought of the frequent comments about how he "kind of walked like he had a load in his pants". He chuckled. Yeah, a load. He turned and approached the urinals. His last ritual before he pulled on his practice mesh over his pads and headed onto the field wais always to take his pre-game piss. He learned his lesson well several seasons before. No pre-game piss and he could be guaranteed to suffer. He needed to take a leak on a fairly regular basis, and the playing field was not a pleasant place to be stuck needing to drain his water.

It was right in the middle of the Armand-Topsfield game that Vinnie first realized the importance of draining yourself out before hitting the field. He had to piss in the worst way, but the game was in play and there was no way he was going anywhere to relieve himself. It was right in the center of the Armand huddle that he got so desperate he pulled out his hog and let it go. Fortunately, he was blocked from view of the stands by the rest of the Armand squad, but he never lived down his whipping out his dong in the huddle. It only took one of Vinnie's intimidating stares to silence any joking team member about the incident, and secretly he was always amused by their playful reminders during his remaining season with the school. But this did teach him the invaluable lesson of hitting the urinals before hitting the field.

Now he paused a moment, untying the string of his football pants and sliding down his ratty jock. He worked the cotton material down over the plastic protection cup. The cup, a football player's best friend, but a pain-in-the-ass when you had to take a leak. He leaned an arm forward onto the wall in front of him, as he let the stream flow. His other hand playfully bounced against the length of the shaft as the piss subsided. He shook his meat dry and pulled his jock back up tightly around his nuts, letting his hog rest against the right side of the plastic cup. *Yep, firmly held in place,* he thought to himself—a nice warm and safe place to house his hog while he plowed the opponents to the ground; crushing bodies beneath him while his equipment was safe and tucked away from harm.

He noticed a few slight drops of urine had escaped onto the front of his jock, as he re-laced the front of the football pants. "No wonder I always have fuckin' piss-stained underwear and jockstraps, fuckin' moron," he said aloud to himself. "The least you could do is empty your goddamn fuckin' hog all the way before you stuff it." He picked up his helmet that had rolled onto its side on the tiled floor while he was in the sink area and returned to the bench in front of his locker. He set the helmet squarely down on the bench and pulled out his mesh top from the top shelf of the locker. Reaching above his head, Vinnie tugged and pulled as he slid the maroon practice jersey down over his shoulder pads. As usual, the mesh was too small. High-school football clothing was not meant for someone already his size. He was too tall and too wide.

The mesh was imprinted with the grey and yellow lettering that was the Northridge colors, but the maroon material that made up the bulk of the shirt was tattered and discolored. The fact that the shirt was ripped in some places at least allowed him to secure it over the shoulder pads, but the length fell a bit short. An inch or so of his stomach hair protruded out between the bottom of the shirt and where his pants were tied. He tightened his stomach muscles and watched the curly hair shift. He smiled to himself again. "Back in the uniform again, Vin ol' pal, back to the field to kick some ass again!" he half-shouted to himself as he slammed the locker door closed.

Vinnie bent down, energetically picked up his helmet and dangled it off one index finger. He walked with a bounce in his step, swinging the helmet in his hand, as he exited the door to the practice field.

*   *   *

"73, you're up for taping!" yelled a voice from across the field. Vinnie looked up from the ground. His right leg was stretched back under his butt, his right arm outreached toward the toes of his left leg. He squinted in the bright sunlight toward the sideline, and focused on the bottom bleacher where the assistant coach and trainer sat amongst piles of pads, unravelled tape, and excess football gear.

"73! Manta... today!" Vinnie jumped to his feet and hustled across the field area between them. His long, quick strides got him there in a flash, an intentional display of his speed. Vinnie approached the two men, swinging his helmet from his outstretched finger.

"Vinnie Manta, this is Billy Ruggiero, our strength trainer. Vinnie here just joined Northridge and has quite the reputation for kicking ass. Ain't that so, Vinnie?" said the assistant coach.

"Yeah, sure, coach, whatever you say." Vinnie's grin began to exhibit the start of a slight sneer. He never liked praise of this type. It always seemed kind of phony or sarcastic.

"Manta. Good ol' Italian boy, eh?" joked Billy. He slapped Vinnie roughly on the shoulder. "We need a few more rugged men like you around here. Must be able to take a hit and keep on charging. Good solid mass. Good for crushing."

Tom Walter, the assistant coach, turned to the trainer. "You get Vin here taped up good, Bill. Strength in those hands... let's protect 'em, okay? They look like they're quite a mess. Last season kind of rough, eh, Manta?"

Vinnie shrugged.

"Right, Tom. No problem," replied the trainer.

Coach Walter turned and walked away in the direction of a group of players gathering at the gate to the field.

"So, Manta, what you think of Northridge here? Guess it's kind of hard to judge, it being summer and all. But, any first impressions?" asked Billy, as he began to gather the white athletic tape.

"I dunno, coach. I guess it's okay. Seems quiet and peaceful. I guess time will tell," responded Vinnie. Small talk. He could never stomach small talk. He just wanted to finish getting taped and get back on the field.

"Yeah, it can be quiet at times. Not in the season though. Those Northridge townies come out in droves to support their team. The Northridge Warriors are their pride and joy. We're one of the top ranked teams in New Jersey. And we aim to keep it that way, too. By the way, drop the 'coach' shit. Reserve it for Morrison, the head coach and Tom there, the assistant. I'm just plain ol' Billy. Not 'Bill' either, Tom's the only one insisting on callin' me that. I'm born and raised in Northridge. I'm a townie myself. Just plain ol' Billy."

"Okay, whatever." Vinnie held out his right hand and allowed the trainer to begin the taping process.

"So, where you from before here?"

"Well, kinda around a few places. We kinda moved around a bit these last years. Played last season at Armand. That's Armand, Pennsylvania. Season before that was in Allentown."

Billy's eyes looked up from the tape wrapping. "Steel towns, eh? Good solid life out that way. Passed through those areas a few times. Nice folk. Steel work is a hard life, builds character."

"Yeah, my father's now working at that steel mill in Trenton. Who woulda thought... New Jersey. This may be a fine suburban town, Billy, but I'm pretty used to the harder life in Armand and Allentown. We kicked ass all around those towns. The aggression went further than just the playin' field, we busted all over town. Me and my pals. Somehow the quiet nights and cricket chirping just ain't gonna cut it."

"Well, give us a chance, Manta. We're a town pretty much of proud Italian families. Along with that comes rivalry and more than our share of brawls. Best for you if you keep your nose clean, though. You're new; you'll be watched and judged. Don't sweat it though, you'll do just fine. A guy your size just has to be there. Nobody in their right mind would mess with you."

Billy finished Vinnie's right hand and pulled his left arm into position for the taping. Vinnie's attention was diverted as he heard increased noise coming from the field gate area. He looked over and watched a small group of players walking in, their attention directed onto one player whom they encircled as he entered. Through the group of the uniformed players, Vinnie was able to see one spike-haired player who noticeably stood out. He walked with assurance and gleamed a constant white-toothed smile. He exhibited the air of "I'm a hot shit", but diverted his attention evenly to all those that surrounded him. He reminded Vinnie of the pied piper leading his flock.

Billy looked up and turned his attention in the direction of Vinnie's gaze. "That's Vuch," mumbled the trainer as he returned to Vinnie's half-completed hand.

"Huh?"

"Vuch. Tony Carvuccio. The QB. The star. We call him Vuch for short. Damn good quarterback. This is his fourth season. Great ability to call plays based on his quick judgement of what the other team has up their sleeves. We joke he's psychic, or ballin' someone with access to playbooks."

Vinnie continued to watch as the parade of players moved over to the sideline area where Tom Walter stood with the others in the squad.

Tony Carvuccio patted the assistant coach on the back and shook his hand. He looked around the squad, his toothy smile steadily directed at each player he acknowledged. His gaze then extended across the field area, taking in the bleacher that Vinnie and Billy occupied. Billy was busy gathering up additional tape for the remaining players that had just entered. Vinnie's eyes locked for an moment on Tony Carvuccio's. In an instant, the gleaming grin was gone from Vuch's face. *Interesting*, thought Vinnie to himself... *interesting*.

The try-outs proved uneventful and offered no surprises. Both Vinnie and Vuch basically watched from opposite ends of the field, their opinions being desired by the coach and trainer. It was the second half of the day, after lunch, that the head coach finally came to the field. He spoke briefly only to the assistant coach and trainer. Vinnie was called in for a few sprints and plays—nothing much, just an easy display of blocking and tackling technique. As he exited the field, he was able to see nods of acceptance between the trainer and coaches. He'd proven himself, he had no doubt, but he also wondered what impression he'd made on Carvuccio. Not that it mattered, but for some reason he wanted acceptance. He switched his gaze from the coaches to the area where Tony sat on the ground, his back firmly against the wire fence. He still had a few players gathered around and they continued to speak to him, oblivious to the plays just completed by Vinnie.

Vuch's eyes stared straight ahead at Vinnie. He had a long piece of grass working around in his mouth, one knee was pulled up toward his chest, with an arm braced across the raised leg. His eyes continued to follow Vinnie off the field, his face devoid of any expression. Throughout the entire day they had sat on opposite ends of the bleachers. No words had been exchanged between them, but their eyes had locked more than once as they assessed the first-year hopefuls. *Yeah, this town has a rivalry alright*, Vinnie thought to himself, *there's one brewing right here on this field*.

* * *

Within a minute of the head coach calling the try-outs officially over for the first day, the players began to group to discuss their own individual assessments of the new guys. Tony Carvuccio again had his flock gathering. Vinnie simply picked up his helmet off the grass and headed back toward the football locker room. Vuch turned his head for a moment and watched the hulking tackle walk off the field, noticing the way he playfully swung his helmet off his finger-tip.

"Fuckin' A!" yelled Vinnie as he violently pushed open the locker-room entrance. The door flew open, crashed hard against the wall and came flying back toward him. He casually held out his arm in anticipation, and caught the door's rebound. "Another season begins!" he yelled.

Vinnie strode into the locker room, pausing a moment for his eyes to adjust to the contrast from being in the bright sunlight all day. He glanced at his watch: four-thirty. He continued on over to the bench in front of his locker and sat down hard. The tape around his hands showed streaks of dirt and sweat, many of the strips of tape beginning to unravel. He dropped his helmet to the ground and placed one leg up on the bench. Leaning forward, he balanced his right arm on the outstretched thigh and began to peel the tape off his hand. Sweat beads dripped from his forehead and further complicated his removal of the athletic tape. He swat at his forehead, attempting to repel the sweat, only making the situation worse by streaking dirt across his face.

"Fuck it!" He quickly stood up and walked toward the sink area, pulling his mesh jersey over his head as he rounded the bank of lockers. He dropped the completely wet shirt on the nearest bench and approached the first sink. Looking into the mirror above, Vinnie saw a familiar sight. His hair was completely matted down with perspiration, his face flushed with the after-effects of a workout. A few lines of dirt were visible above his eyes where he had swiped to clear the sweat. His shoulder pads rested on his grey half-tee, now showing dark stains encircling each of his armpits. Halfway down his torso, where the half-tee ended, dark hair was matted down over his stomach. He flexed his ab muscles again, and watched in the mirror as the hairs gave way to the contrast of muscle definition.

Vinnie smiled his partial sneer at the reflection in the glass. Unhooking the straps that held his shoulder pads in place, he reached his arms above his head and removed them. Tossing them over near the bench where he left his mesh, he quickly pulled off his half-tee and used it to wipe down his hair and face. Vinnie turned on the cold water faucet and peeled the remaining tape off his hands. He dropped the unravelled tape strips onto the tile floor and bent down and splashed water onto his face. Looking up, he again ran the palm of his hand down over his hair, plastering the short black hairs onto his forehead.

At that moment, Vinnie heard the loud yells and hollering as other members of the team hit the entrance door. He finished wiping his face and turned the water off. Returning to the area of his locker, he picked up his pads and mesh jersey, casually hanging the shirt around his neck as he walked over to the bench. "Fuckin' awesome drills, Manta!" said a medium-built hopeful. "Name's Randy. Randy Miller." He extended his hand out to Vinnie.

Vinnie attempted a slight smile and nodded as he shook the kid's hand. "You really know your stuff, huh?" the kid said awkwardly. "I mean it shows you've been playing a lot, huh? Playing the game a lot, I mean... huh?"

Vinnie smiled again. "Yeah, I guess. Fourth year." He turned back to his locker and slung the sweaty half-tee over the top of the open locker door.

"I hope I have a chance... I really do," continued Randy, "I'm a sophomore now and if I don't make the varsity squad this year I can pretty much kiss my chances goodbye. Everybody successful on the team plays sophomore through senior year... I've just gotta make it, man."

"Yeah, well whatever," replied Vinnie, his attention only half hearing what the kid was saying. "You gotta chance, you seemed pretty competent out there."

"Really? You think so? I really did?"

Jesus! You'd think I just gave the kid an award, Vinnie thought to himself. "Yeah, you did okay." He turned his attention back to finishing at the locker. He had cooled off some since coming in from the field, but he still felt confined and hot in the tight football pants and padding. He reached down and undid the ties of the pants. Placing one foot up on the bench, he removed one shoe without bothering to unlace it. He then stripped the wet sock off his leg. His foot showed dirt and sweat caked between his toes. He fingered some of the dirt out from the ridges between his toenails, then set the foot back down on the cold cement floor. He repeated the same process with the other shoe and sock, taking additional care to rub his foot across the top area. The foot was somewhat sore, the discomfort easing when he massaged his toes.

Straightening back up, Vinnie began to slide the pants down over his jock and cup. He seated himself now, his back to Randy and the other players using the lockers behind him. It took a few moments for Vinnie to work the soiled pants down over his thighs. All summer, he had been concentrating on squats to develop his leg muscles, and now that showed as he pulled hard on the damp material to get it to slide down to his ankles. He kicked off the pants and once again stood, half turning toward the bank of lockers behind him.

"You gonna shower?" asked Randy, now clad only in a towel and searching through his gym bag.

"Yeah. I gotta. I always sweat like a fuckin' pig. I didn't even run that many plays or drill that much, but it pours off me," Vinnie replied as he reached an arm into the locker feeling for his towel. "I'd like to just dive straight into a fuckin' cold swimmin' pool right now."

More noise filtered in from outside as the rest of the players stormed in, the same group still surrounding Tony Carvuccio as he led the way into the locker area. Vinnie turned and watched the actions of the quarterback. Carvuccio walked to one of the lockers in the bank occupied by Randy Miller, opened the locker door, and tossed in his helmet. Turning his attention to his hands, he began to peel off his athletic tape in an almost violent way. The crowd that had been following the quarterback had now dispersed around the locker room, busying themselves with their own clean-up.

"You ran some okay drills out there. You're fast and you're able to stop whatever comes at ya... and whatever keeps comin' at ya," muttered Carvuccio, still looking down while peeling the tape from his hand. Vinnie turned toward the back bank of lockers. He chuckled a bit, then draped the towel he had pulled from his locker over his shoulder. He reached with one finger, caught the elastic waistband of his jock and tugged. The jock and cup slid down his left thigh. Pulling harder, he bent over and was able to drop the jockstrap to the floor.

"No, seriously. You looked okay. We need a few big guys like you to mop the bodies off the field. You looked okay," Carvuccio repeated.

Vinnie turned and half-smiled. "Yeah, I looked okay." He chuckled again, turning back in the direction of the sinks, and walked away with just the towel over his shoulder. "Yeah, I looked okay."

Tony Carvuccio watched as Vinnie headed toward the sink and shower area, his dirt-stained butt swaggering as he walked. "Christ, try to give the prick a compliment!" Tony returned his attention to removing his practice uniform and storing his personal gear.

2

Football try-outs continued for two more days, although Coach Walter announced that the senior members of the squad did not have to attend the final selections. Vinnie decided he would use the time to his advantage and make use of the school weight room. He planned on taking a few breaks in his lifting sessions to hit the field and observe some of the new guys, as the final decisions were made. He liked to compare his own assessments to those of the coaching staff; often his insights were similar to the evaluations made.

He got up early and showered quickly, wanting to be at the school right at eight am when the weight room opened and the potential players would be arriving. He glanced at the calendar over his desk just before going down for breakfast. The try-outs would be over tomorrow and the middle of next week they would be leaving for the eleven-day training camp.

Vinnie sat down in his desk chair and pulled on his training shoes. He cushioned his feet with double sweat socks, as they were still a little sore from the beating they took the day before. He picked up the sweat pants he had worn home from the locker room, instinctively held them up to his nose and took a deep whiff. "Yeah, they'll last another day or so," he muttered to himself. He went into his small bathroom and hung them over the shower rod to finish drying out. The bathroom was still steamy from the shower a few minutes before, but he knew that in a few hours they would be totally dry and he would be able to wear them the next day. He took one last look in the mirror, his reflection partially obscured by the mist, and ran his hand one last time down his hair. Satisfied, he bounded down the stairs to the kitchen.

His mother turned from the stove with a frying pan in her hand, as Vinnie hit the last step and came into view. "Vin, take some time this morning and eat, honey. I hate when you just run out of here without having something decent." Vinnie took a few steps over to the refrigerator and opened the door. Bending down, he stuck his head into the middle, leaning on one arm on the door edge.

"Yeah, okay, Ma. I'll have whatever. I'm lifting this morning, so I need all the energy I can get." He pulled his head out and turned toward her, still resting on the open door. "You remember I'm leaving for camp on Wednesday, right?"

His mother placed the pan back on the burner. "Right, honey. Wednesday. How long are you going for?" Vinnie closed the door, walked over to the kitchen table and sat down at the place-setting his mother had set out. He pulled out the chair next to him and put one leg across the seat of the chair, being careful to keep his shoe extended out past the wooden seat. His mother always hated it when he would let his shoe rest directly on the seat of any of the chairs.

"We're goin' for eleven days, Ma." Vinnie picked up the glass filled with orange juice that was always waiting at his place. He downed half the juice in one gulp. "Northridge has a few extra days in their camp. It should be intense. We leave on Wednesday and I think we're back a week from Saturday." He finished the remaining juice in the next swig and put the glass back down. He again ran his hand down his hair — still a little damp.

"Okay. Do you need anything special washed? I'd like to get everything ready as soon as possible. Don't leave me with things to do the last minute, Vincent."

Oh great, he thought to himself, *"Vincent"*. She only calls him Vincent when she gets irritated. "No, Ma, I put everything I need down in the wash basket last night." He shifted in his chair, glancing at his watch. He felt a little impatient to get going, but knew this was not a time to cut out before eating.

"Are the try-outs over?" asked his mother as she placed a well-formed omelet on his plate. She returned to the sink and ran water into the hot pan. Steam rose from the sink as the cold water hit the scorching metal.

"Nope. Two more days. I don't have to go, though. Thought I'd head to the school and pump some iron. I'll try to catch some of the last decisions when I take breaks between body parts." He picked up his fork and cut a large chunk out of the omelet, shoving the piece into his mouth. Still chewing, he looked up. "Some of the guys look pretty good. We got one helluva QB here. Good size on him, considering. And he's fast. Hear he can call plays, too. We'll see. Camp should put him through the paces."

"Good. Armand had a weak quarterback. Couldn't decide fast enough. Your whole game depends on quick thinking and the ability to take charge. A poor quarterback and kiss your game goodbye." She wiped her hands clean and approached the table.

"My mother, the sportscaster," grinned Vinnie, as he finished the last of the egg and dropped his fork down on his plate.

His mother smiled. "Hey, some mothers go to fashion shows, I go to games. What can I say? I'm proud of what you do." She bent down and kissed the top of his head, as she walked by the table and out into the hallway. "Your hair's still wet, Vin," she called back.

He looked in her direction and gave a half-smile. He bounded to his feet, grabbed his gymbag that lay beside the refrigerator, and pushed open the screen door. Stepping out into the sunshine, he immediately felt warmth, even though it was only just after eight. He dropped his bag on the porch floorboards for a moment, reached above his head and pulled his grey tee-shirt off. He welcomed the sunrays hitting his chest. He was glad he'd decided to just wear gym shorts, as he liked to tan his legs. Most days when he was training he would wear full-length sweats; the chance to get some more color on his legs appealed to him. He ran a hand down one side of his right leg. The dark hair acted as a sunscreen for much of the potential color he could get. "Need more sun," he said aloud, as he picked up his gymbag.

Vinnie threaded his tee-shirt through the handle of the bag and went down the porch stairs two at a time. He walked over to the driveway and threw his bag into the passenger side of the small red MG convertible. He opened the door and dropped into the driver's seat. God he loved this car! He had worked hard for it. Boy, had he worked hard. Twelve straight months of flipping burgers, but he had done it. So there were a few rust spots, a few dents; he loved every one of them. Vinnie adjusted the rear-view mirror and ran his hand up and down over his short hair again. Dry enough. Starting the car, he threw it into reverse and backed quickly into the street. Pausing, he reached onto the dash and picked up his sunglasses. Placing them on, he lowered them slightly down his nose, then tapped the stick into first gear and sped off in the direction of Northridge High.

Twenty minutes later, the MG turned into the school parking lot. Vinnie spun quickly around and came to an abrupt halt in a space at the far end of the parking area. Turning the engine off, he sat a moment with one hand still in place on the steering wheel. He leaned all the way back and pressed his hair against the headrest. From this vantage point, he looked out over the football field located just beyond the wire fence at the edge of the lot. He squinted his eyes slightly to adjust for the distance, his sunglasses still perched on the bridge of his nose.

Across the field, there was already quite a bit of action going on. He could see the two coaches and Billy, the trainer, back at the sidelines by the bleachers. On the field in various stages of practice drills were about fifty guys. Vinnie was surprised there would still be this much of a turnout for the second day of trials, an illustration of just how big football really was in this New Jersey town. The sun's rays continued to increase in heat. He was glad he was only wearing the loose shorts. Maybe between the ride over and these few relaxing minutes, he would get a tad darker. He made a mental note to try to catch some sun while he watched the try-outs between his lifting. He ran his right hand down over the hair on his chest, as he continued to watch the players off in the distance. He unconsciously played with the hair across his stomach as he tried to figure out which potential players showed the most promise. Vinnie let his left hand drop off the wheel and fall onto his left thigh, immediately feeling a bit of sweat on the hair of his leg.

He turned his attention away from the field for a moment, and glanced down at his shorts. The white shorts he wore were loose around the leg opening, although he noticed some increased tightness since he'd been working his legs so brutally this summer. Already this early in the day, there was the beginning of a sweat outline where the thick hair went up under his shorts. He felt the dampness for a moment. The combination of the warmth of the sun and his hands on his chest and leg began to stir his crotch. He closed his eyes for a moment and let the intense feeling grow. He heard the coach blow a whistle a couple of times off in the distance, and the continued rising and falling of shouts and grunts from the various players around the field. He let his fingers slide up into the open space that was available in the leg opening. The looseness of the shorts gave him ample room for two of his fingers to slide up far enough just to touch one of his balls. A shot of pleasure went through Vinnie, as his fingers came in contact with the hairy sack. He opened his eyes and drearily re-focused on the football action across the grass. He gently wiggled his fingers slightly to give a ticklish feeling to his nut. He smiled to himself, as he felt his rod expand in the loose shorts. Closing his eyes for another moment, he removed his fingers from the warm leg hole and reached down with both hands, pulling his dick roughly to the right and making it point as downward as was possible.

Looking down at his lap, he realized that because he had his jock still in the gymbag, the outline of his hard prick was more than noticeable. "I should have worn something underneath the shorts," he thought to himself. "No one will be around anyway, everyone's already on the field." He reached over and picked up his gymbag off the passenger seat. Opening the door, he climbed out and stood next to the small sports car. He placed the bag on the hood of the car for a moment, as he again adjusted his dick. "Jesus," he said out loud, "My fuckin' hog's hangin' out for the world to see." He pulled his shorts down all the more, revealing the trail of dark hair that ran from his navel down into the depths of the white material. "Gotta keep my hands off myself. Gotta keep my mind on what I'm doin' here." He grasped the tee-shirt that was looped through the handle of the gymbag. He pulled it over his head and adjusted the length so it partially covered the front area of the shorts.

Pulling his glasses back down the bridge of his nose, Vinnie turned and swung the bag over his shoulder. He started to walk briskly toward the field house that led to the locker rooms. As he walked, his face lapsed into a sneer. "Manta, you gotta get laid! I'm walkin' around half the day with a fuckin' boner. Christ, shoot a fuckin' load once in a while, will ya?" He laughed. Vinnie looked around quickly in all directions as he approached the outside door to the field house — he was glad no one was around to witness him talking to himself. He paused with his hand on the doorhandle, looking once more out toward the action of the football field. "Yeah, I gotta shoot a load." He opened the large wooden door and stepped into the coolness of the gym.

* * *

A few minutes later Vinnie emerged through the door of the small weight room. He had changed into clothes that would allow him to lift comfortably, but were still thick enough to absorb the sweat he knew would be breaking as he worked his body to the max. He still wore his loose shorts, although his Italian pride was now confined in his jock. He had thought twice about putting it on when he saw it was the same one he had used the day before. The small piss stain was still in the front and the odor was already a bit strong from his balls sweating so much on the field yesterday. But he didn't want to chance popping another boner in the gym. He felt bad for his mother having to launder the jock after he got through with it today. He had pulled a hooded sweatshirt over his tee-shirt, intending to wear it until his muscles got properly warmed up. The double socks he had on to help with the soreness of his feet would raise his body temperature pretty quickly, so he knew he would be peeling the sweatshirt off after a few minutes.

He walked into the weight area carrying his weight belt in one hand and a baseball cap in the other. Looking around, he saw there were already several guys pushing iron, even though it was just after nine am. The weight room had been open for an hour, and it appeared that several of the other upperclass players had the same idea — loosen up the muscles and get them ready for the beating at camp next week. Vinnie walked over to a free bench near the dumb bell rack and dropped his belt down on the floor. He pulled the baseball cap down over his head and adjusted it down so the visor rested just above his eyebrows. Looking at the large mirrored wall, Vinnie was pleased with his reflection. His legs looked really large in just the loose shorts. The hair was thick across his thighs, but he was able to see muscle striations, and he watched the muscles jump as he flexed his legs in the mirror. His face took on an even more sinister look with the hood and cap up on his head. His eyes appeared small and menacing, and the sweatshirt showed off his huge shoulders and protruding chest. He looked like he could beat the crap out of anybody. The way he felt today, he could.

Reaching down he picked up his weight belt and placed the leather around his back. He pulled the buckle tight, which lifted his chest up and out even more. He normally wore lifting gloves, but decided against them today as he wanted to toughen up the skin on his hands. As he got into heavier lifting later, he planned on rubbing chalk into his palms. This would give him the same lifting advantage the gloves would have offered and at the same time allow him to strengthen his hands. Vinnie picked up two 60 lb. dumbbells and pressed out a set of fifteen warm-up reps lying flat on his back on the bench. He figured he would work chest first, then break and watch the field action a bit, then pound out some work on his back muscles. He had concentrated quite a bit on chest and back all last season, which had enabled him to put on a good fifteen pounds of rock solid muscle on his upper body. He knew he needed the bulk to continue growing in these areas, to be able to take the hits all season. Dropping the pair of dumbbells to the floor after finishing the sets, Vinnie sat up for a moment to catch his breath. He flexed his chest, enjoying the feel of the pump that was beginning.

His concentration was interrupted by the sound of a loud groan coming from the opposite end of the training room. Turning his head, Vinnie focused his eyes on the squat area, occupied by three guys. One large guy was completing a heavy set of squat reps. Returning to an upright position, the guy slammed the bar of weights back onto the squat rack, the many weight plates clattering on the bar as it came to rest. "Fuckin' A, man!" yelled one guy. "Fuckin' good set!"

The guy completing the squats bent down and tightened his knee wrap on one of his legs, the chalk of his hands smearing across the back of his leg. Sweat was visibly running down his back and soaking the tattered sweatshirt he was wearing. The arms of the shirt had been completely cut off, and his underarms were dripping. He grabbed hold of the side of the rack and leaned his head down to rest. His face was coated in perspiration. He turned his head to the side, still leaning on the rack, his chest heaving as he tried to catch his breath. It was Vuch.

Vinnie turned back to the wall of mirrors in front of him. Sitting on the end of the bench, he looked at the reflection of Vuch and his friends across the room. The two companions were busy loading one more 45 lb. plate on each end of the bar. Vuch still had his head resting on the side of the rack, his gaze now fixed on Vinnie in the mirror.

"Let's go, Vuch!"

"One more, buddy! This is it. Max it out!"

Vuch straightened up and ducked down under the bar, letting it come to rest on his shoulders. A large towel was entwined around the metal bar to give padding between the metal and his body. With the kind of weight he was working with, no way would he have been able to take it directly on his skin. The bar was dipping on each side from the strain of the many 45 lb. plates it housed. Vuch positioned his legs apart and looked slightly upward, carefully watching his reflection and posture in the mirror. He bent his knees and descended toward the floor, his two friends keeping their hands just above the bar as it dropped. Vuch was determined to complete the set unaided. Hitting the lowest point, he let out a very audible yell.

He pushed with all his power and began returning to the standing position. It was slow and difficult.

"Come on Vuch, press it out!"

"All you! All you!"

He hit the full upright stand and began to go down again. He yelled even louder as he pressed out the second rep.

"Do it! Do it! Come on." Vuch was noticeably having difficulty, as he strained to complete the next rep. He looked to be stuck halfway up. His friends positioned their hands closely to the bar, but held off on contact allowing Vuch to attempt the return on his own. "Do it, Vuch. Come on, you pussy!"

"Press it! Right up, Vuch! All you!" Increasing the power of his groaning, Vuch slowly completed the rep. Slamming the weights back into the rack, he seemed to almost lose his balance for a moment. He grabbed the steel supports of the squat rack and leaned his face against it again. His whole upper body was coated in sweat, his face beet-red from the incredible exertion he had just put his body through. A smile came across his face. He reached over to a baseball hat that was hanging from one of the poles that held the unused weight plates. He spun the hat around and placed it backward on his head.

Vuch glanced over toward Vinnie, the look of victory flashed with his white smile. He swiped at the cascading sweat that dripped down his temples. Vinnie caught his gaze and couldn't help but return the wide smile. He was impressive. The quarterback might be smaller... he might not be a huge blocking machine... but he had power! He had speed! He noticeably commanded attention, and gave off an air of superiority. He was okay. Vinnie smiled to himself as he remembered Vuch's attempt at a compliment the day before. Vuch had said Vinnie was okay, too. Vinnie returned the 60 lb. dumbbells to the rack and picked up a set of 80's. Rest over, he laid back and continued with his own assault on his chest. Forty-five minutes passed as Vinnie lashed out at his chest muscles. He worked them hard, and rested only momentarily between the sets and the various exercises — he moved like a man possessed. This was his world.

His motivation was increased as he paralleled Vuch's movements around the training area. Vinnie matched all the power and pushed himself into higher weights and reps than he had previously done. Vuch continued to train with his two buddies, using them to spot when he reached maximum poundage. Vinnie trained alone. His size and strength allowed him to work with the heaviest weights in the gym without the need for spotting. His bulk easily withstood the slamming work of the mighty iron — his body pumping up fuller with each set completed.

After completion of his chest training, Vinnie decided to take his break and catch what was still going on outside with the players. He replaced the set of dumbells he was finishing with and walked toward the door and into the locker room. He would store his belt in his locker and towel off before he hit the field. Just as he reached the door his attention was drawn over to Vuch and his friends, still banging away at the weights. Vuch was down on one knee assisting one of the guys in doing leg extensions on a machine. Vuch used one of his arms to help lift the pad that rested under his buddy's leg. The guy was using a fair amount of weight, and doing a set of high reps. He had pushed himself past the point of failure and now relied on Vuch to assist in the leg lift. Vuch looked up and gave a quick wave to Vinnie, returning his arm immediately back to spot the guy on the machine. Vinnie returned the wave and grinned. He threw his weight belt casually over his shoulder and continued on into the locker room.

* * *

The football action on the field was fairly impressive. At this stage of the try-outs, the coaches had pretty much sifted out the sucky players and what was left were decent guys all vying for the open positions. The camp would further allow the coaching staff to narrow the potentials down to the team of sixty or so that would start the season. Vinnie positioned himself over against the chain-link fence that Vuch and his group had occupied the day before. He pulled his sweatshirt and tee-shirt off together and dropped them down beside him. He turned his "Steelers" hat around backward so the sun would get to his face. Leaning against the fence, he angled his face slightly upward to catch the rays, but still allowing a decent view of the plays. His chest was pumped up due to the intense rush he'd succeeded in obtaining in his workout. He lightly ran one hand down his chest hair. Again he remembered the extra time it takes to get color through the dark hair growth — his Italian ancestry at least helping in making him darker than most guys to begin with. Maybe he would have some free-up time at camp.

Vinnie realized he really didn't know anything about the Northridge camp except that it was somewhere near the mountains, and it was a few days longer than the other camps he had attended. He looked at his watch — 10:15. He would sit out for about forty-five minutes, then go train his back for another hour or so. That would bring him nicely up to lunch. His mother would be happy to actually see him come home for a meal on time for a change. Vinnie reached down and kicked off his training shoes, then pulled off his double sweat socks. His feet still ached and he knew the air and sun would do them good. He spread his legs out and positioned them for maximum ray penetration. He observed his feet had taken quite a beating. Even the rest over the beginning of the summer had not healed them totally. Wearing double socks for a while and getting some new training shoes was definitely needed. The cleats were rough on the soles of his feet all season. With any luck, maybe the coaching staff could recommend something to him at camp.

A whistle blew from off in the distance behind him, and Vinnie turned to see what was going on. Off in a smaller field that was sectioned off were some other players working through some basic moves, or rather, attempting to do so. The ball was fumbled more often than not, and the pass action was fucked.

"Bozo ball!"

Vinnie turned abruptly back and saw the legs of a guy in a football uniform standing right to the side of his head. His exposed calves were caked with dirt. Vinnie squinted up into the sunlight, and could only make out the guy's silhouette framed in the bright light. "Huh?" responded Vinnie.

"Bozo ball. Frosh try-outs. They suck, don't they?" The guy squatted down beside Vinnie, dropping his helmet next to the sweatshirt and tee. "Every year we get a big laugh outta the little fucks trying to play big boy ball. They barely have any dick hair and they're out there trying to act like ball-busters. I guess we all started out there once, but Christ, I hope we were never as backassed as they are. They're all fuckin' thumbs and left feet. They spend more time just runnin' into their own guys then they do makin' any yardage." The guy sat down on the grass. "You're that new guy, Manta, right?" He held out his hand.

"Yeah, Vinnie Manta. Tackle. Senior." Vinnie shook his hand.

"Yeah, we've all heard. I'm Sal Cardone. Center, also a senior. So wassup?"

"Just hangin' out. I was in the gym for awhile. Took a break. Thought I'd just come out and watch and catch some sun for awhile. How come you here? I thought none of the senior guys had to be here for the other two days."

"You mean for the try-outs? Nah... not really. I'm just doin' the coach a favor. Tom Walter, the assistant, has gotta work with the freshmen, so Morrison asked me if I'd help set up some runs today. I kinda like doin' it anyways. I like to see what's up with the cuts."

"What you think?" asked Vinnie. His own assessment in what he had seen was some of the guys had talent.

"They're okay. Actually some of the guys have improved over last year. Some have put on some decent size. Hopefully the power is there behind it. There are still some of the losers that keep trying year after year. They never make it, but ya gotta give 'em credit for havin' balls."

Vinnie sneered. "Yeah, I guess. I don't know, I think if it was me I'd give up. Why keep poundin' your head against the same wall year after year. If you suck... then you suck. Not everybody is meant to be able to play — not well anyways."

"Yeah, but you say that Manta, cause you get to play. They wanna play too. It doesn't come easy to everybody, but they still love the game and want part of the action."

"Yeah well... let 'em have the action from the sidelines. The team is too important to let guys with no fuckin' ability onto the field, just cause they wanna play the game. There's no room out there for half-ass playin'," Vinnie retorted .

"Yeah. But we'll weed 'em out—we always do. The Warriors went undefeated last season. We'll kick ass again this year." Sal Cardone got to his feet. "Gotta get back. Nice to meet you, Vinnie. See ya next week."

"Yeah, Sal. Take it easy. Weed out those candy-asses, huh?"

"Gotta do it. Later." Sal grabbed his helmet and ran off toward the sideline where Coach Morrison stood watching the field. Vinnie glanced back at the freshman section. Someone kicked the ball way offsides, as two little guys ran while watching where the ball was landing. Not seeing each other, they collided. They stayed down for a second, then got to their feet. They shuffled around a bit, obviously trying to make it look like they knew what they were doing. "Bozo ball... yeah," Vinnie smiled and ran his hand down his chest again. This time it was covered in a layer of perspiration; the sun was getting hot. He laid his head back against the wire fence again and closed his eyes. It was really good to be back out on the field again!

*   *   *

When he re-opened his eyes, he was covered in even more sweat. The field had emptied down to just about half a dozen or so guys. The two coaches were sitting together on the lowest seat of the bleachers. Vinnie crammed his neck to the left. The freshman field was empty. He lifted his left arm and looked at the face of his watch — 11:30. "Shit! I fell asleep!" He got up onto one knee and grabbed his sweatshirt and tee-shirt. "So much for my fuckin' back workout." He glanced down at his torso. His entire chest and ab area glistened in the sun. Looking further down he saw his shorts were completly soaked. "Christ!" he muttered. He got to his feet and headed for the entrance to the field house.

Stepping into the locker room, he immediately felt the difference in temperature. He could hear the water running, and assumed that the guys were hitting the showers as they came off the field. He couldn't blame them — the sun was brutal. He could imagine how it felt fully suited up and running your ass off. He walked lazily over toward his bank of lockers. The cool cement floor felt good on his naked feet. The small puddles he encountered as he walked across the floor helped to relieve the burning in his toes. He approached his locker and opened the steel door. He pulled his gymbag from the shelf and dropped it onto the bench. He removed the towel from the bag and slung it over the locker door. A shower is just what he needed to feel right about now. *Need to get this stench off,* he thought to himself.

Vinnie placed his right foot up on the bench and bent down over to examine his toes. They appeared a bit better than the day before, the double socks and air doing them some good. Maybe a good soak is what they need. He briefly planned in his mind that he would soak them in the bathtub when he got home, then remembered the school steamroom. The moist heat of the steam would take the ache out of them. He pulled down his shorts and jock and threw the wet clothing onto the floor in front of the locker. He would wrap them in his towel when he was done and put them right into the laundry. The smell of that jock now could knock somebody out. *Poor Ma,* he thought. He glanced around trying to remember where the steamroom was. He had seen the door the first time he'd been in the locker room, but now he couldn't remember where it was located. He reached his hand around to scratch his bare ass. His fingers probed his butt crack — the hair was matted from moisture. He stuck two fingers up against his hole and tried to relieve the itching feeling. The straps of his jock would often slide over and up into the crack of his ass. After several hours of wearing, he always developed an itchy hole. He pulled slightly on the hair between his ass cheeks and felt better. A good shower after the steam would relieve the discomfort.

He then remembered the steamroom was located in the hallway just outside the inner locker-room door. Although it was still inside the guys' area, Vinnie didn't want to parade out the inner door buck-naked. He also didn't want to get the one towel he had all wet from the steam — he had to be able to dry off with it after showering. He fumbled in his gymbag for anything else he had. At the bottom was a ratty old pair of BVDs. He must have worn them and forgot they were in the bag. Never got laundered. They smelled ripe, but they were dry. He pulled the jockey shorts on. One side of the pouch hung loosely so the hair of his left nut was exposed. *Big fucking deal, it's all guys anyhow.* He threw his bag back in the locker and closed the door. He stuck his hand down into the shorts and adjusted his hog so it hung over to the right side — it was more comfortable that way. Letting the elastic snap back against his stomach, he walked off in the direction of the steam. He passed out of the inner locker area into a large hallway. The hall was empty. Looking both ways, he turned to the left, believing the steamroom was one door down.

He was right. A large glass door marked the entrance into the steam. The handle was warm to his touch — he knew it must be cranked up to a good high temperature. When he opened the steamroom door, he was jarred by the blast of mist that came shooting out at him. It was hot alright. He stepped inside, letting the large glass door close silently behind him. It took a moment for his eyes to adjust to the dim and misty light. He noticed the room was all tile; floors, walls and ceiling. A waist-high platform for seating lined each of the two walls lengthwise. It appeared there was a shower spicket for rinsing off down at the end of the room, opposite where he stood. He fumbled his way along the tiled platform with his hand, until he was about halfway down the length of the room. He climbed up and seated himself with his back against the wall — that immediately felt better. He closed his eyes and let the warmth of the steam overtake the aches in his body.

"That you, Prisco?" asked a voice from across on the opposite platform.

"No, ain't Prisco," replied Vinnie, still keeping his eyes shut and hoping the interruption would stop.

"Manta?... That you, Vinnie?"

"Yeah, who's that?" asked Vinnie, opening his eyes and trying to make out the form that sat across from him.

"It's me. Vuch. Tony Carvuccio." Vinnie heard movement, and then noticed the guy had moved over to his side of the room. "Wassup, Manta?" Vinnie felt a slap on his shoulder. He closed his eyes again.

"Nothin'. Just hangin' around. Thought I'd get some heat."

"Yeah, it's fuckin' the balls for recovering ya muscles. I saw you lifting earlier. Shit, you do enough weight, or what? Man, you're some strong bastard, huh?" The voice sounded enthusiastic.

"Yeah, I guess. I got some decent weights and reps today. Been feelin' pretty strong lately, gotta make use of the time. You were squatting some heavy sets there yourself, Tony," he replied.

"Yeah. Call me Vuch. Yeah, I got myself maxed out today. I'm probably feelin' the psych of getting ready for camp. I was gonna help out on the field today, but decided to kick back instead. The weight set-up at the camp is less than what we got here, so I wanted to get in some heavy stuff this week."

"That's cool," replied Vinnie. "So what's this camp like anyway. Eleven days. That's alot. Why so long?"

"Camp's the tits, man! It's so fuckin' great. It's hard, but it's a fuckin' blast! Yeah, I know most camps only go a week or so. I think ours started out long, cause Northridge takes so long deciding who their starters will be. Now it's kinda spread out to give us some time to ourselves, as well as do the training."

"What you mean, 'time to ourselves'?"

"Well, like there's all the usual drills and scrimmage and shit... but like they give us some free time too. They just kinda started that a few years ago when this island thing started," replied Vuch.

Vinnie reached down and pulled on the underwear pouch. The cotton material had gotten totally wet and now his left nut hung out and lay on the hot tile. He rubbed the hair on the exposed sack, then tucked it back up into the jockeys. "What's this island thing?"

"Ah, that's the tit. See, camp is like sophomore through senior, right? Well, we come down on the stupid sophs all week long. It's brutal. Hazin' up the ass, right? Well, anyways, after givin' it to them all week I guess originally the coaches thought they needed time away from us. One of the upperclass guys that year organized this swim out to this island that sits out about a half a mile from the beach. The camp is on this lake, see? Anyways, the juniors and seniors swam out to the island. It was just supposed to be for the day, but they ended up staying all night. Now it's kinda developed into this big ritual deal each year. The upperclass guys swim out to the island and spend a coupla nights. It's cool. No football. No coaches. No little squirty underclass. Just us top guys. It's pissa!"

"What do you eat?"

"You mean what do *we* eat? You're in it this year, bro. The food and camping gear is rowed out by boat. Before you ask, it's boated out by the sophs. They gladly do it just to get us off their backs for a coupla days. They need the recovery time after we get through with them."

"We do play football somewhere in this camp, right?" Vinnie got a smirk on his face. "I mean there is some serious work done, right?"

"Oh, yeah. You bet your fuckin' ass there is." Vuch stood up, unwrapped the towel he had around his waist and laid it out flat on the tile seat. Sitting down, he turned and lay on his back. His head rested just an inch or so from Vinnie's left leg. He sprawled out, stretching his legs out fully and crossed his ankles. He lifted his right arm up and tucked it under his head. "Yeah, man, we play football alright. Football all day. Strategies all night. Yeah, you'll get enough football. Even for you, Manta. So what you think of our little town here, eh? Been seeing anyone? Get any pussy lately?"

"Funny you should ask. I was cursin' myself out earlier today. Nothin'. Absolutely nothin'. I gotta meet somebody real soon. Once school starts I should meet some, huh?"

"Yeah. The babes all swarm around us football jocks — their heroes! You can dip the stick in just about any girl you want. Summer is kinda tough. If you weren't seein' anybody when last year got over, you're pretty much on your own. Your right hand becomes your girlfriend, know what I mean?" Vuch reached down to his dick. He picked up his pole and gave it a strong squeeze.

Vinnie turned his head slightly toward where Vuch lay. "Who you seein', Vuch?"

"Nobody, either. I broke up with my girlfriend last May. She was a bitch. A bitch and a whore. Her name's Deirdre. We call her 'Deirdre, the wonder slut'! Don't get me started on her. Shit, I hate that fuckin' bitch!"

"Yeah, I guess so! Jesus, man, put it behind ya, huh?"

"Yeah, well I have. Anyways, nothin' since her." Vuch's voiced trailed off. He was silent for a moment. "So what'd you think a' Pennsylvania?"

"It was okay. Kinda too city. We had good football players, but life around the city was kinda tough. I look forward to this suburban life for a while. City girls were wicked stuck-up, too. I wasn't seein' anybody all last year. The girl I was seein' last summer caught me with her sister. I was just fuckin' the girl once, you know? She said my girlfriend was out doin' this other guy, right? So I got wicked pissed off. So the sister offered to help me relieve some of my frustration. She just wanted me to put it to her. She wanted it in the worst way. She started slidin' her hand down the front of my jeans... right there in the fuckin' living room in the afternoon. I couldn't fuckin' believe it! So she reaches down and unzips my fly and pulls my hog out right there. So I got a wicked hard, right? I mean, who wouldn't? So she's pullin' on it and stuff, really yankin' hard. I'm gettin' all hot and grabbin' her blouse and trying to work my way into her tits, you know? So she stops for a minute and reaches up under her skirt and pulls her fuckin' panties off. Right there, man! Jesus! Then she just lays down on the freakin' sofa and exposes her hole to me. I could have shot right there!

"So I pulled down my jeans and underwear real quick, see, an' I just about jump on her real hard. I poked the head of my hog just into her, right, and then bam!.... the fuckin' screen door is opening and in walks my fuckin' girlfriend. She starts screamin' at me, callin' me all these names, and sayin' she gonna call the police and get me locked up for doin' her fourteen-year-old sister, and all this shit. So I jump up and shove my hog, which is still hard and drippin' by the way, back into my jeans. I was so fuckin' horned up by then. I did it so quick I got my underwear all tangled up and got the zipper of my pants screwed up. Anyways I ran outta there so fuckin' fast. I had barely got the tip of my hog in her pussy, man... it was so fuckin' frustrating! I went home and pounded my dick so hard. I had blue-balls, ya know? Anyways, I ain't got nothin' since then. Word spread around Armand and all the girls gave me the cold shoulder all last year — they were all on her side. Jesus, her sister pulled my fuckin' hog out, and *I* turn out to be the bad guy. Shit! So I just let me pop boners all the time and try to forget about it." Vinnie laughed. "Her sister fuckin' wanted it, man."

Vinnie looked over at Vuch. He had a broad smile on his face. His hand was still down at his dick, which now seemed half-hard. He pulled on the head while flopping it side to side against each thigh. "Tough break, Vinnie. At least you got it in for a minute. A split second in a pussy is better than no time at all... guess you gotta learn to shoot faster." He laughed.

"Man, I could shoot these days in one second probably. I don't flog it very often, so I come pretty quick."

"Not me, man, I slap it just about every night. My meat needs attention. You're Italian — you understand. Until I get me a bitch to do it, I'll just fuckin' do it myself. End story."

"Well, whatever. Listen, man, I gotta go. I shoulda had lunch like half an hour ago." Vinnie stood up. "It was nice talkin' to ya. You seem like an okay guy. I think you're a good player, too, man."

Vuch reached up and offered a sweaty hand. Vinnie shook it. "Take care, Vinnie, my friend. If I don't see ya before, see ya on the bus next week. Camp's the balls!" Vuch squeezed Vinnie's hand slightly and smiled his white toothy grin.

"Later," said Vinnie. He pushed open the glass door and headed back toward the showers.

3

Vinnie was startled awake by the clanging alarm. He placed one arm over his face to shield his eyes, and groped with the other hand clumsily to find the "off" lever on the top of the clock. "Shit!" he yelled. He quickly propped himself up on one elbow and turned on his side, hitting the alarm button so quick and hard that the clock went flying off the dresser and landed on the floor. He retreated just as quickly back down and under the covers. He lay on his back again, returning his bare arm across his eyes. The bright sunlight had already begun to cast large slivers of light through the sides of his window shade. He turned toward the dresser and lifted his arm just enough to focus his eyes on the clock. It had come to rest on its side, about three feet from the legs of the dresser. Reading the hands sideways, he was able to figure it was 7:05. He had set the clock early so he would have plenty of time to finish any last minute things before heading for the buses. It was here. Finally.

The week had dragged by; each day seemed endless and boring. Anticipation was running so high down at the school, it was unbearable. Now finally the big day had come. Wednesday — he was finally going off to camp. He closed his eyes, taking in the sounds outside. Cars were already moving fairly loudly out on the main road, and he could hear the voices of some of the kids next door out in the yard. The neighbor, Mrs Gabrini, had three sons: twins aged thirteen and a younger boy of eleven. Each morning since the Manta's had moved in that summer, Vinnie would hear them outside as early as 6:30. They were active kids and just had to get out as soon as they got up; and they always seemed to get up right with the sun. He heard their voices rise, laughing and cursing at each other.

Vinnie kept his eyes closed and tried to figure out what they were doing. It sounded like they were seeing who could run the fastest — they were always trying to outdo each other. Once when

Vinnie was laying out in the sun in the backyard, they were trying to pass a football to each other, taking turns going out long. After watching several lame attempts, Vinnie got up and showed them how to run and judge the ball's descent properly. They thought Vinnie was the greatest. Now anytime he tried to lay out, even for a short while, he always knew he would end up playing with the Gabrini's. They were nice kids and Vinnie often enjoyed being able to show them how to do something properly. He felt kind of like a big brother to them. Their father had died several years ago and Mrs Gabrini often admitted to not knowing how to show them "guy stuff", as she called it. Yeah, they must be testing speed out there. He could hear them calling each other "faggot" — tough kids for their age. Too bad about their dad.

Keeping his arm securely over his face, Vinnie kicked the covers off his torso. He tangled his feet in the blankets as they bunched up, and pulled them down with the power of his legs. They lay all in disarray around his calves, his feet still entwined in the mess. It was already slightly warm in the room. He was still for a moment. He felt an intensity of heat down just below his navel. He concentrated on the feeling. It intensified — it was almost hot. He removed his arm, lifted his head up off the pillow and looked down at his bare body. A path of light coming from the side of the window shade was shining directly on his stomach. The shaft of warmth cut across his midsection along the single trail of hair that went from his navel down to the mass of pubic hair. He put his head back down on the pillow.

He thought about getting up, but decided he could afford to relax for a few more minutes. Once he got to camp, the relaxation would probably be minimal. Then again, from what Vuch had said, maybe there would be some fun times. That island thing sure intrigued him.

He let his eyes wander around the room. He liked the feel of this room — it was his own space. Seldom did his mother or father ever venture up into his room. The Manta's had rented the top floor apartment in a three-family type house right off the main street in Northridge. The best part of this set-up was that Vinnie got to have a converted attic bedroom. It was up a small flight of stairs just off the kitchen. It was very private, and he never heard anything going on downstairs or in the other end of the house. He also had his own bathroom up here. It was small, it actually used to be a storage space next to the chimney, but it contained a toilet, sink and shower stall.

What more did a guy need? It saved him from having to get dressed to go downstairs to take a leak in the middle of the night. His room had posters of his favorite pro teams: the Miami Dolphins, the Steelers, a college banner for the Boston College Eagles. He had some autographed pictures that his Dad had gotten for him: Vince McMahon of the Bears, Doug Flutie the top quarterback from Boston College, and his personal favorite, a large autographed poster of Vinnie Marino. His shelves were filled with pictures of his previous high-school teams and a few MVP trophies he had won. Yeah, this was his private world. His football world.

The sunbeam had shifted down his body. It now brightly illuminated his dick hair, the heat just hitting the head of his flacid manhood. He closed his eyes again. He felt his hog beginning to expand. It grew to full length and vibrated against the trail of hair, the head now stretching past his navel and slapping against his stomach. It ached for attention. He reached down and lightly scratched his nuts. The feeling of the sack hair excited him even more. His hog was rock hard and began to ooze some pre-juice. Vinnie groaned and rolled over on his stomach. This was not good on the day he was supposed to leave for camp. He needed his energy — he needed his aggressiveness... it was not a good idea to shoot his wad now. He closed his eyes very tightly and plowed his hard dick into the sheet under him. He would think of other things. He would make it go away.

Vinnie started to run some football plays through his mind. He pictured himself hitting the defensive tackle opposite him, the guy falling beneath his huge body, chests hitting together, bones making cracking sounds. He remembered the heavy groan of the opponent as his body crushed under Vinnie's immense weight. He pictured blocking and leaving open field for the quarterback to make a completion. He pictured the satisfied face of the quarterback when the touch-down was completed. He pictured Vuch's smile as he jumped and hugged the teammates in victory. All the guys huddled together, rubbing each other's hair, pouring water over their sweating heads; all the rituals of winning. He imagined Vuch walking to him after the victory was over and just hugging Vinnie in appreciation. They were winners together! His mind shifted to Vuch in the weight room. He remembered each detail of his incredible squats, the groans of painful pleasure he let out as he dipped down and pressed the heavily weighted bar with all his power. He remembered his muscled legs and chalk-covered knee wraps, he remembered how the sweat dripped off his face as he lay against the rack and how he turned toward Vinnie and gave his big, white smile.

Vinnie suddenly bucked against the sheets. He threw his body violently into the mattress, over and over. He rubbed his face into the pillow and began a deep, uncontrollable groan. He buried his head in the softness of the pillow, reached down under him and just barely touched the pulsating head of his dick. It began shooting in spasms of warm, sticky fluid. It stopped for an instant, then a second, heavier wave of jism started flooding out. It coated all under him. Vinnie lifted his body up off the mattress just a fraction, as the hot white spray shot up in a stream that hit his chin. The underside of his body was completed soaked — his sheets were a dripping mess.

"Jesus! What the fuck happened?" he cursed to himself. He got up off the bed and stood on the cool wooden floor, looking down his torso at the incredible amount of jism he had sprayed. "God, I musta needed this bad. Even football couldn't get my mind clear. Fuck! Jesus!" He walked in a circle looking back down at his sticky body. "Fuck!" He picked up his jockey shorts that he always dropped on the floor next to the bed as he took them off at night. He wiped some of the spunk off his stomach. He turned and walked into the bathroom, dropped the dirty shorts in the sink and looked at his reflection in the mirror. A small drop of cum was stuck to his chin. "I didn't even think about screwing any pussy. Jesus! I guess I need to shoot a little more often. This is pretty sad, man," he whispered to his face in the mirror. He spit into the sink, then reached over and turned the shower on. He had to rinse this junk off before he could begin to properly clean himself up for the day. He pulled aside the shower curtain, stepped under the warm stream of water and shut his eyes.

Vinnie just stood still and let the steady torrent flow down over his body. He stuck his head outside of the shower stall, and grabbed the small bar of soap that rested on the side of the sink. The spray of the shower reflected off his body and dropped large pools of water on the bathroom floor. With soap in hand, he quickly re-closed the curtain to contain the cascading water. He briskly did a once-over rub with the soap on his entire body. All traces of his "accident" washed away. He shut off the faucet. That would do until he shaved, then he would rinse again and shampoo his hair. He stepped out of the stall and wrapped a towel around his waist.

Still mostly wet, Vinnie stepped back out into the bedroom and opened one of his dresser drawers. He needed clean underwear and some more socks. Remembering his foot problem, he lifted one of his feet up onto the bed, and examined his toes closely. The steam the other day, plus continuing to wear additional socks, were improving his feet steadily each day. He was pleased. They still looked rough, the feet of an active athlete, but the look of their being beat up was subsiding. Vinnie put his foot back down on the floor. He re-wrapped the towel which had loosened around his waist. A loud knock came on his door.

"Vinnie, you up?" It was his father's voice.

"Yeah, Dad, I am."

The door opened slightly. "Mind if I come in?" He paused at the door.

"No, Dad, come on in. How ya doin'?" Vinnie continued to dig through his dresser. He lifted his head and smiled at his father.

"I'm fine. How are you doing? Excited about today? I'm sure you are. I know how excited you get about this every year." His father smiled. He walked over and leaned against the doorframe to the bathroom. "Big day. Got everything you need?"

"Yeah, Dad, thanks." Vinnie closed the dresser and walked past him into the bathroom. He eyed his reflection and ran his hand over the stubble. It had been two days since he shaved, and the growth was thick and dark. He turned his head toward his father. "Yeah, pretty excited. This is supposed to be an awesome camp, Dad. They'll be working us constantly and really pushing us to see what we can do. I can't wait. It's eleven days, you know? That's alot of practice, alot of drilling. They're really putting us to the test. It's supposed to be a helluva lot of fun, too."

Vinnie half smiled and turned back to the mirror. He shook a can of shaving cream and squirted a big mound into his hand. He began to spread the foam onto the black stubble.

"How many going to camp this year? You met many of your teammates?"

"Yeah, some. Someone said there is like about ninety of us goin' up. That means they'll cut around thirty or so. I'm golden, though. They love my ass, Dad. Me and a few of the guys got it made. There's alot of talent in this town. From what I hear, alot of pressure, too. I like that pressure. Some of the guards and backs are pretty big fellas... Tony Carvuccio, the QB, is first-rate. The offense is strong and they seem to work well together. They don't screw each other up. Remember how Armand was always fuckin' up their offense?" His father chuckled and shifted to the other side of the doorframe.

"Yes, that always ticked you off. I remember all too many times having to go down to get you because you got into another brawl. You took the whole thing personally; like you had control. I'm glad if this team is more together, son, but if not... don't get so hot under the collar, okay?"

Vinnie paused his shaving, one side of his face still covered with cream. He put down his razor and wiped his hand on the white towel around his waist. "Yeah, Dad, okay. I'll remember. Thanks." He looked at his father standing in the door and felt pride that his Dad understood him so well, and cared for him so much.

"You take care, Vinnie. Have a good time, get rest. Hope it's everything you want it to be. We'll miss you around here." His father turned and walked toward the door to the stairs.

"I'll miss you too, Dad," Vinnie called after him. The foam was beginning to drip down his neck. He hurried in shaving the other side of his face.

* * *

Vinnie's mother turned her car into the high school parking lot. Vinnie sat restlessly in the passenger seat and glanced at his watch for the third time in the twenty-minute drive — 9:50. The buses were scheduled to leave in ten minutes. As the car rounded the corner, bringing them to the back area of the field house, Vinnie spotted a crowd of players and parents surrounding the four vehicles. A mass of luggage and gymbags cluttered the area. A huge van was parked adjacent to the buses, where Billy Ruggiero and Tom Walter stood supervising the loading of all personal items.

Vinnie assumed all the football gear had already been transferred on to the buses. The van would take up all the luggage and bags, leaving the four buses for just the team members. That was cool. He remembered the fiasco in Allentown when all personal gear had to be on the bus with the players. The ride to that camp had been over three hours and there was literally no room for anyone to move around in the bus. It had sucked big time.

"Now Vin, call if any problems develop. You know to just call collect, right?" asked his mother, as she shut the engine off.

"Yeah, Mom, no problem." Vinnie's eyes searched the area. Many of the seniors were near the door of one bus, he spotted Sal Cardone and some of the guys he had seen in the gym. At another bus was Randy Miller, the sophomore who had been dreading the cuts — obviously he had made the camp cut, but he still had a good chance of being out by the end of the eleven days, though. Vinnie climbed out of the car and opened the back hatch. "Mom, make sure the MG's okay while I'm gone, okay? I put the top up, but check it every day, okay? If Dad has to move it to get into the garage, make sure he locks it, okay?"

"Sure, honey. You got all your stuff?"

Vinnie lifted out two very large duffle-bags, both filled to almost overflowing capacity. He reached into the back seat, lifted out his gymbag and set it down on the ground. He closed the passenger door of the car and walked round to the back, reached his arms up and slammed the hatch down, then walked back up to the open driver's-side window. "Yeah, Mom, I got everything. I fit everything I could into the duffle-bags, but I think they're kinda stuffed. I can't think of anything I'm forgetting. What I don't have I'll just have to do without. No sweat."

"Okay. I did everything you put in the laundry. You should have enough. I hope you brought alot of warm things to wear, the mountains will be cool at night."

"Okay, yeah. I did. I brought warm things. Listen, Mom, I left a few dirty things in my clothes basket. Some underwear and socks and stuff. I pulled my sheets off the bed, too, but just leave all that stuff, okay? They can just be done with the dirty stuff from camp, okay?" Vinnie pressed.

"Okay, honey. Remember, we love you."

Vinnie looked at his watch again — 10:00 exactly. He looked around again — still no Vuch. "Yeah. I love you, too." He bent down and leaned into the window and kissed her on the cheek. "See you next Saturday. Bye." He picked up his gymbag and looped his arm through the shoulder strap. He bent down again and with each hand grasped one of the string ties on the top of the duffles. He half-walked, half-dragged his gear over to the van. He saw he would be waiting in line for a few minutes. Looking up, he watched as his mother drove off. He stepped a few feet forward as the line moved along, kicking his bags, pushing them ahead as each guy finished and his turn grew closer.

"Manta, glad to see ya," said Billy cheerfully, as his turn came up. "You got a couple of big bags here. Sure you filled each of 'em enough?" Billy smiled.

"Yeah, okay, I got a few things. You know how it is. Ready for anything, Billy — that's my motto." Vinnie returned half a grin. Stupid polite talk. *Sure I filled 'em enough? Please, give me a break.* "I'm gonna take my gymbag on the bus. That okay, Billy?"

"Yeah, sure, kid. Whatever you want. I suggest you stow it overhead, eh." Billy lifted one of the sacks up into the air and tossed it into the back of the van. Vinnie picked up the other one and did likewise. "You're set, Manta. See ya there." Billy stood looking as if he wanted Vinnie to move on. Vinnie did. He walked over to the bus that had a number of kids already on it. Randy Miller still stood next to the door, just leaning against the side of the bus. His face brightened as he saw Vinnie approach.

"Hi, Manta. How are you doing? Gee, I haven't seen you since last week in the locker room. How have you been? Isn't this really exciting? I can't believe I didn't get cut. I can't wait to get up there. I can't believe I have this chance." He talked quickly and nervously. He didn't even take a break to inhale.

Christ, it's like this kid is on speed, thought Vinnie. "Yeah, it should be great, Miller." Vinnie turned away and looked around the area. Well, he could get on this bus and get his ear talked off the whole trip, or he could try out one of the other buses.

"Manta! Over here you stupid shit!" Vinnie looked in the direction of the voice. It was coming out the back window of the bus parked first in line. He walked over toward where he had been called from, leaving Randy just standing there watching him walk away. "Don't get on the soph bus, peckerhead. This is the senior bus. Get your sorry ass up in here." It was Vuch. Vinnie climbed up the steps and stood at the front of the aisle.

"Vuch, where the hell ya been?" Vinnie's voice was enthusiastic.

"Been here for about an hour. Got dropped off early. Been catching up on my z's. These fucks woke me up when they boarded." He referred to three guys sprawled out in seats around the back of the bus. Vinnie recognized two of them as the guys who had been working out with Vuch in the gym last week. The other guy took up the very back seat all by himself. He lounged across the width of the back of the bus. He was huge. He looked fuckin' mean, too. His face had at least four days of very heavy growth across it. His forehead jutted out almost unnaturally, giving an ape-like look to his head. His hair was black and a tangled mess. He looked like he desperately needed a shower.

"Vinnie Manta, this is John Kirby and Mike Massella. Kirb's a quarterback and Mikey here's a linebacker. Good guys... okay players." Vuch smiled wide and let it be known he was kidding them. "That there building sittin' across the back seat there is Meat. Meat's a tackle. Surprise, surprise!" Vuch shot another white smile.

Vinnie nodded to Kirby and Massella. He looked back at the monster in the back. "Meat? Did you say Meat?"

"Yeah, Meat." growled the guy. "I got Grade A American beef! Need I say more?"

"No, got it. How ya doin'?" asked Vinnie.

"Meat doesn't need to say much anyway. His fuckin' dong speaks for all he is. Eh, Meat, ol' boy?" Vuch pulled the baseball hat he was wearing off and tipped it to Meat in a sign of praise. Meat just glared back at him, then turned and looked out the window.

A bunch of guys suddenly started boarding the bus all at once. Vinnie looked out the window at the van. Tom was closing up the back, and Billy had gone around to the passenger side door and was loading in a few extra bags. The van must have been filled to capacity. The guys boarding the bus were joking and laughing and all vying for seats. Within a minute, everyone had sectioned off and was lounging in their chosen areas. Many guys were able to spread out across two seats, as it appeared that the bus would not be full.

"How many seniors are goin'?" asked Vinnie. He turned toward Vuch who had pulled his hat down over his eyes and slid down in the seat. He also occupied two seats, his feet spread out over the seat next to him and stuck out into the aisle. He did not reply.

"Twenty-six," responded Kirby. "There are nineteen sophs and forty-eight juniors. A total of ninety-three this year."

"Decent sized camp. Any predictions?" Vinnie directed the question back at Kirby.

"The sophs will start crying by the second day." Vuch had tipped the brim of his hat back up. "And I feel sooooo bad!" he laughed.

Vinnie shot him a wide grin. "And you single-handedly cause that, eh, Vuch?"

"Well, not to blow my own horn, man, but I guess I been known to make a few sophs shit their drawers."

"Shit their drawers? That's an understatement," said Massella. "Vuchie here has been the prince of hazing since he first came to camp our sophomore year. He retaliated and turned the tables on the seniors that first year. He infiltrated the island and swiped all their clothes. They had to come back to camp bare-assed! He never got caught, either. Only a few of us sophomores knew it was him. They never did recover the clothes. What the fuck did you do with them anyways, Vuch?"

"Ah, sorry guys, I keep my secrets, ya know?"

"Anyways, the sophomores are already all nervous and shit about this camp. They know Vuch here is a senior this year and he'll be out for their blood. I heards them a talkin' outside their bus. They'll be lucky if they can get any sleep the first few nights. Hah, the little shits are in for it, eh Vuchie?" Massella started hooting in laughter.

The driver came up into the bus. He closed the door quickly and started the engine. Immediately he leaned into turning the wheel, and the bus started pulling out of the parking lot.

"Let's just say it's gonna be a good year, guys. We'll all get our testosterone flowin' and have a little fun with the new guys." Vinnie looked out the back window, the view partially obsured by Meat's hulking presence. The other three buses fell into line behind them. He turned to the window next to his head, reached his hands up and pulled the latches so he could slide the window down. He locked the glass into its slots, so that the window remained half-open. A cool breeze started blowing across the top of his head. The level of voices and laughing began to increase all throughout the bus. The driver turned the bus onto Route 31 and started to accelerate. They were headed north.

"So where is this camp anyway? How long we gonna be travelin'?" inquired Vinnie.

"Now son, I asked you to make sure you took care of that before we left home!" cracked Vuch. He laughed.

Vinnie tried not to smile. He tried to look blankly at Vuch, but the corners of his mouth started to go up.

"Now son, just hold your little pecker. If you squeeze the tip and hold it hard, no pee-pee can come out." Vuch spoke in a calm, fatherly-type voice. Vinnie's face cracked into a full smile. It was funny.

"Aw Vinnie, just hang it outta the window," joined in Kirby.

"Kirby, you hang it outta the window, you fag. Isn't this about when you pull it outta ya pants and start wackin' it anyways?" Vuch turned to Vinnie and pretended to lower his voice to a whisper, but intentionally made it loud enough for the back of the bus to hear him.

"Kirb here chokes it several times a day. If you think ya feel an earthquake each morning, it's just Kirb humpin' his bed." Vuch winked at Vinnie.

"Hump me, Vuch! Then I won't have ta do it myself. Come on, Vuch, just once. Please. Please!"

"The man's a sex-starved fag! Let this be a lesson to ya, Manta, get it as often as ya can... otherwise you'll end up like this sorry motherfucker." Vuch pulled his hat back down over his eyes and slid further down in the seats.

Massella looked at Vinnie from across the aisle. "The ride takes about two hours. We go up 31, turn onto 94, then off onto 206. The camp's on a lake just about in the corner of where Jersey, Pennsylvania and New York meet."

"Thank you, Mr Map! And our ETA is what?" mumbled Vuch from his reclined position. He had folded his arms across his chest, his face all but hidden by the baseball hat. His feet were pulled up so they rested flat on the seat next to him, his knees sticking up in the air. He spread his legs wide, the cut-off sweat pants he wore opened at the leg holes due to the position of his knees.

Vinnie glanced down, and could see the bright white cloth of Vuch's jockey shorts up in the leg holes. His legs were covered with light brown hair. The muscles in his legs flexed each time he rocked his knees. He playfully opened and closed his legs in a rhythmic pattern as he talked, hitting his knees together each time he closed his legs. Vinnie looked down at the contrast with his own legs. He also wore shorts, but had the baggy type issued by athletic departments. The wording "Allentown High" was inscribed in navy-blue lettering on one side. The shorts used to be pure white, now they were a grayish tint. Vinnie noted that his legs were more heavily muscled than Vuch's, the thick black hair that covered them giving an even larger appearance to the muscles. Though Vinnie's skin was naturally quite dark, it paled in comparison to Vuch's tan. Vuch was obviously Italian, but he had a lighter coloring with medium brown hair. His legs appeared very tanned and the hair was lightened on them from the effects of the sun.

Massella continued, "Our ETA will be about 12:15. That is unless people like Manta here need to make potty stops."

"I think I can handle it. If I have the need, I'll just let it go in this cola can." Vinnie held up an empty soda can that was lodged next to his seat.

"Ah, the new taste of whizz-cola!" smirked Kirby. Meat stood up and pulled his tee-shirt off. He kicked off his sneakers, reached down and untied the string of the yellow sweatpants he was wearing. He slid them down to his ankles, reaching one arm up and grabbing hold of the edge of the overhead rack to keep his balance in the moving bus. He stepped out of the sweats and bent down and bunched them up. He rolled the tee-shirt around them, forming a pillow, jammed the clothing into the corner of the back seat and sprawled back out. All he had left on were paisley boxer shorts. Thick black hair covered his entire body. One solid mass of hair seemed to run from his neck down his torso and into the boxers. The same thickness of hair came back out the bottom of the underwear and went down and across his feet. He was probably the hairiest guy Vinnie had ever seen. As he adjusted himself on the seat trying to get comfortable, curly black hairs would periodically appear through the slit in the crotch of the boxer shorts. He finally settled on his side, with one hand tucked under the make-shift pillow. A very clear outline of his hog was visible through the underwear. Vinnie could see how he had justifiably earned his nickname.

"That's a fuckin' great idea," said Vuch. He slid himself off the seats and stood in the aisle. He peeled off his white tee-shirt and tossed it up into the overhead storage rack. He stretched out his chest muscles while he was standing, then quickly shot back across his seats to his reclining position. He pulled his knees back up in their former prominence, pulled off his baseball cap and replaced it on his head backward.

"No pussy for eleven days, men," groaned Kirby.

"Oh yeah, like you got it at home." Massella swiped his hand across Kirby's head. Laughing, Kirby ducked slightly and slammed his head back against the window glass.

"Ow! You motherfucker!" He rubbed his head where he had hit the glass. "I do get it at home. Jeanann Bornstein. I fuck her all the time."

"Jewish bitch," responded Massella.

"Jewish whore," said Vuch.

"Jewish fuckin' Jew!" grunted Meat. He shifted his position slightly, reaching down into the slit of his underwear and moving the shaft of his immense tool a few inches to the left. It swelled slightly from his touch. *Big fuckin' hog,* Vinnie thought to himself, *this guy's like the biggest fuckin' moose I've ever seen. Fuckin' big and fuckin' hairy.*

"I've done that Bornstein bitch," said Massella.

"You and the whole team," added Meat. "She puts out for any-body."

"Even your hairy, uncut slab, Meat?" asked Vuch. He ran his hand down his hairless chest and rested it on his abs. "She was able to handle that thing?"

"She gave me head out in my car once. I kept pushin' her head down further on it. She was chokin'. I kept at it, though. She couldn't breathe, but I didn't care. The bitch. She kept complainin' about the foreskin. Fuck her! I shoved her head down hard, sinkin' it down her throat as deep as I could and shot a big fuckin' load down her. She started gaggin' and shit. She wanted it in her box... but fuck her! I wasn't gonna give her the satisfaction of havin' my big ol' meat in her. Let her give me some satisfaction, that's what I thought. She's a fuckin' bitch, believe me." Meat closed his eyes and started to nod off.

* * *

The bus had grown quieter. Many of the guys up toward the front had propped their heads against various seats and windows. The quiet was relaxing for a change, after so much noise during the start of the trip. Vinnie looked out the window and watched the scenery go by. The bus began entering a turnoff, the lane turning into an interchange loop. Vinnie watched the road signs. They were passing onto Route 94, a larger three-lane highway. He glanced at his watch — 11:00. They'd been travelling for forty-five minutes already. He shifted in his seat. He remembered the jokes about taking a piss out the window or in the soda can. He tried to think of something else... he was beginning to need to take a leak.

Massella and Kirby suddenly shot upright in their seats. They were leaning to look out the left side of the bus, and starting to get excited. "Hey, guys, the other buses are in the passin' lane," yelled Kirby. "They're gonna go by us!"

Massella pushed his way past Kirby in the seat and jumped up into the aisle. "Vuch! Meat!" Vuch sat up and leaned over toward that side of the bus, peering over Meat and out the back window. Meat sat up. He put his bare feet back down on the floor and stood. He again grabbed onto the overhead, and ducked down so he could get a view out the side window as the first of the three buses approached the back corner of the seniors'. All the guys at the front of the bus started hooting — many of them were trying to quickly get to their feet. Vinnie knew the procedure. He also slid off his seat and got to a standing position. Suddenly everyone was peeling down their shorts and sweats. Underwear came flying off, several briefs being playfully thrown around the bus. One pair of grungy-looking jockeys landed on the side of Massella's head. "Fuckin' moron!" he yelled, casting them quickly back toward where they had come sailing from. Naked bodies were climbing over each other to line the windows on that side of the bus. Vinnie pulled his shorts and underwear off in one quick move and managed to get the window closest to the back. Meat, in all his naked glory, secured the entire large back window of the bus. His hairy monster of a body presented quite a picture out the back.

The first bus came up alongside — it was accelerating past. Half the guys turned backward and lifted their butts up to the window. Sal Cardone, who sat a few rows up, was mooning and fingering his hole to the players in the other bus. The guys who were facing forward in the windows, Vinnie included, started waving their hogs and making jacking-off movements. Everyone on the senior bus was howling. The second of the buses passed by to similar antics. Then the third bus could be seen beginning to approach. This was the sophomore bus and was what everyone had been waiting for. As it got up near the rear end of the seniors' bus, Meat went wild. He shoved his hips up against the large plate glass and started humping his fat, uncut pole into the window pane. He rotated his hips and slapped his foreskin, doing a kind of wagging movement with the enormous piece of dick. Standing behind him, everyone got to see his large butt, hairy as the rest of him, bucking forward.

As the sophomore bus pulled up alongside, the hoots grew in pitch and loudness. Kirby and Massella, at the same window, actually managed to hang both their dongs out the opening. Kirby let shoot a spray of piss, the water streamed out and whipped back against the side of this bus. Vuch scrambled to close the open glass at his window to avoid the urine coming into the back of the bus.

"You fuck, Kirby. Jesus! Your fuckin' piss almost got me in the face. You fag! Why didn't you just shoot a cum load on them. You fuck!" Vuch yelled loudly, laughing at the same time. The expressions of the younger kids on the soph bus were priceless. Vinnie saw Randy Miller sitting in one of the windows of the passing bus, his eyes wide and his mouth dropped open in an expression of disbelief. All the seniors cheered as if victorious. The sophomore bus pulled ahead leaving the senior bus at the back of the line. A scramble began to find the undershorts of those who had thrown them around. Vinnie and the guys in the back pulled their shorts back on and returned to their seats. Each had a wide grin on their face. The guys up the front of the bus continued to move about looking for their lost articles. Sal Cardone walked up and down the aisle looking for his underwear. Two of his friends got him each time he passed by their seats in his search. One of the guys would grab for his dick which was flapping as he walked, Sal would then hunch over to avoid being groped, and the other friend would grab his butt, causing him to lurch up quickly. They all were laughing and calling each other "homo's".

This was the camaraderie and antics that Vinnie knew would be the best part of the trip. Every camp Vinnie had attended had similar rituals and pranks. It was a welcome relief and a definite need, after spending days having your butt kicked around the playing field. The bus had begun to settle down again. A few jokes were being made about the sophs up in the front, but the back area, where Vinnie and his group sat, had grown quiet. Vinnie occupied himself with continuing to look out the window. He crossed his bare feet and pulled his knees up close to his chest. His toes stuck out over the seat next to him, the sunlight coming in from his open window illuminating the tops of his feet. He lazily watched the shadowy reflection of the passing trees, as they formed patterns on his skin. He picked some dirt from between the toes of his right foot, and reached into his shorts to adjust where they had tangled when he pulled them back on after the show for the passing buses.

The bus had grown even quieter, and they drove almost in silence for some fifteen minutes. Vinnie passed the time looking around. Directly across from him, Kirby and Massella sat in seats together. Kirby had his head against the frame of the window, Massella his head back against the headrest and half against Kirby's shoulder. They both had their eyes closed and their mouths open — they were off deep. Vinnie turned to his left and looked at Vuch, lounging in the seat behind him. He was again slumped down in the double seats, his baseball hat still on backward. His spiked, light brown hair shot up through the hole that allowed for the plastic adjustment strap of the hat. He had three notches on the strap used to custom-fit it to his head. His face was turned back into the seat, so Vinnie saw mostly his profile. A smile was still on his face, although he also appeared to be almost asleep. Vinnie watched his long eyelashes move slightly as he blinked, even though his eyes were closed. One hand rested on his tanned stomach, and Vinnie noticed that Vuch did not have a single hair on his chest, stomach or arms. A deep tan covered all these areas, giving him a healthy, but very young appearance.

Looking further back in the bus, Vinnie saw Meat curled up on the back seat. He looked rather unusual; such a huge guy curled in a fetal position on the seat. He had put his paisley boxers back on and was on his side facing toward Vinnie. Meat's eyes were partially open, but did not appear to be focusing on anything particular. Every once in a while, Meat would reach down and pull on the opening slit of his underwear. Vinnie assumed he was adjusting himself, trying to get the monster comfortable. Vinnie looked at his watch again — 11:45. According to Massella, they would be at the camp in about a half an hour. Unfortunately, Vinnie's need to take a whizz was growing in the worst way. He didn't think he'd be able to hold it for the remainder of the ride. He also knew he didn't want to ask the driver to pull over and stop, when they really didn't have that much further to go. He looked out the window again and tried to clear his mind. No way. He had to piss. Real bad. He thought of Kirby hanging his dong out the window. No. That would be too much.

He glanced over and spotted the soda can he'd been joking about earlier. *Well, maybe. Yeah fuck it, why not?* He picked up the can and shook it. Totally empty. He glanced around again at his buddies — they all seemed out of it. He ran his finger slowly around the small opening of the can, where the tab had been popped. No way was his dick going to fit into the opening... he'd probably hack his hog to death, even if he managed to squeeze it into the hole. No, he was going to have to aim it just right and hope the stream went in. Jesus! He put his feet flat down on the floor at the bottom of his seat and locked his toes firmly against the steel reinforcements of the seat in front of him. He didn't want to chance being thrown around in the seat, once he started shooting. He undid the fasten on his shorts and pulled down the zipper.

Vinnie tucked one thumb into the elastic waistband of his jockey shorts and pulled the cloth back, exposing the head and about half the shaft of his dick. He tried to aim the slit hole of his hog at the opening in the can. It wasn't working. His hog was too restrained in the underwear — not enough stuck out to piss correctly. Vinnie looked around again nervously, then lifted his hips up and slid his shorts and briefs halfway down his thighs. The hair on his nuts was pinching him — his legs were still too pressed together. He pulled his clothing down even further, now allowing his legs to spread partially, his nuts hanging freely. Now he could manipulate his dick enough to point it directly at the target. Piss was not flowing. He closed his eyes and tried to relax. He breathed slowly and tried to relax more. Suddenly he felt the warm flow begin. He had to re-open his eyes to make sure he was directing it properly. The piss started flooding the small container. Vinnie couldn't restrain himself. He suddenly had a thought of panic, picturing the can filling to overflowing proportions. As his stream continued, he tried to shake the can very lightly to see if it was nearing the fill point. The movement of the container caused his aim to be off for a second. A small amount of the warm yellow piss shot out and over the top of the can. He quickly re-aimed and continued back into the opening. The can appeared to only be about three-quarters full. His need was subsiding. The last drops spilt out of his dick.

He had managed it. Vinnie let out a small sigh. He couldn't believe he had even tried this stupid idea. It could have been disastrous. He jammed the can very tightly into the space between the seat and the window, making sure it was secure and couldn't move. Reaching down, he grabbed hold of his shorts and underwear and pulled them back up together again. He shifted in his seat, adjusting the pouch of his jockeys. He placed one hand to hold the bottom of the crotch of the shorts, and used the other to pull up his zipper. As he was refastening his button, he turned his head to the left. Kirby and Massella were practically doubled over in silent laughter. They had jammed their hands up to their mouths to cover any noise, tears were running down the side of Kirby's face. Vinnie turned bright red. They had seen the whole thing.

"Oh, shit," Vinnie muttered. He kind of shrugged in a 'what could I do?' message.

Kirby burst out loud. "We thought you was gonna try to jam it in the hole. We'd have to take a side trip to the hospital to get it cut out of the can."

"Man looses dick in vat of diet drink!" Massella joked. "Do me a favor, will ya, Manta, if we bunk together, remind me not to leave a drink beside the bed!"

"Yeah, if it isn't too much trouble, try ta go pee-pee before beddie-bye!"

"Gee, you guys are fuckin' comics," said Vinnie. He was still red. "Do me a favor guys... get bent!"

Everybody started to fully wake up after the noise. Kirby and Massella kept their story to themselves, which Vinnie thought was pretty cool. They were kinda rowdy, but okay guys. The bus turned onto a smaller dirt road directly off Route 206. Within minutes, the air took on the smell of the forest. Trees were thick on both sides of the road, dust rose from the tires of the bus and formed a large cloud trailing them. Off to the right, a lake began to be visible every few seconds between the trees. All the guys started talking and getting excited. Suddenly, the forest opened up into a clearing. The other buses were pulled over to the far side near a log building. Players were already getting their personal gear off the parked vehicles and putting it into large piles. Everyone had arrived. They were ready for the games to begin.

4

It took a good half hour to unload the items that had been brought on the buses and coordinate personal gear that had come up in the van. Once everyone had pretty much been paired with their items, they found themselves just standing around waiting for the one pm designated meeting time. At that hour, everyone would gather in the auditorium and get their cabin assignments.

The seniors all congregated together. A feeling of superiority was already in the air. Fragments of conversation from other groups could be overheard, and as expected, the seniors' show for the passing buses was the hot topic. Vinnie, Vuch, Kirby, Massella and Meat all stood in one area, slightly separated from the larger group.

"Yeah, man. Memories, huh? Vinnie, ya gonna just have the fuckin' time of ya life." Vuch smiled his white grin. "The best, man. The best!"

"Where's that lake we saw from the bus as we drove in?" asked Vinnie, his head turning and scanning what was visible.

"It's over there, man." Massella stopped his pacing and pointed over to the auditorium building. "A path leads down to the beach. It runs right alongside of the big buildin' there. Pissa beach, Vinnie, we do drills down there. Sometimes we go swimmin' at night, too, depends if we can drag our asses outta the cabins. Some nights, ya just wanna crash out, ya know?"

"Vuch, what you thinks gonna be up for today?" Massella started slowly walking around again.

"Same as last year, I'll bet. What you think, Vuch?" Kirby bent down to his suitcase and fastened one latch that had come open. "Cabin assignments, then lunch, eh?"

"Yeah, we'll get our bunks, then something in our stomachs. Bet we hit the field within a coupla hours, though," replied Vuch.

"Right into it, huh?" Vinnie looked surprised.

"Yeah man, no room for pussies here. They wanna start us off right. Your balls will be draggin' on the ground by the first night. Everyone feels that, first day — it takes a couple ta get up to speed. Lot to fit in, in a week and a half." Vuch looked at his watch. The crowd had begun to move in the direction of the auditorium. "Let's go, guys."

Vuch turned and picked up his gear. The others followed his lead. When they entered the main auditorium there was just a mass of guys all looking for direction. Billy Ruggiero stepped up to a mike on the stage. "Hey! Guys! Pipe down!" Everyone quieted right down and turned their attention to the stage. "Very good. That's the way we do things all week. We speak... and you listen — immediately! Got it? Good. Now, here's what we're gonna do. Seniors, you're over here on the far right. See Tom Walter. He'll give you your assignments. You guys lucked out this year, the campground here built a series of new buildings, and you king shits get them. Congratulations from all of us. I'm sure the lower guys who'll still be in cabins with ten guys to a house share my deepest wishes for you to be comfortable."

A slight rumble went through the crowd. Vuch bowed his head in a "thank you" toward the stage. All the seniors had big shit-eating grins on their faces.

"Juniors," Billy continued, "you come see me over here on the left for your assignments. Left... that's the opposite hand you whack off with."

"Uh, coach," Kirby raised his hand. "I whack off with my left hand. Then it feels like somebody else." Everyone broke into laughter.

"Hey!" yelled Billy: "Quiet down! Kirby, I make the jokes around here, got it!" The crowd went silent. Tom Walter walked over and whispered something in Billy's ear. He looked in Kirby's direction and cracked a wide smile. He said something back at Tom and the two men laughed.

"Okay, anyway. Get your assignments. You have an hour to settle in, then two hours for lunch. We want you on the field with half-pads at four o'clock sharp. Sophomores you go see Bob and Teddy in the building next door. They'll give you your cabins, and brief you on camp policies. That's it guys, let's do it!" Billy clapped his hands. "Move!"

The group dispersed into their designated sections. Vuch and Vinnie walked immediately over to Tom Walter. Vuch leaned over the table where Tom sat shuffling through some papers. "We get the new cabins, eh, coach?" Vuch smiled brightly.

"Yeah, Carvuccio, you guys lucked out this season. You won't have to be pent up eight or ten in a cabin this year." He attached some loose papers onto a clipboard, then looked up at Vinnie. "Glad to see you, Manta. I'm gonna put you in with Carvuccio here, he'll be the best player to get you used to the way we do things around here." He turned back to Vuch. "Now, Tony, I'm putting you two in a cabin that holds three. It's up to you what to do about a third. I have John Kirby and Mike Massella in with Anthony Marino in the other cabin of three. We also got five cabins with four guys in each one. I'm doing those on a first-in-line assignment. You choose who you want in the third bunk, but you gotta tell me right now before I move the line."

Vuch crumpled his forehead and squinted his eyes. Vinnie got a smirk on his face. He thought to himself that this must be Vuch's "deep in thought" look. "Give us George Kiriatis," said Vuch. He nodded his head at Coach Walter to indicate he was sure of his decision.

"You got him. Cabin 32. Up on the hill, over the beach. Move. See ya at 4:00." The assistant coach returned to his clipboard.

Vinnie and Vuch moved off to the side. Vuch stuck his head up straight and was looking all around the auditorium. "Who's this George Kiriatis? I haven't met him yet," asked Vinnie, his head following the direction Vuch was looking.

Suddenly Vuch started waving his arm. "Meat, over here," he yelled at the top of his voice and waved his arm again. "Meat! Over here you stupid shit! Come on, man, you're in with us!"

"Jesus!" muttered Vinnie. "We're bunkin' with the missing link." Meat walked over in between Vinnie and Vuch and clapped an arm around each of their shoulders. "Roomies!" This was the first word he'd said since before they flashed the buses. *Well, at least he's quiet,* thought Vinnie. *Huge, but quiet.*

"Let's find our cabin." Vuch walked over to his stuff, which he had dumped in the corner by the door. Vinnie grabbed his duffels, Meat had two suitcases. The three stepped out into the midday August heat. It was 1:20. They had plenty of time to get settled, eat, and be on the field at four.

*   *   *

"This place is so much fuckin' better than the holes we had to live in the last coupla years." Vuch walked around in a circle in the middle of the cabin floor. He looked over at the single bed near the window. Standing in the center of the room, he took his garment bag off his shoulder and tossed it onto the bed. "Mine," he yelled, claiming his spot.

Vinnie and Meat moved from the doorway into the center of the cabin. They looked at the two-tiered bunk bed, then at each other. Meat looked back at the beds. "Top" — he had said his second word at camp.

Vinnie sighed and tossed one duffle onto the small bed on the bottom. He dragged the other over to the opening in the wall, where they could hang clothes. He looked around the room. "Where we put stuff? No dressers or nothin'?"

"I dunno," Vuch replied. "Let's check it out." He walked over to the end of the bunk stack. "Yeah, we gots two dresser things over here in this corner, but that's it. We're gonna have to share. I don't have much stuff, I'll double with whoever."

"Mosta my stuff I'll hang up, I guess. Meat, you got those suitcases filled with shit you need a drawer for?" Vinnie looked at him.

"Yeah."

"Okay, Vuch, me and you." Vinnie and Vuch started unpacking their stuff.

Meat kicked off his training shoes and left them at the foot of the beds. He pulled his tee-shirt over his head, dropped it on top of the shoes, and climbed up on the top bunk. Sitting on the edge, he lay back and slid his shorts and underwear off. He flopped back on the bed, his legs still dangling over the side, his feet hanging in the air between the two levels. "Wake me when we eat." He became silent and motionless.

Vinnie was stooped down at the dresser putting some socks in the bottom drawer as Vuch walked over with a handful of tee-shirts. Vinnie looked up as he approached. He lowered his voice to a whisper, as Vuch started putting the shirts in the side of the same drawer. "Meat always like this? He hasn't said two words all day."

Vuch sat on his heels next to Vinnie. "Yeah, that's Meat. He's kinda quiet. But he's a real good guy. It just takes ya some time to get to know him. It's good to have him on ya side when you need him — both on the field and off. He's saved my butt before. Some of the guys think he's kinda strange, being so big and lookin' the way he does. Most guys are kinda afraid of him and steer clear. But, I'd do anything for him and I know he'd do the same. That's why I put him in with us. You'll like him, Vinnie, after a while."

Vinnie nodded and stood back up. He walked over to his bunk to get the rest of the clothing from the duffle. As he straightened back up from bending over the bed, he had to veer his head to the left, to avoid Meat's dangling feet. Vinnie stood holding an armful of sweat clothes. Just above his head were Meat's hairy balls slightly hanging over the side of his bunk. His famous dick lay to one side against his left thigh and hung down just an inch or so past his nuts. The head was fully retracted in, and a long piece of foreskin hung out past the end of his dong.

Vinnie shook his head in disbelief, as he walked back around the end of the bunks. "And that's soft? I can imagine the size when hard," he mumbled to himself. Vinnie dropped the clothing on the floor in front of the dresser.

Vuch was back sitting on the edge of his bed looking out the window. "What did you say?"

"Nothin'," replied Vinnie. He walked over to a desk that was at the end of Vuch's single bed. "So who gets the desk?"

"Whataya want it for? We can all use it, but not much to do on it."

"What about studying plays?"

"Yeah, maybe," replied Vuch. He turned and lay back on the bed, scooping the pillow up and holding it against his chest. "We do lots of that all day. You'll get them in your head pretty quick. Jeez' it's hot!" He tossed the pillow back to the side of the bed. He kicked his sneakers off using just his feet, then swung his left foot out and pushed the shoes onto the floor. He crossed his ankles, bouncing his bare feet restlessly. Vinnie peered out the window. It looked out into the window of the next cabin. He saw bodies moving about but could not distinguish who anybody was. He looked at his watch. — 2:10. "What time ya wanna go get lunch?"

Vuch lifted his head up and looked over at Meat. He hadn't moved at all. "Let's give him a few more minutes to snooze. If we hit the food line now, everybody will be there and we'll have to wait standing around. If we go about 2:30 or so, we'll miss the rush." Vuch turned one of his legs in and pulled his foot into his hand. He scratched the top of his bare foot. "My feet itch. I like to go around without shoes as much as I can up here. Course sweatin' all day in cleats is what gets 'em this way."

"I got a foot problem, too," Vinnie agreed. "My feet get all hacked up durin' the season. It takes me all spring to get 'em back, get all the dead skin an' shit off 'em. I been wearin' double socks this past week. I sweat like a fuckin' monster, though."

Vuch continued rubbing his foot. "The lake's real good for gettin' all the shit off them. I walk around down there sometimes at the end of practice, just cause it feels so fuckin' good. It's awesome when we do drills in the water."

"I've never done that. We didn't have lakes at Allentown or Armand camps. What we do in the water?"

"It's cool. Half-pad drills. Runnin' and shit. Just pads on your shoulders and shorts. No shirt, no shoes, no helmet. Just wadin' in the water up to your waist. It's the best conditioning we do here, I think." Vinnie walked back over to his bunk. It was getting wicked hot. He peeled his tee-shirt off and tossed it on top of his pillow.

"Man, you're big! You must bench some awesome weight." Vuch turned his face toward the bunk beds and smiled.

"Thanks, Vuch." Vinnie ducked down and sat on the edge of his bunk, leaning his back against the wall behind his pillow. He propped one leg up so he could rest his arm on top of his raised knee, his other leg was hanging off the bed, the heel of his foot resting on the cool floor. One of Meat's legs pulled up onto the bed, then a second later, it was dangling back in the air. Meat jumped down off the upper bunk with a loud thud. He had to catch himself as his momentum propelled him across the room, almost falling onto Vuch, who was still lying on his bed scratching the top of his other foot.

"Jesus, Meat! Get the fuck away from me!" Vuch put his arms up to block, as the huge guy came at him. Meat stopped himself just short of the edge of the bed. He stood there staring blankly at Vuch, still half-asleep. "God, get that fuckin' uncut sausage otta my face!" Vuch's voice raised in pitch.

Meat still stood there blinking, expressionless. He then looked around the cabin, his eyes focusing on Vinnie. "Oh, yeah." Meat reached down and gave a tug to his hog. He turned around and walked slowly back to the end of the bunks. "Yeah, camp... right." The dazed look slowly left his face. He kept one hand down pulling on the hairs around his nuts. "Let's eat, 'kay?"

*   *   *

The guys finished lunch with only a few minutes to spare, leaving
the dining hall at 3:45. They raced back to the cabin and put on
training clothes as fast as they could. Being on the field at four pm
meant being already in half-pads and lined up. Time was expected to
be tightly honored at all football camps. If one member of the squad
showed up even a couple of minutes late, the entire squad could
expect to pay the price. Laps or step drills or push-ups would be
assigned as punishment — and you did not want to be the one to
cause everyone else the extra work, or life would be hell for quite
some time.

Vuch led the three as they hustled up the embankment to the
football field. Most of the entire camp were already there and in
their shoulder pads. They stood around in groups talking quietly.

"Hey, Billy, what's up?" Vinnie walked over and shook his hand.

"Manta. How ya doing? All set to make some sweat?"

"Yeah. I'm ready. Been ready since last December." Vinnie smiled.
"You guys gonna tape us up?"

"Later in the week. Full-pads and contact work only. You aren't
gonna need it these first couple of days." Billy reached into the pile
behind him and grabbed a set of large shoulder pads. "These should
fit. You got your helmet assigned already, right? Well, you don't
need it this afternoon anyway. Vuch! Kiriatis! Pads, guys!" Vuch
and Meat took the pads handed to them. Half-pads meant going in
shorts and a half-tee, the pads sitting over the shirt on your shoulders. Meat looked like a gorilla in his shoulder pads; thick black hair
completely covered his exposed stomach, and a forest of hair cascaded down both arms and legs. He looked menacing in a big way.
Vinnie was far more muscular than anyone else on the field, having
just the right combination of size and definition. While Meat appeared to be more fat in his size, Vinnie was pure muscle.

Vuch had a real lean, fast look about him — his tanned skin and
hairless torso gave him a beautifully sculptured appearance. His abs
were very tight and displayed the six-pack definition. Vinnie stood
off to the side and watched, as Vuch made the rounds and social-
ized. He had a few minutes to spare and wanted to greet his group-
ies. Kirby and Massella were standing with a shorter, muscley guy.
His hair was shaved completely down to nubs and it gave his head a

military appearance. His torso was real thick for his height. His biceps looked huge, even under the partial covering of the shoulder pads. When Vuch reached Kirby and Massella, he shook this new guy's hand enthusiastically. Vinnie did not remember seeing him on the bus. He must be a junior or senior. At his size, no way could he be a sophomore. Vuch looked around until he spotted Vinnie. "Vinnie! Come here, man!"

Vinnie walked over to where they were standing. He nodded in greeting to Kirby and Massella.

"Vinnie Manta, this is Tony Marino," introduced Vuch. "Tony here's a guard. Good size on such a short squirt, huh?" Vuch chuckled. "Tony, wait until you see my man Manta here tackle. He's a crushin' machine."

"Hey, Tony, how's it goin?" Vinnie held out his hand.

"Hi. Good. Thanks." Tony shook his hand.

"Marino's our third in the cabin," said Kirby.

"Us six lucked out in the smaller cabins, huh?" Massella said, as he adjusted his pads. "Kirb... pull this back strap tight for me, will ya?"

Vuch winked at Marino and flashed his trademark smile. Turning, he pulled on Vinnie's shoulder gear. "C'mon man, let's loosen up a bit, before we have to line up." Vuch walked off toward the goal posts that loomed over the end of the field.

Vinnie quickly turned back to Tony Marino. "Hey, guy, I'll catch ya later, huh?" Marino nodded, his eyes tightening. Vinnie jogged over toward Vuch, adjusting his shoulder gear as he moved. Vuch was already seated on the ground stretching as Vinnie approached. "Hey, Vuchie, that Marino seems pretty fuckin' solid, eh? I'll bet he packs a mean punch." Vinnie hit the ground hard, then moved his butt around to get comfortable, as he outstretched his right leg. Vuch leaned forward, lowering his torso between his legs, stretching out his lower back.

"Yeah, Marino can be a mean fuck! But he's a decent guy. Just watch out for him sometimes, he's a wicked horny bastard, and he's been known to jump just about anything that'll move." Vuch looked up from the ground and rolled his eyes. "Massella used to joke that even his dog wasn't safe around the Marino-man!" Vuch returned to his upright position. Vinnie got to his feet and started doing some side-stretches. "Yeah well, there ain't no babes up here to poke anyhows. If you're horny, ya just gotta spank the monkey. What the fuck else, ya know?"

Vuch finished his stretching and sprawled out on his side. Holding his head up by leaning on his arm, he tore a long piece of grass free, and placed it in his mouth. He swirled the blade of grass around between his teeth. "No, bro', ya ain't got it. I said he'd jump just about anything. That includes us." Vuch let out a laugh and fell onto his back. He clasped his hands behind his neck and focused on the clouds that were visible behind Vinnie's head.

Vinnie stopped his movements. He squinted his eyes, his teeth involuntarily clenching. "What the fuck are you talkin' about?" his voice raising slightly.

"Just what I said, guy. No big deal. He just humps anybody and everybody. End story." Vuch's gaze shifted, as he followed a cloud across the field.

"You mean he fucks around with guys?" Vinnie's voice got higher.

"Girls, guys, long-lost little sheep..." Vuch laughed again.

"How the fuck can you find this so fuckin' funny? You're sayin' there's a freakin' freak, queer-ass here in the camp!" Vinnie kicked at the ground with his cleat. "Jesus, man, how can ya laugh at that?"

"Hey, cool it guy. It ain't no big deal. I told ya, he's a great guy. He just leads by his dick, that's all." Vuch jumped to his feet. He ran at Vinnie, playfully charging his right shoulder, the impact causing Vinnie to almost lose his balance. "Besides, he ain't gonna go for your sorry hairy ass, anyways." Vuch laughed harder, punching him again in the shoulder.

Vinnie smirked and relaxed a bit. Lowering his voice, he moved in closer to Vuch. "Yeah, okay, but like...Vuchie, I just gotta know..."

A whistle blew. It was Billy's warning. Four o'clock: line up immediately. The guys stopped their conversation and headed over at once. The field quickly got into lines, six deep. Seniors front, then juniors, sophomores far back; regular set-up for drills. Helmets were placed directly on the ground at the right foot. Even though they wouldn't be needed until the next day, some guys brought their helmets, placing them down as part of their uniform. Feet were spread slightly apart, arms directly down to the sides. Then they waited. It was a regular psychological ploy used by coaches all the time. Make the players stand and wait. Sometimes they waited a long time. Players waited until they, the coaches, were good and ready. A player does not, however, ever make the coaches wait.

Vinnie's face formed into a sneer... he loved this football shit. After about five minutes, the coaches walked up the hill, clipboards in hand. Coach Morrison, the head coach, led the procession.

Directly on his heels were the offense coordinator, Guy Mitchell, and the defensive coordinator, Paul Hayes. Behind them walked the two drill coordinators, Bob Mullavey and Teddy Pina. Bob and Teddy had been assigned the sophomore charges. Each one had to govern a few of the sophs' cabins. Vinnie knew that although they were in flunkey positions, these two guys could be relied on to help with anything, if you got a problem. Drill leads were tough sons of bitches on the field, but they got to know the players pretty personal like, and often would go to bat for you if you needed them. Coach Morrison stood directly center, facing the players. The other five coaches stood lined up behind him.

Morrison stood silent for a minute, just surveying the crowd of players. "So, you want to be football players, eh?" His voice was loud and gruff. "Chip Tollini!"

"Here, coach!" A tall red-haired guy from the front row stepped slightly forward. He stood motionless, as if at attention in the army.

"So, Tollini, you're the captain of this sorry bunch, eh? Well you got your work cut out for you, now don't you?" The coach looked down at his roster on the clipboard. "Yeah, you do, Tollini. You have your work cut out for you." The coach looked back up at the players. "Tollini, how many recruits we got ourselves here?" His voice grew louder.

"Ninety-three, coach!" Chip Tollini yelled back at him.

"Ninety-three. Ninety-three. We'll see how many survive, eh, Tollini?" The coach began to pace across the front row, still keeping his distance. "Who's your quarterbacks, captain?"

"Tony Carvuccio and John Kirby, coach!"

"And who are your tackles, captain?" The coach turned at the end row and began to pace back across in the opposite direction. Chip Tollini straightened, as if tense. He squinted his eyes in thought for a second. "George Kiriatis, senior, Vinnie Manta, senior, Brent White, senior, Pete Taglienti, senior..." Chip paused in thought, "Aaron Carney, junior, Joe Ruggi, junior, Marc Espensio, junior, Greg Alasambra, junior, Mike Nismont, junior, John Pietro, junior... coach!" He looked slightly relieved he had gotten through the list.

"Back in line, Tollini! You seem to know your squad. That's good. Every captain should know his squad. Who's your co-captain, Tollini?"

"Mike Massella, senior, linebacker, coach!" Chip responded in a louder voice trying to match the level of the coach. The coach stopped pacing and moved back into his center position. He looked back at his clipboard, flipping through some of the papers attached. Without looking up he suddenly screamed at the top of his voice: "Hit the ground!"

The senior lines immediately dropped their full weight onto the grass, placing their hands before their chests as they toppled, to catch the brunt of the contact. It took most of the junior lines half a second to respond, then they also dropped. The sophomores looked back and forth at each other and tried to figure out what to do. Within a moment, they knew what was going on, and fell to the grass. The coach dropped his clipboard on the ground and folded his arms across his chest. He started to pace across the front line again, this time moving in closer — to within inches of the faces of the players. He spoke loudly and powerfully.

"When I say hit the ground... I mean **hit the ground!**" he screamed. His foot came within a half inch of Vuch's face. "Back on your feet!"

Everyone scurried to a standing position again. The coach moved in right to Vuch's nose — Vuch continued to just stare ahead. "Carvuccio, when I say 'hit the ground!' when do you do it?" His breath was hot on Vuch's face.

"Immediately! Coach!" Vuch shouted back at him.

"That's it, Carvuccio. Very good." The coach turned away from him and walked back center. "Hit the ground!" he yelled again. This time everyone in the squad went down at once. "Back on your feet!" Everyone scrambled up. The coach picked up his paperwork and did not even watch this last drill, he knew they would respond — immediately. He turned back to Tom Walter and handed him the clipboard, then returned to face front. "At dinner tonight, you will be issued the daily schedule," he boomed loudly. "You will follow this schedule to the letter. You will be up and awake and on this field at 5:45 am. Sharp. I want this understood now! You will be here lined up and suited as required for morning drills at 5:45 on the nose. Not 5:50, Manta! Not 6:00, Kirby! Not 5:46, Taglienti! 5:45! One minute late... and you won't be very popular with your ninety-two friends here! So, I suggest you go nightie-night at a decent hour. They're going to be long, hard days. In order to survive... get your sleep! The schedule you pick up will list the required uniforms for each practice of the day. Read it! Learn it! If you are dressed improperly for a practice, your buddies here will be penalized, while you go get into the correct suit-up! We will run drills from 5:45

until seven. We will break into offense and defense at that time. We will run tackles and blocking for a half hour. At 7:30 we will run laps on the camp course — you'll get to know that layout shortly. We will break for breakfast at eight o'clock. I suggest you make use of your first break by getting some food for energy. If you choose to rest, make well sure you eat something, I don't want anyone passing out on the field here before noon. Got it? At 9:30 you will be back here lined up in full-pads — we'll break down for contact drills and runs at that point. At twelve noon you get a two-hour lunch.

"At two pm sharp you will again be here in half-pads and we will run plays. Your two drill instructors will take over at four and run you until six. You get your dinner after that. Pay attention to the schedule, some nights we're going to run plays in chalk in the auditorium. Be there. You will, for those of you panicking right now, have some nights free. If you have the energy, the assistants here will line up a couple of social things to do. They'll tell you more about that later. Some of you will just want to rest... you may be the smarter ones! Before I turn you over to the drills, anybody got questions?"

The squad was silent. Even the sophomores were smart enough to know not to ask anything right now. Any questions could be answered by the assistants later. "Good! Men, I hope for each of you that you do well and learn here. We are making a team! That means we work together. It may take a while to get our shit together and act like a team, but it will come — that's what this camp is for. To see if you can take it, and to see if you can be part of the whole. In ten more days... we'll have our answers."

The coach turned to the assistants and nodded. Without another word he walked off the field. Everyone continued to keep their heads straight ahead. Many sets of eyes, however, followed the coach off the field. The two drill leaders, Mullavey and Pina, started everyone right the first day. They drilled for two and a half hours straight — no break. Vinnie assumed they were trying to make a point about the serious work involved in the camp, as well as make good use of the short period they had on the first day. The beginning drills they had everyone run were pretty standard football issue. They started off with jumping jacks and basic stretching. They ran sprints up and down the field, non-stop for well over an hour. Vinnie began to feel the energy mount, as they repeated drill sequences over and over: Karioka cross-leg runs, Tennessee Walking Horse drills, Crossover side steps and then up/downs to a whistle. Then the squad repeated the line again.

Normally, these type drills are done regularly at practice, so most guys were used to them... but these instructors were brutal! Vinnie finished a sprint sequence at the end of the field. It would be a few minutes before his rotation began again. He bent over and placed his hands on his knees breathing heavily, swiping at the sweat on his forehead. Vuch ran past him and slapped him on the back, then continued to run off. He turned back toward Vinnie, the big white smile across his face. "Fuckin' A, huh Manta!" He ran out of voice range. Vinnie straightened up and walked back into waiting line to run the next series. There were still a good twenty guys up before his turn.

The guy in line in front of him turned around and looked at Vinnie, but still paid attention to the movement of the line. "You're Vinnie Manta. I'm Pete Taglienti, the guys call me Tag. Also a senior tackle. How ya doin?" Taglienti turned his attention back to moving up in line, then turned to face Vinnie again.

"Okay, thanks."

Taglienti moved up a few more feet. "I heard of your reputation. Hope you can live up to it. You're offense, right?"

"Yeah." Vinnie was trying to concentrate on the action of the drills and was turned away from Taglienti. His face tightened into a sneer. He turned back, and noticed Taglienti was watching Vinnie's face and not paying attention to the line. Vinnie slapped him on the back and gave him a push. "Move, man. Christ, pay fuckin' attention!" He pushed him again. Taglienti moved and spun his head back around at the same time. He collided with Kirby who was passing back the other way.

"Aw, sorry, Kirb," he mumbled. *Fuck*! He looked back at Vinnie and growled, as he got down in position to run. He took off in the sprint. Vinnie saw the look Taglienti had given him, and flipped him the finger as the guy ran past.

* * *

By the time the drill instructors called dinner break, all the guys were worn down. It would definitely take a few days to get back into the routine of daily workouts. Vinnie walked over under a tree at the edge of the field and sat down and pulled his cleats off — his feet were fucking killing him. He pulled one foot over, rested it on his thigh and worked the sock down his calf and off the end of his toes. He massaged the sore foot roughly.

"Whatsamatta, Manta? Can't take it already?" Massella said with glee in his voice, as he walked over and dropped himself down next to Vinnie.

"Screw you, man. I ain't even got started yet!"

"Me neither, Vinnie. You ain't seen nothin'." Mike turned and looked directly at Vinnie's face. He broke into laughter and fell backward, sprawling himself flat on the grass. "Jesus, I can't do it! It's fuckin' brutal! Aaaaa!"

Vinnie turned his head and looked down at Massella. "Mikey, you wimp! You faggot! Get up and run two laps! I won't hear any talk like that."

Massella lifted his head and looked in disbelief. Vinnie was rubbing his foot and had a look of pain across his face. "You feel the same way, eh Vinnie?"

"Fuckin' right, man. My feet can't take this anymore! It *is* fuckin' brutal. Aaaaa!" he mimicked Massella.

Vinnie and Mike Massella walked into the dinner hall together — screw Vuch's theory of waiting until the line went down. They were hungry and needed food now. They had piled their pads back into the equipment area, and decided to go right into the hall in their shorts and half-tees. Fuck the sweat. Fuck the smell.

Massella spotted Vuch, Meat and Kirby already in the food line. "Those shits! Hey, Vuchie! Cut us in!" Massella motioned for Vinnie to follow him. They walked over to where Vuch stood with his tray. Massella turned to three sophomores who stood behind Meat. "Fuck off, sophs! This is our place in line." He looked at them with a blank expression, just waiting for them to put up an argument. None came. The three smaller kids stepped back and let him and Vinnie into line. "Good sophs. Good little sophs." Mike turned back and faced his friends. The line moved along quickly. All the guys were just grabbing food, no one was being picky.

Vuch led his group over to a long table. The only guys sitting at it were two small guys Vinnie had never seen before. Vuch stood over them, tray in hand. "Bye!" he said loudly. The two guys grabbed their trays and darted out of the chairs. "I do believe this table is free!" Vuch made himself comfortable in the end chair. He put down his tray and held out his arms pointing at either side of the table. The guys in the group all took seats.

"Man, my ass hurts! And it's only the first day," said Kirby.

"We all shoulda stayed in better shape through the spring and summer, man. I spent too much time hangin' at the beach," added Massella.

"Gentlemen, gentlemen. Give it some time. We will work these bodies back into the primo fightin' machines they were last year," said Vuch. "Remember the first day of camp last year? We was sayin' the same thing. And what did we say at the end of camp?"

"That my ass hurt," cracked Kirby.

Everyone started laughing. Tony Marino walked over to the table with his tray. He dropped it loudly on the table and slid into a seat.

"Marino, my good man, what you thinks of our little group of ninety-three misfits this year?" asked Vuch as he piled a forkful of spaghetti into his mouth. He continued to talk with his mouth stuffed, the words coming out garbled. "Tony here is good with the early predictions," he explained to Vinnie. Spaghetti fell out of Vuch's mouth as he talked. Vinnie eyed Marino cautiously.

"Nobody has speed. You see those sprints? Christ, let's get it together, huh," replied Marino. He gulped down half a glass of milk at once. "You see Jones and Peterson, those are the only two sophs I give any possiblity to. The rest are just pussies. No speed. No size. No thought in anything they do. The coach better not rely on new blood... cause they is gonna have their blood spilled all over the freakin' field... and I'm not being taken down with 'em." He stabbed at a meatball.

Vinnie nodded in agreement. "We got some big juniors here, though," he offered, relaxing with Marino for the time, and getting into the football talk.

"Yeah, you're right, Manta." Marino lifted the whole meatball up to his mouth. "Vuch, you notice the extra size Espensio and Nismont put on?" He shoved the meatball into his mouth, his cheeks bulging as he chewed it.

"Yeah." Vuch swallowed. "I've seen them over at Mike's Power Gym over in Glendale. They got real serious about liftin' all last year."

"Big tackles. We got ourselves a crew of big mother tackles," said Meat. He didn't look up, but kept a steady pace of shoveling the pasta into his mouth.

Vinnie looked up at the big dining-hall clock — 7:30. "We got anything scheduled for tonight? Playin' wise?"

"Naw. They let us just settle in the first night," replied Kirby. "Mikey, you gonna eat that meatball?"

"Yeah. Keep you fuckin' hands off it. Go get some more, you lazy bastard!"

Vinnie finished, and was just sitting there listening. "I'm gonna go back to the cabin and relax for a while. Let me know if you guys are gonna do anything." He picked up his tray and nodded to the group. "Later." He walked off.

The cabin had cooled off some, now that it was nearing sundown. Vinnie walked over to the window above Vuch's bed, stood in front of it and allowed the cool breeze to blow over him. He pulled his half-tee over his head, laying it over his shoulder. The air cooled against his chest hair. He ran his hand down across his chest and stomach. Vinnie had a fair amount of hair, but it wasn't the thick brush of hair that Meat had on practically every inch of his body. Vinnie's body hair was soft and not very curly. Most of the girls he'd dated had always liked running their hands over his chest. He often caught himself absentmindedly running his hand over his torso, whenever he wasn't wearing a shirt — and that was quite often, especially at home.

One of the things Vinnie enjoyed most was the privacy of his attic bedroom. Whenever he was studying or just watching television, he would sit around in just his jockey shorts. Ever since he was a little kid, he was in the habit of peeling off his clothes as soon as he got home. He knew here at the camp he would be able to relax and sit around the same way. In the presence of Meat, Vinnie might actually seemed overdressed in his underwear. He turned and walked away from the window, and hung his damp shirt over a wooden chair that was next to the door. Turning back to his bunk, he removed his shoes and flopped face down on the bed. He buried his nose in the pillow. He was really tired... but a damn good tired.

Vinnie awoke to the noise of the door being opened. Vuch and Kirby were laughing as they walked in. Vinnie turned on his side to face them, as the overhead light was flicked on. "Hey, what time is it?" he asked, as he rubbed his eyes.

"9:30, bro." replied Vuch. He tumbled onto his bed. "Kirb, pull up a chair or somethin'."

"Manta, you been asleep?" Kirby sat down on the floor and leaned against the leg of the desk. He propped an arm up on the seat of the desk chair. "You better be able to sleep later, man. Five am comes pretty fuckin' early."

Vinnie scratched his balls through his shorts. "Man, I could sleep another eight hours, no problem. I didn't sleep much last night, ya know?"

"Me neither, never do the night before we leave for camp. Too excited, I guess," said Vuch.

"You know, I swear it's the mountain air or somethin', but I sleep like a baby up here," added Kirby.

"Kirb, that's just cause ya draggin' ass. That's all."

Vinnie got up off the bed and stretched. He brushed his hair flat against his forehead with his hand. "Where's Meat, Vuch?"

"Don't know. He wandered off somewhere. He goes for walks or somethin'. I don't know. Haven't seen him since dinner."

"I tell ya, man, Meat's gettin' stranger every fuckin' year." Kirby rubbed his eyes with his hands. "I swear, it's the juice or somethin', but he's not only gettin' bigger and meaner, he hardly talks anymore." Vuch looked over at Vinnie. Their eyes met, and Vinnie understood what Kirby was talking about.

"How much juicin' he doin?" asked Vinnie.

"I don't know. And anyways, it's his business. Alot of the team have been known to take a steroid or two. It's no big deal. I stay out of his business," said Vuch firmly.

"Man, I'm gonna get going. I'm gonna wash up and shit, and then probably just sack out." Kirby got to his feet. "Guys, listen, whichever cabin gets up first tommorrow, let's check the other and make sure we're all awake. Okay?"

"Yeah, good idea, Kirb." Vuch half sat up on the bed and started unlacing his shoes.

"Gentlemen... sweet fuckin' dreams." Kirby headed out the cabin door, slamming it loudly behind him.

Vinnie continued to look at Vuch, watching him finish with his shoes and then toss them across the room. They landed against the corner dresser. "Vuchie, you do any juice?"

"Naw, I thought about it sometimes, but I haven't done nothin' yet. I might sometime this season, though. I don't know. I don't have anything against it or nothin'." He undid his shorts and lifted his butt off the bed so he could pull them down his legs. He dropped them down on the floor next to him. He reached back and tugged at the pouch of his white undershorts.

"I done some," said Vinnie. He sat back down on the edge of his bed facing Vuch. He pulled one leg up under himself and sat on his foot.

"Seriously? Wow. Whatcha take? Didn't the needle hurt, man?"

"I only took orals. I took some Dianabol to put on some size. I also did some Anavar, but that's a cuttin' drug, not good for strength or size."

"No shit! Wow! How long did you do 'em?"

"Just one cycle. About sixteen weeks. But I'd do them again. Not the Anavar, but the Dianabol. Real hard to get though, ya know."

"Would you ever do injectables?" Vuch's eyes were wide with interest.

"Yeah, I guess so. Yeah, I would. But Meat must be stackin' alot a shit to get the moodiness and irritability."

"What's stackin' mean?"

"Doin' a lot of different kinds all at once. You can get good results, but man, watch out for the bastards doin' that! Mood city!"

"Well, I don't think Meat is much more moody than he was before. As I said, most guys don't know him. He doesn't say much unless he knows ya kinda well." They heard the sound of the door opening. "Hey ya Meatman! Where you been hidin'?" asked Vuch cheerfully.

"I been around," Meat mumbled. He walked over to his dresser and opened the bottom drawer. He pulled his shirt off and dropped it in on top of all his other clothes. Vinnie could smell his sweat all over the room. Obviously, Meat hadn't taken any time to clean up since practice. He tugged his shorts down. They stuck to his immense thighs, and he had to sit in the desk chair to get them all the way down to his ankles. He wasn't wearing any underwear, just the cup and his jock.

Vinnie glanced back over at Vuch, still just laying in his white underwear. "Vuchie, didn't you wear a cup at drills?"

"Yeah, of course. Man, I wouldn't chance havin' my jewels broke. I came back here and changed before dinner. What, did you go right from the field?"

"Yeah. I thought you did, too. Man, you musta hauled ass off that field today."

Meat stood up and pulled down his jock. He kept the cup inside the pouch and strung the leg band of the jock over his bed post. He then stepped back a few feet and came running at the beds, aiming to propel himself up onto the top bunk. Vinnie slid sideways, and moved back against his pillow and the wall — he wanted to keep out of Meat's way. Meat's large appendage flapped against his legs as he

69

ran and lifted himself up onto the mattress. The top bunk sagged for a second under his huge weight.

"That was amazing, Meat. You should join the circus. George Kiriatis and his amazing flying meat!" joked Vuch.

Meat layed face down on the bed, his bubble-butt rising high above the level of his back. "Fuck you." His final words of the day.

Vuch took his tee-shirt off and laid it over the knob of his bedpost. He lifted himself up on one arm and peered out the window. You could hear noise through the window, coming from the cabin next to them.

"What's going on?" asked Vinnie, as he got up from his bunk and walked over near Vuch's bed. He leaned over and looked out the window.

"Sal Cardone is over there wrestling Espensio and Nismont. Jesus, come on! Cardone may be quick, but he can't beat guys their size."

Meat started snoring.

"Vinnie, you mind if we call it a night? I'm kinda tired and wound up. I just wanna crash."

"No, that's cool. I gotta just step outside and take a piss. You want me to shut the light off now?"

"Will ya have enough light to get back in?"

"Yeah, look at that moon. Shit... watch," he turned off the overhead light. The room was still flooded with moonlight.

"Okay... night, Vinnie. Don't fall in any ditches out there, man."

"'kay. Night." Vinnie opened the cabin door and stepped outside. The pine needles felt good on his bare feet. He closed the cabin door behind him and walked around to the side, standing between the window of their cabin and the window of the next. The light was still on inside Sal Cardone's cabin. From where he stood, Vinnie could clearly see Sal and Marc Espensio grappling in a choke hold. Sal was definitely losing the battle. They jousted around the inside of the cabin, falling into the edges of the bed and desk. A chair fell over as they tumbled to the floor. Sal got hold of Espensio's shirt and tore the side, as they tried to pin each other down. Espensio put all his weight over on top of Sal and pinned his shoulders. Sal had lost. They got to their feet laughing.

Vinnie reached down and tugged at his shorts. The button came undone and he worked the zipper loose. Rather than chance another post-piss leakage into his jock, Vinnie pulled the cup and jock down to his ankles with his shorts. He was going to make sure he drained every drop out this time, before he got dressed again.

A cool breeze stirred the hairs on his nuts. Reaching down, he pulled roughly on his testicles, loosening them up after the confinement in the hot plastic cup. His dick bounced freely in anticipation, as he awaited his piss stream to shoot. He loved this sensation. His calloused fingers held his cockhead tightly, as the urine shot out. He drained quickly. When he finished taking his leak, he took his time to adjust his dick back into place. He was in no hurry. The night air felt so good. He turned toward his cabin, so he could make the way back along the wall to the door.

From this position, he was now able to look into the window over Vuch's bed. The moonlight really did light up the whole inside of the cabin. He continued to look in for a moment. Vuch was lying on top of his blankets, his head tipped back on the pillow, his mouth open and emitting a low groan. He had slid his undershorts down to his ankles, although he had not bothered to totally remove them. His hands were rubbing his crotch area frantically. One hand pulled on his ball sack repeatedly, while the other was sliding up and down the shaft of his hard hog, twisting the skin on it back and forth in quick jerks. He wrapped his hand all the way around it tightly and started pumping the length in rhythm. His legs spread out wider, as he let one foot come loose from the confines of his tangled underwear. He then reached his free hand down under and past his nuts, searching below to massage the area where his butt hole began. His groans grew slightly louder. The pace of beating his dick increased, as his hand now flew up and down the shaft wildly. His fingers probed his butt deeper, responding to the increase in the tempo of his stroking. Suddenly, he arched his back up off the bed, raised his head and looked down at his pounding meat. White spasms shot out of the tip and flew up and hit the wall behind his head. The spunk continued to shoot, now spurting globs onto his hairless stomach. He settled back down on the bed breathing very hard.

5

Vinnie's alarm clock went off on schedule: five am on the dot. The loud clanging stirred him immediately, his hand shooting out to try and turn it off, as if it were on his bedside table. He was confused for a moment — his arm was only hitting air, no table was within his reach. The noise continued to blast. He raised his head and looked around trying to get his bearings.

"Shut that fuckin' thing off!" shouted Vuch from across the room. Vinnie sat up in bed quickly, his eyes darting around trying to locate the clock. Then he remembered. He had placed the alarm on the floor next to his bed. He bent down and tried to find where the noise was coming from. The clock was not where he had left it. "I'm gonna fuckin' break that thing, Manta, if you don't get it shut off... now!" Vuch's face was half buried in his pillow, his one visible eye glaring strongly in Vinnie's direction.

"I'm lookin'. I'm lookin'." Vinnie jumped up out of the bed. He kicked his undershorts he had dropped beside the bed as he got in the night before. No clock. He got down on his hands and knees and stuck his head under the bed. There it was. He reached in and pulled the clock out, finally bringing the bell to silence.

"Christ, Manta... I think the camp is awake now, thank you very fuckin' much!" Vuch sat up and scratched the top of his head. "Couldn't you have brought Big Ben? I think it would have been a little quieter."

"Alright, Vuch. I get the point. It's early... shut the fuck up about it, already." Vinnie shivered. The floor was cold against his knees. His dick shriveled a little from the temperature. He grabbed his underwear, put them on, and hopped back under the covers. He sat up in bed, allowing his bare chest to get used to the cold air first.

Vuch looked over at Vinnie. "Gee, it's early, huh?"

"No shit."

Vuch looked up and tried to see Meat's bunk from where he sat in bed. "Manta, is Meat movin' around at all?"

"Nope."

"Meatman! Get up!" yelled Vuch. No response. Vinnie pulled his right foot out from under the blankets and reached it up to the middle of the mattress above. He kicked against where the big sag was in the center. Still no response. "Vinnie, get up and shake him."

"You get up and shake him. I'm fuckin' cold, man. I'm sittin' in these blankets for a minute." Vuch pulled the blankets back and hesitantly got up out of his bed. He quickly walked across the cold floor. Vinnie noticed he slept in his jockey shorts and a tee-shirt. "See man, you got some clothes on. I'd be a lot fuckin' colder out there," said Vinnie as Vuch approached.

"Oh yeah, Manta, cotton underwear and a tee-shirt. Yeah, arctic-type clothing. You're a moron." Vuch reached the edge of Vinnie's bed, placed one foot on the mattress and boosted himself up so his face came up to the bunk level. He shook Meat. "Meat! Get the fuck up, man! Meat!" Meat stirred a little. "Christ Vinnie, this moose is sleepin' up here naked as a baby, no blankets or nothin'. Just lyin' on top of the bed bare-assed."

Meat picked his head up and turned slightly to look at Vuch. "Whaaa?"

"Up, Meat. It's mornin', man," said Vuch quietly, as he jumped back down onto the floor. He quickly retreated back into his bed. Meat sat right up and turned so his legs dangled off the side of the bed. He held onto the post of the bunk as he jumped down to the floor. This time he did not get flung across the room. He let go of the post, and turned around to face Vinnie underneath.

"Mornin'," said Meat.

"Yeah, hi Meat. Mornin'." Vinnie saw that Meat had a partial hard-on, the giant foreskin was mostly retracted back from the end, exposing the big red head of his dick.

Meat shook his dick and started walking toward the cabin door. "I gotta piss out somethin' fierce!" He pulled open the door and stepped halfway out, turning to the side — not bothering to go all the way out the door.

Vinnie heard Meat letting it go. "Yeah, that's okay, Meat, don't bother getting dressed. Don't bother going around the side. Just piss on our doorstep. No problem." Vinnie knew that he was speaking too softly for Meat to be able to hear him. He looked over at Vuch, who just shrugged.

"We have to be on the field in half an hour."

"Shit," said Vinnie. "This getting up is the one and only part of this I could do without."

"It's just your lazy summer ass talkin', man. By the day after tommorrow, you'll be jumpin' up."

"Especially if I keep kickin' the alarm under the bed. I musta done it when I came back in from outside last night."

"Whatever. But... we're up now!" Vuch threw the blankets off and jumped up onto the floor. He looked at Vinnie expectantly.

"Oh, alright!" Vinnie slowly got out from the blankets and stood up. "Happy?"

"Yeah, bro... it's a new day. Football day!" He mussed Vinnie's hair with his hand. The short hair didn't move much.

"Don't do that." Vinnie already had a sneer on his face. Vuch smiled his white grin. His teeth were slightly coated from sleeping, but he still had a cheerful look. "Are you always this peppy every fuckin' morning?"

"Yeah man, and I like to share it. We're playing ball. Come on, Vinnie, we're playing football!" Vuch walked with a bounce over to the dresser.

"I hate to clue you Vuchie, but we're runnin' drills. And then, when we're done doin' that, guess what? We're runnin' more drills. We won't be playin' ball for days more, man." Vinnie walked slowly over to the dresser. He leaned an arm on Vuch's shoulder.

"Drills... playing... it's still all football!" Vuch turned and looked directly in his eyes and smiled again.

"Okay, it's all football. Let's get goin'," said Vinnie. He still had a sneer as he pulled out some clothes. "And, Vuch..."

"Yeah?"

"Your breath could kill somebody."

* * *

Twenty minutes later everyone was lined up in position. Fortunately, all the new guys had taken the warnings to heart and were all there on time — in correct uniform. Sleepiness was still visible on many of the faces. It was also apparent that no one had taken the time to shower or do much about their appearance. Being there on time, in line, was quite enough to expect. The squad stood silent and still, as the group of coaches walked up the hill to the field.

The coaches stood in the same formation as the previous day. Coach Morrison stood center, his clipboard in hand, his whistle now hanging about his neck. "Well, girls, today we start working. It's gonna be a hell of a day! We'll see what you are made of, we'll see what you can take. Those of you itchin' to actually play ball will be happy to hear the following announcement. This year in addition to the end of camp game we play against Revere, we've arranged for some scrimmage action with them. They have some field problems this year, so they're gonna come by and run some plays against us at the beginning of next week. The rival camp game against Revere is going to be on Saturday. See the assistants for more information on that. Tonight will be the first of several nights we run chalk plays in the auditorium. That means everyone is there at eight pm sharp! We'll break for dinner right at six tonight. When we break for breakfast this morning, you can pick up a written schedule of how the days are gonna run. See Coach Walter to obtain that — everyone needs one."

Coach Morrison began his pacing across the front row. "I'm sure some of you new guys, and those of you who slacked off too much over the spring and summer, are already kinda sore from yesterday. You know who you are. We know who you are, too." He chuckled to himself and glanced back at the line of assistants. Tom Walter returned the grin. "You'll loosen up within a day, count on it," Morrison added. "I'll be turning you over to the assistants today, but I'll be here. I'm gonna be watchin' to see where your strengths are and where your weaknesses are." He stood up straight and his eyes searched over the entire squad. "Put everything you got into this, boys! You want to play football this year?"

Everyone yelled, "Yes, coach!"

"You're gonna have to show us what you're made of!" he yelled. "Coach Walter?"

Tom stepped forward. "Yes, coach!"

"Show me what these women can do!"

"Yes, coach!"

And so it began. The drills. Massella and Tollini led the stretching. Following a series of individual stretches with the group remaining in formation, the captains had the squad pair off to do doubles. Vinnie and Vuch paired together.

"Guys, hit the grass! We're gonna do seated stretches. Remember, loosen the muscles, don't try to pull them beyond where they can naturally go. Ease them," said Tollini.

Vuch and Vinnie sat on the ground facing each other. They extended their legs completely out, their feet pushing against each other. They reached out their arms and grabbed each other's hands. Leaning in toward each other, they pulled further on their arms and bent in, fully stretching out their lower back muscles. They held their stretched position for a moment. "Coach Morrison is just standing over offsides and watchin' every move everyone makes," whispered Vinnie.

"Yeah. He does this every year. He's evaluating," replied Vuch.

"Yeah, but stretches? He's evaluating how we stretch?" said Vinnie, in amazement.

"No. He's watchin' how we respond to commands. How quick, and everything." Vuch pulled harder on Vinnie's arms. "Easy, man... Yeah, better. I feel the stretch." Vinnie pulled harder on Vuch's arms, Vuch bending further into the center.

A whistle blew. Everyone stopped and turned toward the coaches. Massella dropped the whistle from his mouth. "Alright guys! Stay in the same pairs... standing stretches. Let's go... up!" Everyone hurried to their feet. Vinnie turned so his back was to Vuch, and raised his right arm over his head. Bending his arm at the elbow, he positioned himself so Vuch could grasp his elbow and slowly begin to stretch the muscles out.

"Hey, asshole... work the kinks out, don't rip them out!" said Vinnie in a low voice.

"Take it easy... you puss! I'm just workin' it to the point of resistance," replied Vuch. Vinnie switched arms. He could feel Vuch's warm breath on his neck. Vuch worked each area in the arm, concentrating on the muscles that gave him the most protest. They then switched positions, and Vinnie had his turn at Vuch. Upon completion of their arms, under Massella's guidance, they switched to legs. Each worked on the tight areas they found in each other.

Massella blew his whistle. "Alright, guys, you should be sufficiently stretched out for now." He turned to get his next instruction from Coach Walter. "Okay, captain. Thank you. Men return to line for sprints."

The squad returned to their original places. Tom Walter started the sprint sequence the same as the day before. For the next forty-five minutes, the squad ran a series of sprints up and down the field. Combinations again consisted of Cross-Leg Kariokas, Tennessee Walking Horse moves, Side-Stepping Crossovers and concluded with up-downs to the whistle. This last drill gave the group additional practice in being ready for Coach Morrison's unexpected whistle drills for up-downs. At the blow of the whistle, the entire field of men would hit the grass. At the next blow, they returned to their feet. The sequence was repeated endlessly. At seven am on the nose, the field was given a five minute break. The offense and defense would divide into their respective groupings when the action resumed.

"Man, I'm gonna start hurling if I don't get some fuckin' food in me soon," said Tony Marino, as he walked over to Vuch and Vinnie. Vuch was stooped over with his hands resting on his knees. He was panting, trying to regain control of his breathing. All he could do was nod in agreement.

Vinnie turned and gave Marino a grin. "Whatsamatta, Marino, can't take it already?"

"Screw you, Manta, I just need food. I'll still be kickin' ass out here, long after you have your sorry ass dragged back in the cabin." He grinned back at him and ran off to get back into formation.

Vinnie patted Vuch gently on the back and bent down to the level of his face. "Come on, roomie, we're up in offense." Vuch stood up straight, and the two sprinted off to the offensive area. The exhilaration of the game began to come together, once the offense and defense were separated. Although they would still be running drills for the remainder of the morning, anticipation was running high. They knew that once lunch was over, they would begin the long awaited plays. All the members of camp had been issued the playbook once the try-outs had been completed. Vinnie had immersed himself in studying the plays. He knew it would be well to his advantage if he had as much of the book in his head before camp as he could handle. The chalk plays at night would be a good review.

Vinnie caught up to Vuch as they circled the field in laps. "Hey, man, you been studyin' the playbook this week?" Vinnie panted, his heavier frame straining to keep up with Vuch.

"Yeah." Vuch slowed his speed slightly to accommodate Vinnie. "They made some major changes since last season. I hope they have a lot of review of the plays in the auditorium. They had us all confused last year until we ran the plays in wicked slow motion. That's the thing that makes the night work all worthwhile."

Vinnie dropped back and slowed his pace. He could feel the ache starting in his feet. He looked at his watch. They would be breaking for some food shortly. His stomach felt in knots from all the exertion without having eaten first. *Discipline. They were trying to instill discipline,* he thought. Guy Mitchell, the offensive coordinator, signaled for them to end the laps and line back up. Vinnie was relieved.

"Okay, guys," said Mitchell, "I know you're about to drop. This is how it's gonna work the rest of the day. We're gonna break for some eats now. You'll return here right at 9:30 in half-pads. Don't bother to line up field full for Coach Morrison. We're going to stay sectioned off from the defense for the rest of the day. When we get back together this morning, I want to do some short sprints just to get your heart rates back up. Then we split the offense line from the backs and receivers. I'll be working with the line, Billy Ruggiero will take the B's and R's. We'll do some slow motion work until lunch." Mitchell began to turn away and then added, "I suggest you eat now! In formation, your teammates will not appreciate your breakfast all over them, so give yourself some time to digest. Understand?"

"Yes, coach!" came the unified response.

"Okay, break. See you at 9:30." Mitchell started to head over toward the defense section. Vinnie immediately sat down on the ground and pulled his cleats off. He yanked his socks down and tossed them on top of the shoes.

"Feet hurt again, huh?" asked Vuch, as he stood above where Vinnie sat.

"Man, they're fuckin' killin' me. Those laps did 'em in."

"Let's head down to the water for a short while, before we eat. You up for it?" asked Vuch.

"Oh yeah. Christ, that's what I need. Cool water on these." Vinnie got to his feet, bent down and retrieved his shoes and socks. He walked with them in one hand, swinging his helmet off a finger of the other hand. The gravel along the walkway of the field felt good on Vinnie's feet after sweating so much in the double socks and cleats. The rest of the squad was hurrying past them to get to the dining hall.

Vuch slowed his pace, to allow Vinnie to keep up. "Man, you gotta soak them feet tonight," he said as he eyed the way Vinnie slightly limped.

"Yeah, whatever." Vinnie hated the attention on something that kept him behind anyone else. His face changed into a tight sneer. He looked around as they walked.

"You'll get to work more with some of the other offense tackles this afternoon, Vin. Ruggi and Hurley are big fucks, huh? Hurley can be an insane mother, too." They passed by the auditorium and started down the path that led to the beach area. The gravel changed to a soft moss. The cool, damp feeling of the moss felt great on Vinnie's bare feet.

"Hold up, man." Vuch sat down against a tree stump that was sticking up in the air. He pulled off his shoes and socks, then resumed walking. He tried to balance the shoes and helmet as they continued down the slope. "Shit, we shoulda left the helmets back up at the field. Hold on." Vuch paused and looked around. He walked over to some underbrush and set down his shoes and socks. He waved his hand for Vinnie to follow suit. "They'll be fine here. We'll pick 'em back up on the way to eat. No one will bother 'em."

Vinnie tucked his socks deep into the shoes and stashed them alongside Vuch's in the underbrush. They continued down the path, which now began to dip sharply downward. Vinnie could see the sun reflecting off the water through the dense leaves of the trees below them, the path winding along a high ridge. As they passed an embankment that was covered with old dead stumps, the water came fully into view. The path now turned into loose sand and gravel, and they had to proceed carefully, watching their footing on the rocks that stuck up out of the dirt. The beach widened out to their left. The sand was a nice clean quality. About two hundred yards down from where they stood, a dock led out into the water that ended in a platform, giving the structure a T-shape.

Vinnie stepped right into the shallow water. The cold immediately felt soothing. He walked along parallel to the beach, still swinging his helmet off the end of his finger. Vuch set his helmet down on the sand and pulled his half-tee off, dropping it on the sand. He waded into the water, trudging along knee deep, a few paces behind Vinnie.

"Workin' on that tan, eh?" called Vinnie from the lead. He continued to walk straight, but turned his head around to glance at Vuch.

Vuch smiled broadly. "Yeah, man. It's still summer. Gotta get dark."

Vinnie stopped in the water and pulled his own tee off. He tucked it into the waist of his shorts.

Vuch caught up to him. "I guess you're lucky to be naturally dark. That forest of hair must be a bitch to get the rays past." He laughed and plowed ahead of Vinnie in the water.

"Well, we can't all be baby smooth like you. Ya sure you're Italian? I ain't never seen a true Italian that hairless."

"I'm not. I shave it off. I have some hair on my upper body and stomach.... I just take it off."

"Why the fuck you do that?"

"I like the look. And believe me, the chicks love the feel."

"It sounds kinda strange. I can't see myself shavin' my body." Vinnie stopped and eyed him closely. "Ya really shave ya chest and abs, man?"

"Chest, stomach, and arms. Look, it isn't that queer. I used to go to a liftin' gym last spring. A lot of the guys there do it. I was trainin' with this guy who was gettin' ready for a competition — I used to shave him sometimes, cause some of the places are hard to reach, ya know? Anyways, he was always tellin' me I should compete in a few years and shit. I don't know, he just kept tellin' me how I had the genetics and stuff. One day when I was shavin' his back, he just suggested I'd look better that way. So I tried it. On my own, ya know? Anyways, I just liked it and kept doin' it."

Vuch started walking along again. Vinnie squinted at him, trying to understand what he was saying. He followed along in the water. Vuch added, "But, if I had that much hair, man, no way would I be able to shave it all. I have some, but not as much as you. Can you imagine Meat shavin'? God, it would take him like, all day, and probably three razors."

Vinnie caught up with him and walked alongside. He kept looking over at Vuch's hairless chest. It was so tanned. He had to admit it did look good — the muscles were so clearly defined. In his mind, he pictured Vuch with hair on his upper body. He decided it would detract from the appearance.

Vuch spun around in the water and started to head back. "Come on, Vinnie," he called. "I gotta eat. Let's get up to the hall, while there's still some food, eh?"

Vinnie squinted in the bright sunlight and watched him plowing back through the water. Yeah, he definitely looked better without hair.

* * *

The late morning session consisted of running some basic formations in slow motion. As was always the case, the best way to get the players able to run plays up to speed was to take them one step at a time. Even in slow motion, many of the guys were screwing up. The obvious reason was they didn't know the playbook at all. After a series of blatant screw-ups, Guy Mitchell called the line over for a talk. All the guys got down on one knee on the grass.

Coach Mitchell stood impatiently shifting from one foot to the other as he spoke. "Look... you guys are the offensive line! That means the entire play is based on your coordinating with each other and not getting in each other's way, for Christ sake! We're running rudimentary plays here, guys! This is not hard!" He ran his hand up through his hair, pulling on the top as he let it go. His eyes narrowed, as he looked to each face before him. "Okay, we're gonna try it all again. We best get some of this down. Coach Morrison wants some scrimmage action in the afternoon segment. Carvuccio?"

"Yes, coach." Vuch got to his feet.

"We're gonna do slow motion for a Pro-right, Sweep right."

"Yes, coach."

"Now, we're going to do this slowly. Got it... slowly. Line up in formation." The line got into the required pattern. "Carvuccio, run it once. Second offense, watch the sweep. On Two!" Vuch got into position. His hands ready for the snap from Sal Cardone. He looked left. "Blue 52!" He looked right. "Blue 52!... Hut! Hut!" The ball was snapped. Vuch dropped back, the line correctly moving to the right in a sweep. Guy Mitchell blew the whistle. "Good!" He walked to the edge, to where the line had stopped advancing. "Carvuccio, out. Peterson, in. McEvoy, replace Cardone. Let's run it again. Slow it down this time. One-quarter speed. Espensio and Nismont go in for Manta and Kiriatis." Vinnie and Meat looked at each other. "Now!" yelled Mitchell. They hustled to change positions.

Meat leaned over to Vinnie's face, as they came off the field. "Why the fuck is he puttin' in soph players for QB. I can see a junior like McEvoy in as second for center. But, come on... Peterson sucks!" His voice grew louder as he finished his analysis. Several of the guys around where Meat stood looked in his direction.

"Give the guy a chance, Meat. Besides, we ain't doin' nothin' complicated. We're just runnin' the simple shit."

"Yeah, well..." He lowered his voice so only Vinnie could hear. "Well, why get a guy like Peterson even in there, when he sucks at everythin', huh?" He snorted. Vinnie felt his mouth begin a sneer. *Let the guy try, for Christ sakes!* he thought. Now he was defending the lower players, just like Sal Cardone had been doing with the freshmen the week before. Vinnie looked down at the ground.

The line got into position. "Okay, again... on Two!" called Coach Mitchell. Peterson, the sophomore quarterback, looked nervously around. He got his hands in position for the snap. "Blue 52!" He looked left. "Blue 52!" He looked right. "Hut! Hut!" The ball was snapped. He cut back to the right and collided with the guard, before he had moved.

"Jesus!" whispered Vinnie to himself.

The coach blew the whistle. "Okay... Okay... Look, Peterson. You gotta drop back straight. Your guys are sweeping off to the right... you can't go ahead of them. Okay, look... Peterson back out...Vuch, in there. Run it again. Keep McEvoy as center. McEvoy, snap on two! Don't jump the gun! Come on, boys... run it again!"

The rest of the morning session was all running of slow-motion plays. The guys didn't tire out much, as the action was so slow; it was mainly standing around watching. Vuch was in for most of it, as he knew the plays well. Kirby was in when the coach wanted to try the second offense. It all progressed slower than was expected. As it approached noon, Mitchell went off to confer with the defensive coordinator and the assistant coaches. The offensive guys again knelt in a circle, and waited for his return.

"You sophs suck!" said Meat loudly. He directed his comment to no one in particular.

"Shut up, Meat. That ain't gonna help no one!" replied Vuch quickly — his voice had a definite tone of anger in it. Meat grew instantly silent. Vuch turned to where the sophomores were sitting. "It takes time, okay? You'll get it. Just pay attention," he said softly.

Peterson looked up and nodded, then looked back down at the ground and kept his eyes fixed. Coach Mitchell walked back up to the circle, and stood in the center of the group. "Okay, guys. We're going to break for lunch now. We're behind in formation drills, so this is what we're gonna do. You have to be back on the field at two o'clock. Eat, and then I expect you to spend some time studying the formations. We aren't gonna get to pass-plays until late afternoon. We need to get these formations down first, got it?"

The group nodded. Some voices loudly replied with "Yes, coach!"

Mitchell looked around the group. "When we are back together, I expect you to know the basic formation and moves for Twins, Traps, Dives and Counter... got it? So do some reviewing."

"Yes, coach!" This time everyone spoke up.

"Okay, guys... break. See you at two."

* * *

After lunch, everyone stayed in their cabins and read about or discussed the plays they would run in the afternoon. Vuch sat in the desk chair — already dressed in his football pants and lower body pads. His cleats and socks were neatly arranged beside his bed. He aimed the chair toward the window so that some of the sun came in and hit him on his bare chest.

Vinnie walked in from the outside, still in his morning half-pad uniform. He looked toward the bunks as he approached Vuch's desk. "Meat is asleep again? Man, shouldn't he be studying the plays?"

"Don't worry about Meatman. He's a natural. All last year I swear, he didn't review the playbook at all and he was never called for an error. He knows his shit. He listens."

Vinnie sat down on Vuch's bed. He leaned back against the wall and laid his legs out straight. He crossed his bare feet at the ankles, placing them next to where Vuch had propped up his feet.

Vuch looked up from his book. "Manta, you should see how black the bottom of your feet are. I think you're crazy for walkin' around without any shoes. It's probably gonna make 'em worse."

Vinnie bent one foot up and brushed some of the dirt off. Clumps of gravel fell onto Vuch's blanket.

"Hey, you fuck! Not on my bed, huh?" Vuch raised his voice slightly.

"Sorry." Vinnie swept the dirt off the blanket with his hand. "No, I think they're gettin' better cause I walk around like this. I'm gonna soak 'em tonight. Yeah, they're gettin' better," he eyed his foot, "you shoulda seen 'em last week." He extended his leg back out, crossing his ankles again.

Vuch flipped through the playbook. "Okay, explain a Trap to me." He looked up at Vinnie.

"Fuck that, man, I ain't stupid. I know my shit."

"You best know these. The coach was serious about us havin' to review."

Vinnie kept his gaze out the window. He tried to focus on what was going on in the next cabin. "Hey... I'm fuckin' good out on that field. You don't gotta worry about me, okay?" Vinnie turned his head back to Vuch. He looked carefully at Vuch's chest, lit brightly from the sunshine coming in the window.

"Vuchie, you got nubs on your chest, ya know that?"

Vuch looked down and ran his hand across his pectoral muscles. "Yeah, I know. Every few days when I don't shave it starts to show up. I'll shave it off tonight." He looked back down at the playbook, then tossed it onto the desk.

"Fuck this!" Vinnie got to his feet and walked over to the corner near the dressers. He pulled off his half-tee, and with one movement pulled down his shorts and jock. The plastic cup bounced off the side of the dresser, as he kicked the jock off from his ankle. He pulled slightly on his dick, to loosen it up after being confined in the cup. "Hey, Vuchie, we're the fuckin' best out there. Let the dipshits study... the pussies who screw up." Vinnie paused before he put on his pads for the afternoon session. He looked over at Vuch who was still buried in the book. "Vuch, ya think I oughta shave off the hair I got on my back? I mean, ya think it will look any better if I shave it off?" He turned around so his back was facing Vuch.

Vuch looked up. He rubbed his hand across his chin, then got up, walked over to Vinnie and ran his hand lightly over his back. "Yeah, man, you don't got too much on it, but it is dark and kinda noticeable. It would probably be better if ya took it off." He reached down and playfully pulled some of the hair on Vinnie's butt. "You could take some of that off too, if you want."

Vinnie laughed. "Fuck you! My ass stays like it is. How do I do my back, if I wanted to?"

Vuch walked back to the window and glanced out. "I'll do it for you." He sat back down in the desk chair and lay his legs back across the bed. "Later tonight. I have to do my upper body... I'll do your back for you at the same time."

Vinnie fished around in the dresser for his football pants. They were due back on the field in twenty minutes.

*　*　*

The afternoon was more of the same running of basic formations. Despite having the Football Playbook given out a week earlier, many of the rudimentary moves had to be worked through in slow motion. The sophomore players in the first offense seemed to have gained some confidence; their moves were more in line. After running the basics of the Traps and Counters, the defense lined opposite to give contact to some of the offense plays. Vinnie began to feel the intensity of contact again. His tackles were strong, his face gaining the look of intimidation that was his pride. By late afternoon the squad was dirty, but cheerful. They had begun to feel the unity within the team, and gave verbal encouragement as formations were set correctly.

At 5:30, Mitchell blew the whistle and called the guys back into their kneeling circle. "Okay. We saw some good things out here this afternoon." He shifted from one foot to the other again, but now had a tone of satisfaction in his voice. "You've demonstrated better abilities. That's good. Remember, we're playing off each other here, not against each other. Watch and work with the guys around you. Keep a mindset of where everyone is going. We're gonna need to work with that tomorrow, as we go into pass plays." He bent down and retrieved his clipboard, jotting down a note. "To finish this afternoon, I'm gonna have your captains run the whole field of players through the course we got set up here. It's an easy two-mile run through the woods and down onto the beach. I'll meet you down there for some water drills. You'll be up for dinner by about 6:15." He looked around to locate the captains. Massella was off with the defense. Mitchell's eyes found Chip Tollini. "Tollini?"

"Yes, coach?" Chip scrambled to his feet.

"You start these guys off on the course. The defense and sophomores will fall into place once the coaches over there see us start out. I'll meet you down by the water."

"Yes, coach! Squad... on your feet!" Everyone immediately stood. Tollini started the run, taking the lead out around the field. The team all fell into a line; the other players joining them as they passed by. Vuch sprinted out ahead of Vinnie, his lighter weight allowing him ease in his speed. Vinnie slowly trotted along, his 230 lb. frame pounding down on his feet with every stride. Chip Tollini took them off the edge of the field and down onto a grassy path that led into the woods. As the lighter players passed by, the squad fell into a pace with the heavier muscled players pulling up the end of the line.

Mike Nismont came up beside Vinnie and fell into his stride. "Hey ya, Manta, how's it goin'?" He glanced over at Vinnie and nodded, quickly returning his view to the ground and the uneven terrain.

Vinnie took a deep breath in, expanding his chest. "Good. Thanks, Mike. You?"

Mike ducked down to miss a tree branch as the path turned. "I'm feelin' great. Pissa day, huh? You seniors are playin' like you got all the plays already in your head. I'm still strugglin', you know?" Nismont stumbled with one foot and started to lose his balance, he put out one arm quickly to catch himself. Vinnie stepped sideways and let him fall against his shoulder, at the same time uprighting Nismont with his left arm. "Thanks, Vinnie." Nismont shot back upright and returned to the pace.

"You and some of the other juniors are real good. You're first offense, right?" Vinnie asked.

Nismont nodded, although they were both watching the pathway ahead.

"Yeah, you should be a starter. You got good size on you." Vinnie slowed a bit, his breathing more strained.

"You got the size, man. I gotta get a good twenty-five pounds on me to hit like you do. I saw the way you just pounded into the sleds today. Man, you got power!"

Vinnie half smiled. "Yeah, I guess. Thanks. Hey, anyways, where's this path go anyhow?"

Mike Nismont pointed with his chin. "We break out into the lake area just ahead. I'm droppin' back to the end of the line. Later, Vinnie, huh?" Nismont fell back a few guys, just as the water appeared through the leaves of the trees. Once on the beach, everyone had to pull off their shoes and socks. They remained in full pants, shirts and pads.

The two coordinators, offense and defense, stood together on the edge of the beach. Paul Hayes, the defensive coordinator, blew his whistle to get everyone's attention. "Okay!" he shouted, "Helmets on for the water drills. Since this is the last uniformed action for the day, I'm sure you girls don't have a problem with getting your pants all wet. I want two lines formed, one at each end of the beach area here. Offense, down to the dock area down here to the left. Defense, stay here at this end. I want you up to above the knees in water. Keep that depth. Lines run at each other, pass, and continue on to the opposite end. Then turn around and come on back. Run until we blow you in." He smiled and held out his arm in the direction of the docks. "Move offense!"

Everyone in the line moved down the beach on land. Guy Mitchell followed them down to their mark. It was a good two-hundred yard distance each way. Vinnie and Tony Marino were the first to walk into the water. Again, Vinnie immediately felt the relief of the cold water, although the temperature seemed quite a bit warmer than when he and Vuch had waded in before breakfast. Tony positioned himself almost waist deep, Vinnie stood right behind him. Due to Vinnie's height, the water on him only came to just above his knees. The rest of the offense fell in line behind them, many still standing on the edge of the shore, waiting for the front guys to move along before they had room to get into the water.

"Man, this is great," said Tony, as he turned back to Vinnie. "I hadda take a leak real bad. I just pissed through my pants here, and now they'll get rinsed out as we run!" He laughed fully out loud.

"Gee, thanks, Marino! I thought I felt a warm stream pass by me!" Vinnie flexed out his chest fully and tapped into the back of Tony, causing him to go down on one knee in the water. His face just touched the top of the water before he was able to regain his balance and stand back up.

"Hey, you fuck! Suck me, man!" Tony wiped his face through his helmet with the back of his hand.

"Drink that piss, Tony! Yeah, come on, take a deep gulp! Yum! Yum!" Vinnie laughed.

Tony turned back and smiled. "Suck my piss right otta my pud, Manta... come on, I know you want it!" Tony scooped up some water with the palm of his hand and flung it in Vinnie's direction. Vinnie ducked and laughed. *Yeah, Marino is okay*, he thought. The whistle blew. Tony turned forward and started trudging through the water. Vinnie fell in right behind him, as the offense started working their way back toward where the defense was starting out.

Promptly at eight everyone gathered in the auditorium for the first night of chalk talk. The only requirement for dress was that you had your helmet and shoes — most guys were in just shorts and tee-shirts. As the night was hot Vinnie wore his mesh top, without bothering to wear any tee underneath. The coaches had not yet come in, so everyone was just sitting around waiting. It was a very informal atmosphere, many of the squad sitting on the edge of the stage. Vinnie and Vuch, with some of the other guys, sat cross-legged on the floor along one wall. Vinnie bounced his helmet in his lap as he looked around at everyone. He reached up and rubbed his hair down his forehead.

Vuch lifted an arm and gave a sniff. "Man, I smell! We gots to shower up after this, huh?"

Vinnie turned and gave a grin. "Yeah. We ain't showered since we got here yesterday. We're gonna have ta get in the habit of showerin' at night, cause man, I ain't in no shape at five in the mornin'."

"Vin, you need it bad, man. I can smell ya over here. It's all that hair," said Vuch. He held his nose and squished up his face.

"Fuck you. I ain't got that much hair. Screw you, Vuchie."

The coaches filed in. Everyone started to get seated, mostly on the floor, giving the coaches room to gather in the center of the room. Coach Morrison took charge. "Alright, boys, those of you behind the chalkboard here, scoot around so you can get a good view." He paused while some of the guys shifted position. "Okay, we saw some good things on the field today. We saw alot of screw-ups too. Mostly, you seemed to pull it together better in the afternoon. I have to attribute that to the fact that Coach Mitchell here insisted on some playbook work in your free time. That's good. Defense, we still got a long way to go... you need the studying also." He paused and looked around at the group. His eyes seemed to meet those of each of the guys. "I want to instill the importance of getting the playbook down cold. Without your knowledge of the plays backward and forward, you're gonna screw up. And that affects everyone! You screw up, and others have to suffer the consequences! Understand?"

Most guys nodded, a few gave out a loud "Yes, coach!"

"Okay, let's run some plays on the board here." He began to draw out formations. Within an hour, the coach had the first offense line up and standing in place in the center of the room. The point was to run plays very slowly, miming the action. Each player moved slowly, walking through the motions and just touching the opponents. In this slower paced study, it was easier to watch how the movement of all the players affected the play as a whole. It was fun... and definitely a good learning tool.

* * *

The coaches finally dismissed the team at 10:15. Meat and Vinnie walked back to the cabin, Vuch stayed and talked to some of the defensive players, giving his opinion on some blocking moves.

Meat flicked on the light switch as they entered the cabin. He silently walked over to the dresser area and began removing his socks and shoes. "Meat, you gonna shower tonight?" asked Vinnie, as he pulled the mesh top off, folded it, and laid it on the chair next to the desk.

"Nope," grunted Meat. He pulled his tee-shirt off over his head.

Vinnie scowled. "Meat, it's been a long two days. I think we all need to clean up a bit, huh?" Vinnie could just imagine the odor Meat would have within another day.

Meat slammed his dresser drawer shut. He stood up straight, his eyes glaring at Vinnie. "You know... you fucks think you know me. And you think just cause I'm big... and just cause I'm hairy... and just cause my sausage is uncut... that I'm dirty and shit. Well, fuck you!" He pulled open another drawer of the dresser, the angry force pulling the drawer out of its track. The drawer slammed onto the floor, clothes spilling out everywhere. He stooped down to put them back into the drawer.

"Meat, I'm sorry... it's just that..."

"Fuck you, Manta! You guys don't know jack shit!" He picked up the drawer and slammed it back into the track of the dresser. It awkwardly hung down to one side as it closed, part of the side had broken off in the force. "If my showering is any of your business, which it ain't... I showered yesterday after dinner, and today before I ate dinner." He rubbed the stubble on his face angrily. "Yeah, you motherfuckers... I've showered twice since we got here. And how many have you taken? So fuck you all!" He pulled off his shorts and hung them on the bedpost of the bunks. He boosted himself up onto his top bunk, still wearing his jock and cup.

"Meat..." Vinnie stammered, "I'm sorry. You're right, it's none of our business. I'm sorry, man."

Meat gave no reply. He just lay on his back on the bunk staring at the ceiling.

Vinnie felt like a total asshole. Vuch had been right. Everyone based their judgements on Meat's appearance, and didn't give him any credit for being a decent human being. Vinnie dug in his gymbag for a towel. He slung it over his shoulder, grabbed the bag, and walked out of the cabin — slamming the door behind him. He was angry at himself.

It took his eyes a second to adjust to the darkness outside again. He waited on the step until he could see the path clearly. Next door he heard the shouts coming from Sal and some of the other guys.

They were horsing around like last night. As Vinnie started on the path that led past the auditorium, Vuch rounded the corner running. They almost collided.

"Manta, where you goin', bro?" Vuch smiled. He was in a very happy mood. He bounced around pulling on the branches of a pine tree. "You goin' to shower now?"

"Yeah. I gotta. I had to get outta the cabin, anyways. I think I just pissed Meat off somethin' fierce." He rolled his eyes and scratched his head. "I didn't mean to. It just kinda came out wrong, ya know?"

Vuch smiled again. He pulled off a small branch from the pine tree and wagged it in Vinnie's face. Vinnie pulled back from the branch.

"Yeah, that can kinda happen alot with Meat. Don't worry, he forgives and forgets easily. You'll see." Vuch turned back down the path in the direction Vinnie had been going. "Come on... I'll go too." He started bounding down the path taking large strides. He called back to Vinnie, "You don't mind if I share your towel, 'eh?"

Vinnie stood a moment watching Vuch drop down the descent of the path. He shook his head. "No problem, you mooch," he muttered to himself, as he started down the trail.

* * *

The showerhouse was lit brightly. They both squinted as they walked in. "Jesus. Let's have some light, huh?" said Vuch.

Vinnie smirked. "Yeah, it's a little bright after bein' outside... like walkin' into the fuckin' sunlight." Urinals and stalls lined both sides of the walls of the large room. Down the far end past the toilets, an opening led to a tiled area with sinks and mirrors. Opposite the sinks was a large wooden door. Vinnie figured this was the dry sauna.

"I gotta take a shit." Vuch walked into one of the stalls and slammed the door behind him. Vinnie walked in further past the stalls, and now could see where the room opened up into the large group-shower area. He could hear water running. He walked over to one of the white sinks that hung from the wall. He dropped his gymbag into the sink and unzipped the top of the bag.

Vuch made farting sounds from the stall. "Shit, I gotta load to come out, man," he yelled.

"Gee, Vuch, I really wanted to know that!" Vinnie pulled out a can of shaving cream and a razor from the bag. He turned on the next sink and splashed water across his face. Shaking the can of shaving cream, he sprayed some into the palm of his hand and began to lather his chin. The water that had been running in the shower area shut off. Vinnie started the razor down his cheek.

"Manta! How's it hangin'?"

Vinnie shifted his eyes in the mirror. From the side, he could see Sal Cardone standing in the drying area of the shower room. He was briskly rubbing a towel over his chest and stomach. "Hey, Sal. Okay, thanks." He returned his gaze to his shaving.

"Isn't this the balls? Showering this late, nobody is stacked up in here waitin' for their turn."

"Yeah," Vinnie responded. He started down the other cheek with the razor. Looking back toward where Sal was standing, he noticed the thick coating of hair that covered his butt when he turned his back to Vinnie. It covered each of his ass cheeks and went up in a line to the small of his back, where a large patch of curly hair grew. Above that point, his back was totally bare and smooth. The odd difference was quite noticeable.

Vuch flushed the toilet. A moment later, he came bounding out of the stall. "Sal, ol' buddy. Same idea as us, huh?"

"Yeah, Vuchie, get the showers while we can." Sal wrapped the towel around his waist, walked over to the edge of the shower wall and slipped some shower thongs onto his feet. "Vuch, ya made some good formation work today." He patted Vuch on the shoulder as he walked toward the door. "Can't wait 'til tomorrow, we'll see how ya throwin' arm did over the summer." He stopped and tied his towel tighter and opened the outside door. "See ya guys bright and early!" He laughed.

"Later, Sal," said Vinnie. He bent down and wiped the remainder of shaving cream off his face, then stuck the can of shaving cream and the razor back in his bag.

"Hey, no man, keep that razor out. We're gonna need it." Vuch kicked off his shoes and pulled his shorts and jock down. He tossed them all aside, and rubbed his hand up under his shirt. "Yeah, I gotta do all my chest and abs. Nubs, man, no good!" He pulled the shirt over his head. "Hey, you got any soap in there too, Vin?"

Vinnie shook his head in disbelief. "Vuch... ya want me to wipe your ass, too?" he sneered, as he fumbled through the bag for soap.

"No. Thanks for offering though, Vin," he said sarcastically. "I took care of that after I took my dump." He patted Vinnie lightly on the cheek. "Maybe next time though, huh?"

"Don't do that," said Vinnie impatiently. He kicked off his own shoes and started to get out of his clothes.

Vuch pulled open the sauna door and stuck his head inside. "Hello? Nope, nobody home." He slammed the wooden door shut. He walked into the shower room and started one of the sprays. "We actually get to have hot water, too. Man, if ya come down here during the time when everybody's here, ya run outta hot water after a while. That sucks!" He stuck his head under the shower spicket and dowsed his hair.

Vinnie walked into the shower room, shampoo and soap balanced in one hand, the razor in the other. He turned on the shower next to Vuch.

"Hey ya, Manta, not hung so badly, huh?" Vuch cackled and playfully reached toward Vinnie's crotch.

"Cut it out, you homo!" Vinnie tried not to smile, but one side of his mouth began to turn up. He pulled away from Vuch's reach and turned his back, letting the spray cascade down over his head.

"You don't have that much hair on your back, Vinnie." Vuch reached out and ran a hand down Vinnie's shoulder blade. "We can take it off, but it ain't much."

"Yeah, well... whatever." Vinnie grabbed the soap and started to lather up his chest and down his stomach. He pushed the bar of soap over his dick hair and worked it in.

"Give me a little soap."

Vinnie stuck out his hand with the bar. Vuch took it and lightly soaped his chest and ab area. He set the soap into one of the wall holders, then bent down and picked up the razor. Vinnie turned and watched, as Vuch began to carefully run the razor over his chest. "Don't you ever cut yaself? What happens if ya cut a tit off or somethin'?" Vinnie stood still and watched, as Vuch held his nipple area firmly and worked the razor around it.

"I ain't never cut myself badly yet. See, I just gotta be real careful around this area. The trick is to get the hair in the direction it grows. That makes me the smoothest." Vinnie continued to lather himself all under his crotch. He spread his legs apart and let the soap get up into his butt crack. Turning, he let the water rinse off the front part of him. "Vinnie, here, get my shoulderblade area will ya?"

"Come on, Vuch... I ain't never done that. I might screw up and cut ya or somethin'," Vinnie protested.

"Don't worry about it. Here. Come on. I can't reach it right."

Vinnie took the razor. Vuch turned around so his back was to him. Vinnie put one hand against Vuch's shoulder to hold it still, then carefully ran the blade over the top of his shoulder. He worked the blade in the opposite direction that the hair grew. It came off easily. He repeated the same to the other shoulder. "Okay, it's done." He slapped Vuch on the back to indicate he was finished. Vuch took the blade back and started to do his stomach. He bent partway over to get a good aim at the area. He ran the blade dangerously close to his dick hair.

"Hey, man... watch out, or you're gonna chop your hog off!" Vinnie rinsed the soap off his legs, spinning around a couple of times to get totally clean.

"I ain't gonna chop it off. Anyways, I got some to spare here, huh?" He looked up from shaving and flashed his big white smile. "Granted, not what you got there... but, I ain't had no complaints."

It flashed in Vinnie's mind how Vuch had pounded his meat the night before. He closed his eyes as he rinsed the shampoo out of his hair. The image of standing next to the window of the cabin and seeing Vuch wailing on his dick flooded his thoughts. He pulled on his dick forcefully under the stream of water, feeling it swell slightly. *No*, he thought, *I'm sure you haven't had any complaints.*

"Vinnie!" Vuch was saying loudly.

"Whaaa?" He turned back to Vuch. "Hey, man... you in another world? I been talkin' to ya."

"Oh, sorry." Vinnie removed his hand from his crotch and moved his head out from under the flow of water. He wiped his hand down his head, again flattening the hair to his forehead.

"I said... let me do your back now. Turn around." Vuch picked up the razor.

"You sure about this?" asked Vinnie hesitantly.

"Turn around, chicken shit. It don't hurt none."

Vinnie turned his back, and Vuch began to spread the soap across his muscles. "Hey, ya got real good definition here, Vinnie boy." He lathered up all across Vinnie's shoulders and down to his waist, and began to coat the hair of Vinnie's butt.

"You slide that soap up my ass Vuch, and I'm gonna shove my fist down ya throat! Got it?"

"Oh, I'm really scared! Shut up you fag, that's not what I'm doin', alright?" He began to slide the razor against the hair on the shoulderblades. Vinnie tensed. Vuch moved a bit closer and wrapped his arm around Vinnie's front, placing his open hand against Vinnie's abs to hold him steady. "You can't move around while I'm doin' this, okay? That's when I cut somethin' important off, see?"

"I don't know about this, Vuchie... it feels strange." Vinnie tried to move away, but Vuch's hand held him firmly.

"Manta, take it easy. It's no big deal. Nobody's around, calm down." He continued to wipe the blade down Vinnie's back. "This is comin' out good. Just stay put." Vinnie shifted his weight onto the other foot. He could feel the tightness in his back from being uneasy. He consciously tried to relax.

Vuch released his hand and rinsed the blade under the shower. He stooped down and sat back on his heels, the height of his face in line with Vinnie's waist. He ran the razor across the small of Vinnie's back; the hair skimmed off and stuck to the sharp blade. Vuch rinsed it again.

"I thought you said you were just gonna do some of my back."

"I am. I am. Don't worry, I'm almost done." Vuch spoke through gritted teeth, his concentration on the movement of the razor.

"Hey, why ya puttin' ya hands everywhere. Stop movin' 'em around. I can't tell what the fuck ya doin'."

Vuch moved the path down across Vinnie's butt cheek; Vinnie pulled sharply away. Vuch reached out around him and grasped his stomach again, pulling him back into position. This time, as Vuch opened his hand to secure hold of Vinnie, his fingers fanned out down into Vinnie's dick hair. "This'll be it. Come on, Vinnie, just hold still another minute." Vuch had a plead in his voice.

"Vuchie... hey! Vuchie, what ya doin' down there? Just my back hair, right? Hey... right?"

Vinnie closed his eyes. He felt the pressure of Vuch's hand against his crotch area. He tipped his head so the shower stream would flow down over his face. This was fuckin' intense! He felt a slight swelling in his hog again.

Vuch finished the other cheek of his ass. "Okay, Manta... all done! Good job if I do say so myself!" Vuch laughed and dropped the razor to the floor. He shoved himself under the hot stream of water and started to rinse off all leftover traces of soap. He smiled widely, eyeing his work. Vinnie rinsed quickly, then shut his shower off and walked over to where he had hung his towel. He dried himself as he walked out to the mirror area by the sinks. He turned his back to the glass, and cocked his head around to view his backside. All traces of hair had been removed. He ran his hand lightly over his butt — everything had been carefully shaved.

Vuch stepped into the sink area. "Lemme use that towel when you're done, okay?" He walked over to where Vinnie stood. "Smooth as a baby's butt, huh?" He laughed and patted Vinnie's ass lightly.

Vinnie whipped his head around, glaring at Vuch. He felt a head rush of anger. "You fuck! You stupid, faggot fuck!" He grabbed his towel from Vuch's shoulder and stormed off to where he had left his clothes.

Vuch watched as his hair-free butt swaggered away. "Christ!" he called out, smiling brightly. "Try to give the prick a compliment!" He fell against the tile wall laughing.

6

"Aw, c'mon Vinnie! Jesus, ya can't fuckin' really be that pissed about it." Vuch whispered loudly in the dark. "Vinnie... c'mon!"

Only the rustling of Vinnie's sheets responded to his plea.

"Vin!" he raised his whisper in volume. "I think it looks pretty much better anyways." He laughed a bit, trying to keep a serious tone. "No, really... aw, c'mon... I was just clownin' around, Manta. Jeez."

Vinnie had been ignoring Vuch since they'd returned from the showers. Once back in the cabin, he had quickly gotten undressed and climbed into his bunk. In the last couple of hours the temperature had shot up at least ten degrees and the humidity was high. His anger at Vuch had grown in degrees along with the thermometer. Vinnie pulled the sheet over his shoulder, as he turned on his side and faced Vuch's bed. "Christ, Vuch... a really funny joke... asshole." He kicked at the sheets with his foot in anger. "Fuck, it's hot!"

"Okay, okay... I shouldn'ta done it without tellin' ya first... I admit that... but hey, it really was just a fucking joke. I don't see why ya gotta be mad at me."

"I just feel fuckin' stupid lookin' like this now, ya know? Yeah, I guess me and some of the guys at Allentown have held down a soph or two and shaved 'em down... but, I thought we's was friends, Vuchie. I didn't think you'd do anything like this to me." Vinnie continued in a tone that showed he was feeling sorry for himself. He again kicked at the sheet, wrapping it around his foot and pulling it down his torso. He tangled the crumpled sheet around both ankles. Even totally uncovered, his body was overheating. Not so much as a breeze was coming in through the window above Vuch's bed. "I just think I look fuckin' stupid."

Vuch propped himself up on one elbow, straining to see Vinnie through the darkness. He could only slightly make out his form on the bed. "No, Vinnie... honest, it don't look bad, man. Honest, I wouldn'ta done it if it had looked bad, honest, buddy... I wouldn't." He spoke in a quieter, calming voice. "Besides, bro', who's gonna be seein' ya ass anyways. Probably just me and Meatman."

"Yeah, ya got a point there, Vuchie. But don't fuckin' pull anything like this again! I'm just irritable in this fuckin' goddamn heat!" He kicked violently at the sheet, now sending it flying off the end of his bunk. He tossed himself up in the air for a second, then crashed back onto the mattress. His chest hair was matted down with sweat.

"It is pretty fuckin' sticky, huh?" Vuch lowered his head back onto the pillow. "I think I'll be able to sleep only cause I'm so dead tired."

Vinnie wiped his hand down his chest and onto his stomach; it dripped from the pool forming on his body. He flicked the liquid from his fingers. "Night, Vuchie," he whispered into the darkness, turning onto his opposite side. His eyes focused on the blank wall in front of him, as he waited for Vuch to respond. Within a few seconds he heard Vuch's breathing change rhythm. He closed his eyes and tried to bring on sleep.

Vinnie awoke some time later in the darkness. The night heat had gotten worse. His face was mashed into the pillow as he lay on his stomach. Vinnie could feel the layer of sweat that ran fully down his back and onto his newly shaved butt-cheeks. He bucked his hips into the mattress below. His dick was fully erect and warm. Sighing, he flipped onto his back, opened his eyes and focused on the sagging form that lay in the bed above him. He turned and raised himself up and sat on the edge of the bed, his bare feet finding even the boards of the cabin floor warm. He sat still and listened to the sounds of the night.

Meat's familiar snoring was coming in the usual waves from above. Turning his attention across the room, Vinnie could hear Vuch's heavy breathing, signaling his deep sleep state. "Well, at least some of us can get some rest," he whispered to himself. He reached down and scatched his wet balls, causing his hard hog to slap against the slippery hairs of his stomach. He wrapped the fingers of his right hand tightly around the shaft and slid it up and down a few times. The callouses on his fingers gave a good, tough sensation that ran through his dickhead. Sighing again, he stood up and stretched in the darkness. Thrusting his chest out, he arched his back and yawned. His hand unconsciously stroked his dick a few more times as he padded over to the window. He peered out into the stillness, keeping himself balanced over Vuch's bed, one arm propped against the window frame holding him in place as he gazed out. Vinnie smiled to himself as he looked down and saw his full standing cock hovering over Vuch's closed eyes. He immediately stepped back, fearful that Vuch might awaken in the night heat and get the wrong idea. He walked slowly into the center of the cabin, the humid air causing more sweat to break out. He felt a trickle begin down the inside of his thighs.

"Fuck this!" he said out loud. He stepped over to his bed and retrieved his undershorts that lay piled next to the alarm clock. He gazed at the dial — 1:10 am. "Fuck," he mumbled. Clumping the shorts in his fist, he opened the cabin door and went out into the night, his dick springing freely as he bounded down the path toward the beach. By the time Vinnie got to the edge of the lake, his hog had deflated to a semi-erect state. "Fuckin' mother heat, man!" he yelled out across the water. He used the underwear in his fist to swipe down over his torso, removing most of the sweat. A slight breeze came off the lake, giving a cooling feeling to the matted hair on his body. "Yeah!" he whispered, relaxing in the pleasure of the wind. Tossing the shorts on the sand, he waded out deep into the water, plunging his hair under the surface, then throwing his head back. The cool water flowed down over the muscles of his back. He closed his eyes and stood still. Off in the distance, he heard what he figured must be the hoot of an owl. "Come on in, guy!" he shouted out to the unseen bird. He chuckled as he dipped himself under again, then standing, he dove in deep and swam out further into the lake.

* * *

Vinnie lay back and floated on the surface of the water, slowly moving his hands to paddle himself gently along. The moon was bright overhead, the lake expanse sufficient to allow light without being blocked by trees. He gazed at the reflection of the light as it danced on the surface of the ripples. His eyes scanned down his body as it bobbed partially submerged. Laying in the floating position, his body hair would soak wet, then clear as he breathed in and allowed his torso to rise up slightly out of the water.

His gaze focused on his dick, the large head jutting up out of the depth of the water. He reached down and slapped his hog roughly.

Again it expanded in immediate reply to his assault. He smiled to himself as he watched his hog grow up across his stomach again. Suddenly Vinnie's attention was diverted back to the path along the shoreline. He first heard voices laughing, but as he scanned the land, he could not immediately make out any forms. He swept his arms under the water, spinning his body along the surface so he could obtain a better view of the shore. Squinting, after a moment, he saw two dark shapes moving up along the ridge. He pulled his head fully up out of the water and tried to distinguish any conversation. His ears were partially blocked from being under water, and all Vinnie could detect was that they were two team members. Obviously, others could not sleep in this heat, he thought to himself. He watched as they disappeared again into the darkness.

That part of the path only went off to one area — the showers. It made sense that they must think a shower would cool them off and get rid of some of the sweat. He heard one of them laughing, as their voices faded into the trees. Vinnie closed his eyes and floated. He wasn't sure, but he thought when he opened his eyes again that some time had passed. He must have actually fallen asleep in the enjoyment of the lake. He raised his head again up out of the water and listened, but he did not hear any voices. He might have been asleep long enough for them to have showered and gone back to their cabins. He felt confused. It was still pitch dark, except for the moonlight, so it wasn't nearing morning quite yet. He spread out on his stomach and swam back to the shore. He picked his way along the beach, a few times stubbing his toes on rocks. "Okay, now where the fuck is my underwear," he spoke out loud to himself. Seeing a white clump, he bent down and grabbed the damp shorts. "Great... they're wet." He lifted them to his face. "Sweat wet, great. Fuckin' great." He walked down to the edge of the water again and dunked them. He squeezed them out, then pulled them on. He adjusted his dick and balls in the material. "Better," he mumbled.

Vinnie returned his gaze up the path to where the two guys had swerved off toward the showerhouse. Looking back down at his bare feet, he realized they were covered with a coating of sand that clung to the wetness of his skin. "Okay, I'll just go up and rinse off, too," he instructed himself. The hardness of the underwear cotton seemed to scrape against his hog, as he slowly moved through the darkness and up the hill. He paused a moment to pull the wet cotton away from his balls. Tucking his shaft firmly against one thigh, he tried to limit the friction of the wet material. The darkness made following the trail difficult, and it took Vinnie a good few minutes to make his way over to the showerhouse. Had the moonlight been able to penetrate through the trees, the hike would have progressed more quickly. He finally crested the hill and spotted the familiar lights of the showers. Vinnie entered the door and was immediately flooded in the bright fluorescent glare. He stomped his feet, clearing them of most of the sand, as the walk had pretty much dried out the sand that clung to his legs. He stepped deeper into the building, taking quick note that there was no noise coming from the showerroom.

* * *

Vinnie stuck his head around the corner and looked into the tiled area. It was empty. Overhead, he noticed that several of the incandescent bulbs in the shower area had been turned off, it being so late at night. The showers now had a murky, almost hazy quality of light, compared to the bright contrast out in the toilet and sink area. Vinnie walked back out the main door, further convinced that he had lost some time by dropping off into sleep while he had floated on the water. If the guys that he had seen along the water's edge were in fact heading for showers, they must have finished while he snoozed. Or perhaps they changed their minds and went off to another portion of the camp. But just as Vinnie got to the corner of the showerhouse and turned to head back up the path toward his cabin, he heard laughter coming from inside the building he had just exited. "What the fuck?" he mumbled to himself. He paused and listened. Inside he now heard a voice, distinctly calling out to someone: "Man, I'm gonna fuckin' piss myself here." Again laughter followed.

Curious, Vinnie stepped further around to the side and looked up at the screen window area that connected with the eave of the roof. A two-foot window area circled around the showerhouse, allowing air to circulate from within. "Honest, Tag... I swear this sweat and piss all coming outta me is gonna dehydrate me in no time." Again the voice was calling out loudly. "Taglienti?" Vinnie hissed under his breath. The image of Taglienti screwing him up when they were running drills flooded his mind. "But who's talkin' to him?" he whispered to no one. Vinnie worked his way along to the back of the building and noticed several trees that leaned right up against the wall of the shower area. He approached a low-limbed tree, gazing up at the configuration of branches. Without a moment of thought, Vinnie hoisted himself up into the first of the low branches. Carefully picking his way, he climbed up further, bringing himself up in line with the screened area at the top of the building.

Vinnie paused and looked down. He was probably twelve feet off the ground, his bare feet nestled into a niche between the main trunk of the tree and a large outgrowth branch. He leaned back against the trunk and positioned his head so he could see clearly in through the screening. From this vantage point, he could actually look through the showers and out into the main sink area. Again, the light appeared darker in the showerroom. But he could clearly see the back of someone at the sinks, the fluorescent lights brightly illuminating his form. He had a towel wrapped tightly around his waist. It appeared he was frantically pulling it off and heading toward the urinals. Vinnie leaned further against the screen to get a better view. As the guy tossed the towel into one of the sinks and approached the nearest urinal, Vinnie saw his reflection in one of the sink mirrors. It was Tony Marino.

Marino had just begun to shoot his stream, when Vinnie noticed the wooden sauna door open and Taglienti walk out. He approached the urinal next to Marino. "Yeah! Oh shit, yeah!" Marino whispered. Cocking his head to the left, he saw Taglienti had his own dick out and was hosing down in one of the troughs. His towel was slung over his shoulder as he pointed his dong at the porcelain. Taglienti turned his head slightly and looked at Marino. He smirked as he groaned in relief. "Honest to God, Tony, I didn't think I was gonna make it to the pisser," he laughed, the sweat dripping down into his eyes.

"Ya gotta be careful, man, ya can get wicked dehydrated sittin' around in that sweat box." Marino finished and shook his dick. He walked over to the sink that contained his towel. He picked up the towel and wiped it across the mirror over the sink. "Piss builds up real easy when ya so hot and sweatin'." He eyed his reflection. Taglienti pulled the towel off his shoulder and wrapped it back around his waist. He paced toward the entrance to the showers, flicking sweat off his chest and arms.

"No shit! But I just fuckin' love this feelin' of havin' all my muscles gettin' hot and shit, ya know? It just revives me somethin' fierce!" Taglienti stopped and leaned his shoulder against the tile corner of the shower area. He reached down and yanked on the towel where it surrounded his butt, the hair in his crack straining against the pull from his fingers. Vinnie adjusted himself in his tree perch. He had a full view of Taglienti's backside. He moved his torso flat against a shorter trunk that shot out and up over the showerhouse roof; not only did his new position give him a clear view of Taglienti's back, he could also now see Marino standing at the sink.

"Ass-picker," Vinnie muttered under his breath, observing Taglienti's adjustment of his towel.

Taglienti watched as Marino pulled at an ingrown hair on his chin. "Ya still goin' back in for another rounda heat?"

Marino turned his gaze in the mirror so his eyes fell on Taglienti. He continued to pick at his beard. "Yeah, I don't know. I guess so. Yeah." He returned his focus to his reflection.

Taglienti restlessly crossed his ankles and leaned harder against the white tiles. He waited a few more seconds, then realized Marino was immersed in the mirror. "Hey man, how 'bout that field action, huh? It's gettin' pretty fuckin' intense out there, huh?" He bounced his shoulder against the wall as he spoke. Marino did not shift his view.

"Yeah, seems so, huh?" He pulled hard on a short hair in his stubble. "Yeah! Pretty fuckin' intense. That's why this sauna stuff is so darn good for ya muscles."

Taglienti massaged his shoulder with his hand. "I'm takin' quite the beatin' out there, man."

"Yeah, well it seems ya been askin' for quite the beatin' out there." Marino yanked on the same hair again. "Ow! Fuck!" He dug his fingers harder against his skin. "So what's the fuckin' deal with you and Manta? Jeez, you two look likes ya hate each other's fuckin' guts." This time Marino successfully removed the irritated hair. "Yes!" he smiled at himself in the glass, as he dropped the offending hair down the drain.

"Fuck him!" Taglienti straightened up and planted both bare feet firmly on the tiled floor. "He's just a panty-wadding little sissy. Honest to Christ, I swear he just can't handle himself on the field, so he like... takes it out on me. Like I'm to fuckin' blame that he can't handle a football!"

Vinnie tightened his eyes. He turned and spit violently into the air. "Screw you," he hissed. He placed his ear closer to the screen so he could hear better.

"That's it, huh?" Marino finished the appraisal of his reflection and turned to face Taglienti. "He can't play football. That's the bottom line here, huh?"

"Yeah. Exactly." Taglienti shifted on his feet. He avoided Marino's eyes.

"Yeah." Marino picked his towel up off the sink and began to rub some of the sweat off his chest. "Seems to me he can play." His eyes fixed on what might be another ingrown hair on his chest. "In fact, it seems like he can play pretty fuckin' well, if ya ask me." He dropped the towel to the floor and began examining his chest in the bright light. Vinnie smiled to himself in the darkness.

"Yeah well, who the fuck asked ya anyways!" Taglienti ripped the towel from around his waist and stormed over to the sauna. He yanked open the door and tossed his towel onto the wooden seats inside. "I'm goin' in for another dose." He disappeared into the heat, closing the door behind him.

*　*　*

Marino smiled to himself and walked over to the entrance to the showers. He kicked at his towel, sending it across the tiles and coming to rest against the corner where Taglienti had been leaning. Walking into the large empty showerroom, Marino headed over to the spicket in the far corner. Positioning himself, he turned the dial and let the cold water cascade down over his body, his skin still heated from his time in the sauna. "Jesus!" he yelled, throwing himself away from the invading spray. He quickly spun the dial toward the hot water indicator. "Fuckin' goddamn," he muttered to himself, holding his hand under the stream as he awaited a tolerable temperature.

Vinnie leaned back, adjusting himself once again in the tree. His position now looked directly down onto Marino through the screen window, the shower spicket only a few feet below his seat in the branches. Satisfied with the warmth coming through the nozzle, Marino stepped back under the flow. His hand immediately fell to his dick, pulling absently on the excessive skin that made up his shaft. Marino started to lather all under his crotch. He spread his legs apart and let the soap slide over his ballsack. Turning, he made the water rinse off the front of his torso, then closed his eyes and let his hand begin to roughly pull on the skin of his hog again. He rinsed the soap off his legs, spinning around a couple of times to get totally clean. Aiming his face into the water, Marino opened his mouth and let it fill with the warm liquid, then tipped his head down and shot a pulsating stream out onto the dark tiles. He reached up and cranked the dial into the "off" position, abruptly ending the echo of the spilling water. He shook his body violently to rid the excess water, performing a kind of grotesque dance in the empty stillness.

Suddenly he threw himself down on the wet tiles, spreading his hands wide and holding his body weight at arms length. He crossed his ankles, suspending his torso on the muscled toes of his right foot. He dipped his body down slowly, striating his back muscles in response to the action. Marino let his nose touch the floor tiles, exhaling and spitting out as he prepared to raise himself back up. Slowly he began the ascent. Upon his return to arm's length position, he again began to dip down, his speed becoming even slower. With each passing second of effort, veins became more defined across his shoulders and back. The pump that Marino was producing in his body was incredibly intense due to the extreme effort of the exercise and the lasting effects of the sauna. He was a mass of huge pumped muscle. Marino completed his great set of push-ups and returned to a standing position. He moved quickly to retrieve his towel, wrapping it tightly around his waist without bothering to dry himself off. He picked up his soap dish and shampoo and walked quickly toward the showerhouse exit. He silently gave the finger to the closed sauna door, smiling to himself as he headed off without Taglienti.

Vinnie watched quietly as Marino passed the corner of the building, sitting still so that he wouldn't call attention to himself overhead. He leaned his head back against the rough bark of the trunk, the light from inside the shower area illuminating his face. He smiled to himself in thought. *So, Taglienti's all alone. Interesting.* He replayed the conversation between Taglienti and Marino in his mind. Taglienti's comments about him not being able to play well flooded his thoughts. "What a fuckin' A-hole!" he whispered. He looked down, then began to adjust onto the lower branches and bring himself down toward the ground. "Screw you, Tag... we'll just take care of this right now," he said under his breath, as his bare feet found their mark. The pine needles crunched between his toes as his weight came down fully with a thud.

He paused and adjusted his underwear. They were almost dry now. Then, moving carefully, Vinnie slid slowly along the edge of the wall and entered the door without making a sound. The bright glare of the lights made him wait a moment for his eyes to adjust. After a pause, he continued along the inside wall, taking care not to come into view of the sauna door. He stopped once he got to a toilet stall entrance, then stepped inside and partially closed the steel gate. He peered out the opening, his view directly looking across the room to the small window in the sauna. He could clearly see Taglienti sitting on the two-level bench, his towel plastered over his head, obscuring any view he would have to the outside area. Looking more intently at the wooden door, an idea came to mind. Vinnie smiled again as he darted back along the wall and slipped back out into the night. He moved quickly along, peering down as his bare feet guided him. Within a minute he had completed his search. He bent down and grabbed the end of a pine branch that lay on the ground. "Not too thick. Just right," he whispered to himself, as he headed back toward the showerhouse. Once back inside, Vinnie made sure that Taglienti remained in a position that blocked his view. Although he had pulled the towel off his head, Taglienti was now sprawled on his back on the wooden bench, his gaze directed straight up at the ceiling. Vinnie took his time in moving toward the sauna — he did not want to call attention to himself in any way. He pressed his back against the tile, his skin feeling the heat that the sauna gave out through the smooth surface of the wall. How could Taglienti possibly stand being in that furnace on a hot night like this?

Vinnie slowly slid his hand toward the handle of the wooden door. It was closed tightly, the handle jutted out, its large circular opening matched by a wood support next to it on the door jamb. Vinnie smiled again, he knew this support was attached to the jamb to allow a chain and lock to be put in place when the sauna was out of order, or for any other time to prevent access. He paused one beat, then quietly slipped the stick through the support and handle, trapping Taglienti within. He moved back along the wall until he reached the exit door. Rather then go out, he slid his hand up to the light switch. With a chuckle, he flipped the switch off, plunging the main part of the building into darkness.

"You gonna be pretty hot for a short while, ass-wipe," Vinnie chuckled. He stepped back away from the doorway and moved back into the toilet stall. He leaned against the jamb, watching Taglienti's movements. A few minutes passed without Taglienti changing his position. He remained on his back, his towel now tucked behind his head forming a pillow on the hard wood bench. Finally, Taglienti sighed loudly. He lifted his feet up and propped them against the hot wooden walls, then pressed his soles into the steamy boards, the heat shooting through his feet and up his legs. He curled his toes and squeezed them into the wood, tensing his leg muscles tightly. A moment later he relaxed, letting the warmth penetrate the soreness that he had been feeling from his work on the football field. He closed his eyes again, luxuriating in the calmness of the sizzling room.

"Hey, Marino! You're missin' all this heat, man. I'm tellin' ya, it's the balls!" he yelled loudly, his voice echoing off the low ceiling. Taglienti lifted his head and shoulders off the bench for a moment. Remaining on his back, he scooted his butt further down toward the wall. His knees now came up almost to his chest. He once again closed his eyes and let the heat work on his muscles in this new reclined position. He started to quietly sing a tune, the echo of his voice sounding pleasant. "Touch me, baby. Touch me, touch me... all night long, baby..." Beads of sweat from his feet ran down his calves and pooled on his knees. He reached up and let his fingers play with the puddle that was forming. He tapped his long fingers, watching the sweat plop off his legs into the air. His ass was getting hot as it lay flat against the boards. He could feel the more intense heat from a few nails whose heads were elevated to the same level as the surface of the bench. He adjusted himself slightly to his side, sliding his feet to a new location on the wall. Another surge of warmth shot through the skin of his toes. He tapped them slowly to attune to the intense feeling, the hairs of his toes each holding their own small reservoir of perspiration.

Taglienti moved his hands from his knees and let them fall into the wet hair of his crotch. He was momentarily surprised by the extent of the saturation around his dick and balls. He shut his eyes tightly and slid his long fingers down to surround his ballsack. The heat and wetness shot a shiver through his spine. He pushed his butt slightly more toward the wall, his knees now rising further up his chest. Sliding his fingers back down over his saturated testicles, he let the fingertips of his right hand explore the ridge between his butt and balls. Drenched hairs tangled together, their soft blackness responding with a tickling sensation as he slowly prodded the skin lightly with his thumb. His finger extended a little more, moving further under and finding his tight entrance. He jumped as his large thumb found its mark. He pulsated his digit ever so slightly against the sealed opening. A strong pressure was given back, letting him know his body was battling any kind of intrusion. He gasped with the poweful feeling that was sent right down into his toes. He turned his head fully to the side, arching his shoulders in response to the growing excitement he was feeling. He half-opened his eyes, his vision slowly adjusting to the light again. The lights were off in the main sink area! He pulled his hands away quickly, as his thoughts returned to where he was. He remained curled on the bench, blinking his eyes to clear the sweat.

"Hey ya, Marino!" he yelled. He paused a moment. No response. "Marino!" he yelled again with more force. Again no response. He pulled himself up to a sitting position and swung his legs out onto the floor. He sat staring ahead at the darkness out in the main area. "What the fu..." he stood and took a step forward, pushing his hand out against the door. His effort was met by resistance, the door did not move. He took a step back, his hand unconsciously raising and scratching his head. "What the fuck?" he said more forcefully. He moved and pushed against the wooden door again. No movement. "Hey, Marino! Okay, fuckhead... very funny! Now open the fuckin' door before I open ya fuckin' head!" his voice contained a slight tremor. "Hey! Motherfucker!" he screamed, panic beginning to set in. Taglienti's eyes widened as he pushed again and again on the small door, each time getting the same resistance. He grabbed his towel and wiped the sweat from his forehead, forming more from his nerves than from the heat. He stood still, quietly praying in his mind that he would be able to get out. "Tony?" he yelled again, his voice sounding more strained and quivering. Throwing the towel back down on the bench, he noticed that his dick had shrunken down fully in his terror, his nuts pulling up tightly in their sack.

Taglienti's eyes swelled with tears. "Aw, c'mon, Tony..." his voice trailed off. He shivered in a panic that ran down his back. He turned and stepped back toward the bench, picking up his towel and wiping his face. Suddenly he hurled his weight fully against the door, sending it slamming back against the wall, swinging slightly and remaining open. He was free! He paused a moment to look at the door. No lock had been in place. The door had swung easily open this time! He quickly tied his towel around his waist. Glancing for a moment at the unobstructed handle, he half-ran to the showerhouse door and darted off into the night. He did not see Vinnie exit the showerhouse a minute later, throwing the branch in the bushes with a laugh. Vinnie headed off toward his cabin. For some reason, the night heat didn't seem so bad now.

7

By late Saturday afternoon everyone agreed that the team had begun to come together. Many were already worrying that the coaches were making lists of intended cuts, so all the guys were trying their best at working toward a team effort. The performances of Vinnie and Vuch had escalated to an almost playfully competitive game between them. The adverse feelings that Vinnie had felt for Vuch, due to his shaved butt, quickly were forgotten once they were back on the football field. As the offensive line developed, Vinnie knew he was able to keep holes open for Vuch to complete passes to the receivers. They worked off each other; and worked for each other. A true sense of brotherhood was being seen in the players. Vinnie was developing quite a reputation already, for the thunderous tackles and blocks he made. No mercy was shown when he was working for the team. He wanted open field for rushing and passing, and no man was going to stand in his way. The intimidating sneer and powerful drive with which he propelled his body was a force not many wanted to encounter. Vuch worked on his throwing arm. The receivers working hard at following Vuch's calls. He knew the playbook well, and was taking control of his offense, expecting they too would study the required moves and be ready for his passing.

Late Saturday afternoon, as the squad continued running drills, form tackling and form blocking, the sky began to cloud up. The coaches still had a series of sled drills to run and everyone knew that if they hung in there, dinner would come soon; it had been announced that they would have the night free to socialize or rest. Many of the seniors were already laughing and joking about their intended "socializing". Vinnie knew all too well to what extent that could go. He smiled to himself as he readied for the sled. He was wicked psyched about the possibilities for the evening.

"73! Let's go!"

Vinnie snapped back to reality. He positioned himself down to charge at the sled.

"Let's go!" Billy Ruggiero called from his stance on the backside of the single-sled. "Come on, Manta, give it all ya got!" he yelled. Vinnie took off and plowed into the large padded area of the sled, his shoulder pounding solidly into the upright supports. The sled moved off a few feet. "Down again, Manta! Come on! Hit it!" The coach's voice grew in authority. Vinnie crouched down, letting the power and intensity build in his mind. He pictured easily thundering over some defensive tackle. He paused, took aim at the obstruction and then charged at it with all his force. He hit the sled with a fierce display of power. The sled came up and moved across the grass, the coach riding on the rear. "Yeah, Vinnie, yeah!" Billy shouted in enthusiasm. Vinnie came up at it a third time, hitting the barrier and sliding it further across the field. Several of the team had stopped as they were walking past. They cheered his success and brawn. Vinnie was demonstrating what he did best. Hit. And hit fucking hard.

"Okay, I wanna see Manta and Taglienti. On the double-sled... together, guys!" Vinnie looked over at Taglienti who was standing off to the side with a few of his friends. He'd had no expression on his face as he listened to the group praising Vinnie's hitting power. Taglienti returned the stare at Vinnie, his face taking on a look of disgust. He slowly walked over and stood in place at one side of the sled. Vinnie looked up, standing in place, not getting into charging position.

"Today, 73! Let's get set here!" Billy called. Vinnie continued to stand in place, a sneer growing across his lips at the thought of working with Taglienti. Since the start of camp, Taglienti remained the only guy he had any problem with. Whenever he saw him, all Vinnie could think of was the first day in drill line and Taglienti's piss of an attitude. That kind of attitude undermined all they were trying to do as a team. He didn't seem to be a team player. Vinnie closed his eyes and replayed Taglienti's words to Marino. It was obvious to him now that Marino's opinion was on target, despite what Vuch had said that Marino did when he got horned up. Yeah, Marino was decent, definitely one of the guys. But, Taglienti! Jesus, that A-hole bastard needs to be put in his fuckin' place!

"Manta!" Vinnie looked up at the coach. "We're waiting, Manta!"

"Wassamatta, Vinnie?" Taglienti said in a sarcastic voice. "Too tired? Wanna rest a while?"

Vinnie glared back at him. He immediately crouched down in charging position. He turned his head to the side and faced Taglienti again, he could feel the pressure building in his head. He wished it was Taglienti he would be slamming into.

"On the whistle!" The coach paused for them to ready, then blew the whistle. Vinnie and Taglienti charged the sled. Contact was made at the same time. The sled flew out several feet. They crouched immediately down again, waiting for the whistle signal. It blew. Vinnie and Taglienti charged again, this time Taglienti holding back a slight amount in his force. The offset was just enough to give an imbalance in the drive of the sled when Vinnie hit it with all his power.

The sled turned and started to tip offsides. Billy had to jump off, as the structure turned quickly to the side. "Christ, Manta! You're supposed to work with him here, not try to outdo him!" Billy glared, obviously pissed off at what he perceived to be a blatant attempt by Vinnie to show up Taglienti. "73, off the sled. Taglienti and White get in position!"

Vinnie looked at the coach in amazement. *What the fuck just happened here?* he thought to himself. Jesus! He got to a standing position and turned to walk away. In an almost inaudible whisper, Taglienti said, "Gee Vinnie, that's too bad!" The sarcasm in his voice was obvious. Vinnie turned and looked at Taglienti, his eyes felt as if they were burning with anger. He ground his teeth and tried to hold his temper; he was ready to deck Taglienti. He kept his rage in check, turning and walking off to the side of the field. He looked back in time to see Taglienti and White plowing together into the sled.

* * *

"You know Manta, you gotta just fuckin' sit down and calm down." Vuch was watching Vinnie pace back and forth in the cabin.

Vinnie spun around from in front of the door. "No, man, you have no idea how fuckin' stupid he made me look! He's a fuckin' A-hole!" Vinnie walked back toward his bunk, pounding his fist into the palm of his left hand. "I don't like it when someone makes me look stupid. I fuckin' hate it, okay? I know football, man. I don't need some halfwit cocksucker trying to make me look bad!" He hit the wall with his right fist.

Meat stuck his head over the edge from the top of his bunk. "Vinnie, I was a watchin' ya today. You didn't look stupid. Don't let some pencil-dick like Tag get ya this worked up." Meat stuck his bare legs over the side of the bunk and let them dangle in the air.

"Yeah, really, Vin. You looked good," Vuch added. Meat hoisted himself down off his bed. He grabbed the shorts he had dropped on the floor earlier and pulled them on over his jock. "I'm gonna go take a dump... you okay?" he asked, looking at Vinnie as he paced by.

Vinnie shrugged. "Yeah. I'm okay," he said through clenched teeth.

Meat looked over at Vuch, who nodded. He then continued past Vinnie and went out the cabin door. "Relax, Vinnie. The night is young. We're gonna have ourselves a good fuckin' time tonight, okay?" Vuch sat up and moved over to the edge of his bed. He placed his bare feet on the floor. He was still wearing his football pants, leg pads and mesh top from earlier — he had even gone to dinner in the clothes. He started to unbuckle the pants, pulled them down to his knees and began undoing the ties around the pads.

Vinnie finally sat down in the chair in front of the desk. He silently watched Vuch trying to undo the ties. "Yeah, man, tonight we gonna have ourselves some fun with those little shits, huh? Yup, this is what I live for at these camps." Vuch pulled his leg pads off, then pulled the pants down and off his ankles. He threw them over in the corner by the dresser. He sat back on the bed, still wearing the mesh and cup. He pulled one foot up and rubbed it with his hands.

"What you guys do at the other camps you went to?"

Vinnie continued to watch him, slowly sighing and sitting back further in the chair. "Well, we got... yeah. One year at Allentown it got outta hand. One kid got hurt. Not bad or nothin', but enough that he went cryin' to the coaches and then word got back to the school and all this shit. Anyways, the principal of the school called an assembly the first week a school and said there would never be any more away camps for the team and all this other crap." Vinnie crossed his arms across his chest and flattened out his hair. He continued to swipe the hair down his forehead as he talked. "Fortunately I left Allentown at the end of that year, so I didn't miss out on anything, cause Armand had a camp I went to the next summer.

It woulda really sucked though, to stay at Allentown and only be able to do a dorky day football camp at the high school." He put a hand over his eyes and pressed against them, he had quite a headache — courtesy of Pete Taglienti.

Vuch switched his foot and began to rub the other, his leg crossed up over his raised knee. "Yeah, that would suck. We've been lucky here, man. We have fun, the sophs get a good scare... but nobody's been hurt. Not really." He dropped the leg back down onto the mattress. "How's your feet doin'?"

Vinnie moved his hand from across his eyes. "Okay, I guess." He stuck his feet out straight and looked at them. "Yeah, okay. The double socks do good, but they sweat so much like that, you know?" He dropped his feet back down to the floor.

"I told ya a couple a days ago, ya should soak 'em," said Vuch.

Vinnie put his hand back up to his eyes and pressed his fingers firmly against his closed eyelids. "Yeah, whatever," he muttered.

"Here, lie down on my bed, here," said Vuch. He pushed himself to the edge and got up. He held out his arm toward the bed to indicate Vinnie should lay on it.

"What?" Vinnie looked at him, not understanding.

"I said, lie down, fool." Vuch walked past him over to the dresser.

"What for?" asked Vinnie, not moving.

"Just lie down. I got some stuff here that might help your feet. Maybe that headache you keep rubbing, too." He opened his top dresser drawer. "Just lie down, okay. Come on, Manta."

Vinnie slowly got up and flopped over onto the mattress. He propped the pillow up against the wall so his head was raised up and watched Vuch move around. He smiled. "You know, Vuchie, last time I did what you said, I ended up with no hair on my butt!" He flattened his hair again.

"Yeah, well, it looks better, doesn't it?" Vuch closed the drawer and returned to the bedside with a bottle of lotion in his hand.

"It might look better, my butt I mean, but it itches like a fuck right now."

Vuch sat on the edge of the bed and smiled at him. "Well, that's cause it's been a coupla days now. Might have to do it again soon, huh? Gotta keep up on these things." He laughed.

"Yeah, sure. Like I'd let you near me with a razor again." Vinnie leaned forward and changed his tone to a sarcastic whisper. "If you're smart, Carvuccio, you won't let me near you with a razor again either!" He leaned back against the pillow, grinning.

"Such hostility, Manta!" Vuch uncapped the lotion and began to pour a little into his open palm. "Maybe you should save it for our little sophomore friends, 'eh?" he smiled back. He lifted one of Vinnie's feet and placed it in his lap bending a little closer to look at the foot. "Well, I've seen worse. There's no infection or nothin' like that." He squeezed some of the lotion into his hand and rubbed his two hands together.

"What is that shit, anyways?" Vinnie asked, his eyes squinting as he tried to read the bottle from the distance.

"Ah... old family recipe," Vuch chuckled. "No, actually just some stuff my father once dumped all together for me when I got a real bad sunburn one time. It's got hand lotion and that aloe vera shit and some sort of antibacterial cream. My father just sticks all the stuff in the bottle together. It works, I know that's hard to believe, but it does." Vuch began to massage the lotion into Vinnie's foot.

Vinnie flexed his toes as Vuch rubbed the lotion into them. "It feels good anyways," he said, closing his eyes.

"Yeah, I know," Vuch continued to massage, "Christ, Vin, you even got muscley feet. I can feel the power in 'em. Strong, ya know?"

Vinnie opened his eyes and shrugged. "Yeah. Whatever." He closed his eyes again. Vuch ran his fingers down the underside of the foot. Vinnie jumped a bit. It tickled.

"Ah, sensitivity. I didn't think you had it in you."

"Fuck you."

Vuch rubbed more lotion into the big toe, gently working the soothing moisture into the cracked skin. Vinnie moaned softly. "See, under this hulk of an exterior, you're just a pussycat, Manta," Vuch said softly. He smiled widely and laughed.

"And you're just a pussy, Carvuccio." Vinnie returned the smile, even though it still resembled a sneer.

"You know, you can't smile, Manta. You know that?" Vuch picked up the other foot and went to work on it. "You ever look in a mirror? Your smile is like the gleeful look of a Hell's Angel at a gang fight." Voices were heard outside and suddenly the door of the cabin burst open. A gang of the guys were piled up on the step and came bounding in, laughing and pushing each other.

"Vuchie, it's Hell Night! It's here man!" shouted Kirby as he danced into the center of the room. He waved his arms in excitement. Vinnie instinctively moved his foot off Vuch's lap. The group of guys continued to stream into the cabin — within moments all floor space was occupied by someone either standing or sitting.

Vuch smiled widely, his bright white teeth shining. "Yes, men, it's an important job we undertake tonight... difficult... dangerous... but somebody's gotta do it!" He reached back to grab Vinnie's foot, returned it to his lap and began to massage it again. Vinnie tensed. He felt really strange doing this in front of so many of the guys. *But what was he uncomfortable about?* he wondered. *It was no big deal.* He shifted uneasily on the bed. Vinnie looked around the room at all the visitors. The only ones he really knew were Kirb, Mike Massella, Sal Cardone and Tony Marino. He recognized many of the other seniors, but had not really gotten to know them personally. Many of the guys were those who had grouped around Vuch when the try-outs were going on. Massella and Marino had brought two large coolers in with them. They each sat leaning against the containers.

"Vinnie, you still havin' problems with your feet?" asked Kirby. Vinnie felt wicked uncomfortable. Vuch continued to massage his foot, working more lotion into the toes.

"Yeah. They're okay, though." He looked at Vuch, mentally wishing him to stop the massage.

"So, Kirb. What's in the coolers?" asked Vuch smiling.

"Hey, man, you even have to ask?" Kirby laughed back.

"Well, let's pop 'em. We got a long night ahead of us."

Kirby moved and opened the lid of the cooler. It was packed with cans of beer.

"Oh, yes!" said Sal. "I've been a waitin' for this!" He reached out his hand to Kirby, who tossed him one. "Line up. Here we go." He started tossing the cans out, a couple of them missing their intended marks and hitting the floor. Tony Marino made the mistake of picking up one of the cans that had rolled across the floor and immediately opening it. The beer sprayed up over his head. He waved his hand across his face, wiping up some foam that had landed on his cheek.

"Real swift, Marino," Massella started laughing.

"Suck me, alright?" Tony smiled.

"Yeah, you wish," responded Massella.

"Maybe we should get one of his suck buddys in here, huh?" chided Sal. Playful looks were quickly exchanged amongst the guys.

"Maybe we'll get some sophs to suck me!" Marino played along.

Vinnie's mind raced back to what Vuch had said about Marino. It just did not seem possible. Marino seemed like a regular guy. How was it possible he did fag things? Vuch held out a hand. Kirby tossed a can to him, then sent one through the air to Vinnie. Marino squeezed the can that had just showered him. He crushed the empty metal and popped it into the trash can beside the desk.

"Whoa! A real man! Check it out. Tony, here's another." Kirby sent another through the air.

"Try not to bathe in it," joked Vuch.

Within minutes empty cans were flying into the trash as fast as they were being passed around. Vinnie was handed his second beer and opened the top. He lifted his foot from Vuch's lap and leaned forward so Vuch would be able to hear him. The noise in the room had increased as everyone was talking back and forth to each other at the same time.

"Hey, Vuchie. These are gonna be kinda hard on us come five o'clock. We're gonna be one fucked-up team on the field first thing in the morning." Vinnie made his comments in a low voice.

"No, problem, bro," replied Vuch. He opened his second beer. "We always got this covered each year. Saturday night is always Hell Night. We don't have to be on the field until noon tomorrow."

"So, what we got goin' tonight, Vuch?" asked Massella. "We gonna make the little shits pee their pants, or what?"

Vuch leaned back on the bed, his back braced against the corner of the desk. He squinted up his forehead. "Well, gentlemen... as I see it, we gotta give these pussies a night they won't ever forget." He took a gulp from the can. "Now we got ourselves a lot of ground to cover tonight. Mikey, where's our numero uno captain?"

Massella looked up from playing with the beer tab. "Chip? Ah, he's around. He ain't gonna miss it. I think he's showerin' or somethin'. I don't know."

"You know the set-up of the cabins?"

"Yeah, sure. Let's see, we got like nineteen sophs here, right. And they're in two cabins. The ones up next to the access road by the field." Massella dug down into the bottom of the cooler for another can.

"They ain't in just two cabins, Mikey. Think about it, ya stupid shit, they can't fit nineteen guys in two cabins!" Kirby sprayed some beer over onto him.

"Cut it out, you fuck!" He tried to move quickly to get out of the way of the fizz. His reflexes were beginning to slow down and some of it caught him on the arm.

"I dunno. But, there ain't no nineteen guys stuffed into two cabins." Mike opened the can and poured half of it down his throat in one swig. "We gots the Minority House. We ain't accounted for the Minority House," said one of the guys next to Sal. His voice had already begun to slur. Vinnie looked over at him. "What's the Minority House?"

"You know. Where they put all the guys who aren't white," the guy replied. He belched loudly and looked back over at Vuch. "Some a thems gotta be sophs." He belched again.

Vuch nodded. "Yeah, I think so. They got eight guys in there." He laughed and sat up, crossing and folding his legs underneath him. His voice got excited. "You wouldn't believe what they did this year. It's so fucked!" He howled with laughter, taking another big slug of beer. "They got this new kid, Santiago, he's a sophomore, right? Well anyways, the Minority House has always been black, right?" He turned in Vinnie's direction. "Well they stuck this kid who's Spanish, I don't know... Puerto Rican or one of those, anyways, they stick him in with all the black guys. Like he's dark skinned kinda, right? So they assume he'll just fit in with the blacks." Vuch rolled back and leaned against the corner of the desk again. "I mean, is that fucked, or what!"

Vinnie shook his head in disbelief.

"I mean, like the blacks don't want the Spanish guy in there. And Santiago don't wanna be in with all the blacks. It's fucked!" Vuch finished his beer and stuck out a hand for another. Vinnie did the same.

Massella opened the second chest of beer. "So like who are sophs in there?"

"Oh yeah. Well, Brent White, a senior. We got Lucas and Fitzy who are juniors..." Vuch counted on his fingers. "Santiago is a soph and we must got two other sophs, cause Mark Nolan is a senior this year." He counted again on his hand. "So we gots three sophs there. Yeah, that would be right... nineteen total, two cabins of eight each and the three in Minority House." He smiled proudly that he had figured out the list, and chugged the newly opened brew.

The cabin door opened suddenly and Meat came bounding in, carrying a large watermelon in his arms. He stopped just inside the door and set the melon down, then rubbed his hair which was dripping wet. All eyes in the room turned to him. He was wearing boxer shorts, which were also wet and caked to his body, and his bare feet had mud almost completely covering them.

Vuch held his beer up in salute. "Hey, Meatman, we been wonderin' where you been. Glad you could join us."

Meat nodded, but didn't say anything. He held out a hand toward the open cooler and nodded again. Massella took out a beer and chucked it to him. With one hand Meat popped the tab and chugged the beer down in one drink. He dropped the empty can on the floor. He bent down and picked up the large melon and started to walk toward his bunk. The guys sitting around the room all shifted their positions to make way for him. The mud on his feet tracked behind him as he walked. He grunted and lifted the heavy melon up onto his mattress.

"Hey, Meat, you're all wet," said Vinnie.

Meat turned and looked over at him. "No shit. It's rainin'"

"What?" Vuch bent back further on his bed and looked out the window into the darkness. "Guys, shut up a minute!" The room started to quiet down.

"Whatsamatta?" asked Marino. He staggered to his feet and walked slowly over toward the window. With each step he swayed.

"Shut up, man!" Vuch yelled again. The room went quiet. Drops of rain could be heard through the trees. "Shit, it is rainin'!" he yelled.

"That's what I said," grunted Meat.

"Well, the better to get 'em, I guess. Kinda makes throwin' 'em in the water pointless, huh?" Marino staggered back to where he had been sitting, and fell back down into the spot. Meat walked over to the clear area near the dressers. He stood there, his wet shorts plastered against his legs and hips. He raised his arms over his head and pulled his tank top off, casually throwing it in a pile in the corner of the room, water spraying on the wall as it hit the spot.

"What's the melon for, Meat?" asked Vinnie. He raised himself up on his elbows and tried to see up onto Meat's bunk. Vuch's bed sat too low for him to get a view. The melon had sank down in the center of the mattress.

"Don't ask," said Vuch. "You don't want to know."

"Huh?" Vinnie looked at Vuch.

"Hell Night tradition for Meat." He lowered his voice so only Vinnie could hear him. "Believe me! You don't want to know!" He belched.

Vinnie shrugged. "Whatever, man." He finished off another beer.

* * *

By about eleven pm, as they started heading out for the night, most of the guys who has gathered in the cabin were pretty tanked. The rain had continued to come down, although most of the path areas were shielded by the heavy growth of trees above. Many of the guys were stumbling as they walked along over the dirt pathways. Vinnie spun around and poked Tony Marino solidly in the center of his chest. "Hey, man, quit fallin' into me!" his voice rose in anger.

"What?"

"I said, quit fallin' into me. Jesus, Marino, you're walkin' into everybody."

Marino swayed as Vinnie spoke to him. Again his shoulder banged into Vinnie, as he stood there trying to listen.

"See! Stand up, you shit!" Vinnie pushed him up with his arm. Vuch came back to where they stood in the group.

"Christ, Tony, you is a little shit-faced, 'eh?"

Marino looked at him, his eyes not focusing very well. He turned toward the side of the path, still remaining on the walkway, and clumsily stuck his hand down the front of his shorts. He yanked the fabric aside quickly, as a stream of piss started shooting out. He staggered in place as he aimed the flow of urine onto the ground.

Vinnie jumped aside quickly, so as not to get hit. "Marino! Keep your fuckin' piss off me, okay?" Vinnie laughed and walked up to the front of the group.

Vuch stood a moment and watched Marino, making sure he was somewhat in control of what he did. "Tony, you're fucked." Vuch turned and left Marino to finish his business. The group was laughing and hooting, as they made their way up the hillside toward where the sophomore cabins were.

Vuch and Massella stopped just before they hit the rise, and Massella turned back to the parade of guys that were coming up the hill. "Shut up! Jesus!" He tried to speak in undertones and waved his arms signaling for everyone to quiet down. Vuch walked back into the boisterous group. "Hey, look! We wanna surprise 'em, okay? Shut the fuck up!"

Mike Nismont and Greg Alasambra were leaning into each other, holding each other up. Both were taking a piss at the same time. "Mikey, hold my weenie for me!" Greg nearly fell down laughing.

"Shut up, you fuckin' queer boy!" Nismont whispered back. He turned so his stream came in Alasambra's direction. "Greg! Here, man, suck me off, will ya?" he laughed back.

Vuch walked over to them. "Excuse me, girls... but would you kindly shut the fuck up! We're tryin' to surprise 'em, try to keep your queerness under control for a few minutes, will ya?" He patted Nismont on the back.

"Oh, yeah, never mind Greg, I'll get a soph to blow me," Nismont hooted and zipped up his fly. The group all crouched down and continued up the last of the slope. They slowly circled around the pathway in front of the cabins that were occupied by the sophomores — at times stumbling into the guy walking in front of them. The group of seniors, and some select juniors, had grown in number to about thirty. They encircled the two cabins that were containing sophomores. The lights were out in one, the other was still dimly lit, but neither appeared to have any movement within them.

Vuch leaned over to John Kirby, who was standing next to him. "The little shits are all asleep already!" he whispered. "Isn't that cute!" He belched loudly, then looked around in apology. Tony Marino was the first to lead the group around the cabin that was in darkness. He slowly crept up to the cabin door and tried the doorhandle. It did not open. He turned back to the group and signaled by shaking his head: "No." Pete Taglienti bounded up the steps of the other cabin and gently tried that door. He nodded a "Yes" back to the group. For a moment everyone stood still, not knowing what to do next, then Meat walked up the steps of the first cabin and positioned his arms around the doorframe. He looked over at Taglienti, who got his hands back on the handle. With his free arm, Taglienti counted off three seconds, then at the same time he opened the one cabin door, as Meat pulled hard on the other locked one. Everyone outside started hooting, as the door easily came off in Meat's huge arms. Both groups rushed the cabins at the same time.

Within seconds, each cabin had a fill of drunken players ready for some games. The group storming the darkened cabin all started falling over each other once they got inside. As Vinnie came through the door, he fished on the wall for the light switch. His arm flew randomly across the boards of the wall, his drunken state making it difficult to control the movement of his hand. Finally, he came across the plate and flicked the overhead light on. The light revealed a stack of guys piled in the center of the floor, all trying to regain their balance and get to their feet. Vinnie looked around the room of the cabin. Each of the eight beds was occupied, most having a kid sitting up suddenly whose eyes were wide with surprise.

Meat reached down and pulled Vuch up from the pile of bodies, steadying him on his feet as he stood. Vuch tilted into Meat's shoulder, trying to balance himself. He waved his arm around, pointing at each of the faces in the beds. "Good evening, girls!" He stumbled against Meat. Meat lifted him easily back into a standing position. He balanced for a moment before continuing to speak. "Girls, we have quite the treat for you tonight. Yes, indeed!" he shouted. The rest of the group had managed to get to their feet, or were leaning against a wall or piece of furniture, each looking around at the sophomores.

Massella stood up straight and continued the address to them. Vuch stopped talking and put his arm around Meat to steady himself. "Tonight, girls, you will address each of us as 'sir', and only 'sir'." His gaze went from bed to bed. "Now get the fuck up and line up!" he shouted. "Now!" Massella smiled in victory.

The sophomores nervously looked around at each other, then quickly scurried to their feet and formed a line on each side of the room in front of their beds. Each were in various levels of dress: a couple in full pajamas, most in undershorts and one stood nervously completely naked — frantically looking next to his bed for something to put on. He knew not to move from the line. After a moment he gave up and looked straight ahead.

Vinnie moved from where he stood just inside the door over next to Meat. Vuch turned and smiled at him, his wide grin somewhat lopsided, his eyes glazed.

Massella walked up the length of the cabin, then turned and walked back down the other side, looking intently into the face of each of the shaking boys. "Quite a sorry group here, don't you think, men?" Various comments of agreement were heard from the upperclassmen. Vuch began to walk down the line of boys, stopping in front of the sophomore who stood naked. Vuch slowly looked up and down his body. He stopped right at eye level and leaned into the boy's face.

"What is your name, dear?" he said sarcastically. The boy froze.

"Mr Carvuccio asked you a question!" yelled Massella. "Jeff Tobin," he replied weakly. He was starting to shake badly.

"Jeff Tobin... what?" yelled Massella.

The boy swallowed, his eyes darting nervously about. "Jeff Tobin, sir," he said faintly.

Vuch leaned closer to his face, his breath right against Tobin's nose. He glared into the boy's eyes. "You think you got a piece o' meat there?" He spit as he spoke, wetting Tobin's face.

The boy blinked and inhaled. "No... sir, I... I just sleep... this way. Er, sir." The boy shook more.

"You just sleep that way." Vuch turned and started to walk away. After moving a few feet, he turned back. "You just sleep that way."

"Yes... sir," said Tobin weakly. He looked like he was going to faint.

"You don't got no meat there. You don't got nothin'." Vuch turned and continued to walk back to where Meat and Vinnie stood. "You ain't nothin' but one of the girls." He reached the edge of a dresser, turned and leaned back against it, folding his arms across his chest. "Isn't that right, Tobin?"

Tobin looked at him nervously. He didn't know what to do. He stared blankly at Vuch.

"You were asked a question, boy!" yelled Massella.

Tobin nodded slowly. "Yes, sir." he said very softly.

"Yes, sir... what?" asked Vuch very softly, each word coming our slowly and viciously.

The boy started to stammer. "I'm... ju... justttt... one... of... the... the..." He turned pale and his legs were noticeably shaking.

"Girls," said Vuch softly. "Just one of our... girls." He leaned his head back and laughed loudly. All the other guys in Vuch's group started to laugh also. "Mr Massella, why don't you get our friends here ready." Vuch lifted up the front of his tee-shirt and scratched his stomach.

"Yes, sir!" replied Massella. He walked down the line of boys, looking into the eyes of each. "Alright, I want you to strip! All of you! Now!" he yelled. Each boy looked back and forth at each other. "We're waiting!" screamed Massella. He walked right up to the head of the shortest sophomore in the cabin. The boy's face only came up to Massella's chest. Massella stood so his chest was firmly against the boy's nose, lowering his voice to a whisper. "Take 'em off, boy."

Each of the sophomores began removing their clothing, as the upperclassmen moved around the room. John Kirby had brought along a large suitcase, which he now placed in the middle of the floor and opened it. Each of the upperclassmen paired off and stood near one of the sophomores. Vinnie and Vuch stood next to the increasingly nervous Jeff Tobin, who stood silently still as the rest of the cabin of sophomores undressed. Vinnie noticed for the first time that the boy who was nearest to Mike Nismont and Greg Alasambra was Randy Miller. He felt slightly guilty for what he knew they would be put through. Randy was annoying, but he seemed like an okay kid. Then again, this was part of getting on the team, he himself had gone through similar things a couple of years ago. Randy would just have to grin and bear it.

Massella returned to the center of the room. Each boy now stood fully naked in line. Massella smiled and turned to where Vuch stood. "You were right. They don't got nothin' hangin' between their legs, do they?" he laughed, as his eyes scanned the crotches of the boys.

Vuch left his spot and walked over to Kirby who was still digging through the suitcase. "What do we have to start our little games with, Mr Kirby?"

"Well, sir, I would suggest the record," replied Kirb. He held a record album up for Vuch to see.

Vuch turned back and spoke to the group. "Ah, yes... the record. Good idea, Mr Kirby." He started to pace back and forth in front of the sophomores. The rest of the upperclassmen seated themselves on the beds. "For your information... and our amusement, we will start with a little test of your speed." He paused again in front of the suitcase. "Your speed... and your agility. Because, my friends, both are most important to a football player. Isn't that right, Mr Meat." He turned and looked at Meat sitting on one of the beds. He still only wore his boxers, although they were almost dry. He sat in a half-drunken state, the head of his dick sticking out through the slit of the shorts, and nodded in response to Vuch's question. He grabbed at his dick and pulled on it, then belched. The other seniors all started to break up in laughter. "Very wise response, Mr Meat. Thank you for that input." Vuch smiled widely and bowed to him. He looked back at the line of sophomores. "The object of the game is to hold a greased record while you duck-walk across the floor." He looked at the short guy. "Duck-walk, for those of you who do not know, is stooping down and grabbing your ankles. You walk across the room... er... like a duck!" He paused and walked over to the short sophomore. "What is your name, young lady?"

"Anthony Marvetti, sir!" The voice came out loud and booming.

Vuch jumped a little in surprise at the power behind the little guy. He leaned down slightly so he was face-to-face. "Well, Anthony Marvetti..." his voice became a whisper again, "I strongly suggest... you don't... drop... the record!" He stood up straight.

"No problem, sir!" boomed the voice.

"Well then, Anthony Marvetti, you should be our first contestant!" Vuch walked back and sat on the bed next to Vinnie. He nodded for Marvetti to go over to where Kirby stood rubbing petroleum jelly on the record.

The sophomore walked confidently over and took the greased record from Kirby, then looked back at Vuch. "From where to where, sir?" he spoke loudly. Vuch motioned with his hand. "From the corner there, to the end of this bed here." Vuch bent over to Vinnie and whispered directly in his ear. "Well, the little shit's got balls, I'll give him that." Vinnie leaned over and looked across to where Marvetti was standing. Vuch rolled his eyes and flopped drunkedly back on the bed against Vinnie's chest. "No, you stupid shit!" He tried to keep his voice low, but he started to laugh and get louder. "I mean, he's got nerve! Don't look at his balls, you fuck!" Tears of laughter started coming out of his eyes, and he buried his face against Vinnie's chest.

Vinnie shoved his head away, embarrassed. "I know what you meant." He pushed his arm against Vuch again. "Sit up, you queer." His face turned red.

Vuch fell back down against him, still laughing. He mimicked Vinnie's protest, "I know what you meant!" He rubbed at the tears in his eyes. "Yeah, sure, Manta. You just wanted to look at his balls!"

Vinnie pushed Vuch's head down his torso slightly, so Vuch's head now rested on his stomach. He reached inside the leg opening of his shorts and pulled them back so his balls fell out. "Yeah, look at these, you homo!" Vinnie whispered.

Vuch lifted his head off Vinnie and turned to him with a huge grin. He then turned his head and spoke to Marvetti who was still waiting for instructions. "Go ahead, Mr Marvetti. We await a demonstration of your abilities."

Marvetti stooped down and grasped his ankles, his dick hanging down toward the floor between his open legs. He held the slippery record in one of his hands, the album scraping the wooden floor. He looked questionally at Vuch for the word to move ahead. All the upperclassmen started laughing. A few whistled in approval. Vuch got to his feet and slowly walked toward the crouched Marvetti, shaking his head as he approached. "Oh, no. Stupid me. No, no, Marvetti." He stopped in front of the boy, Marvetti's face right at Vuch's crotch level. "Didn't I mention the agility part? Perhaps I just wasn't clear enough. You see, Mr Marvetti, we don't want you to carry that record across the room." He paused and smiled at all the seniors scattered on the beds. "We want you to hold that record firmly in place... between those cute little butt cheeks of yours." Vuch smiled broadly at him. "And don't drop it, Mr Marvetti."

Marvetti looked up at him with wide eyes. His mouth dropped slightly open. He acted like he didn't know what to do or how to respond. Then just as quickly, he lifted the record and spread his butt slightly, then closed his legs tighter. The record stayed in place. He looked back up at Vuch with a slight smile. Vuch stepped aside, and Marvetti began to waddle across the floor. The seniors cheered. Massella turned to Meat and said, "Five bucks says he drops it."

Meat looked back at him and gestured a pumping-on-his-dick movement. "You're on. I say the little fuck's got a virgin hole that keeps it there," he shouted over the loud cheers.

Marvetti paused for a moment, halfway across the room. He tensed his ass tighter, then even more slowly continued his trek. He passed the edge of the bed that marked the end, sucessfully completing the waddle without dropping the record. The group cheered. Marvetti slightly relaxed and the record fell to the floor. Vuch clapped his hands in approval. Marvetti stood and smiled, then silently returned to his spot in line.

Massella waved his arm for the cheering to cease. He pointed at the sophomore standing next in line. "You! You're next... move!" The sophomore hesitantly walked to the end of the beds and picked up the record from the floor. "And before you begin..." said Massella slowly — the sophomore looked nervously back at him — "...lick the edge of the album." All the upperclassmen fell back against each other howling in laughter.

*   *   *

The next hour was spent totally humiliating as many of the sophomores as they could. Each had to participate in the duck-walk, many failing to keep the record in their butt crack as they went across the room. The ones who unfortunately dropped the record were made to feel even more embarrassed. The upperclassmen made full use of their control; having the boys perform dances for them, coating their jock straps with itch cream, making them wrestle fully naked; whatever they desired, the sophomores had to do. The initial nervousness of most of the boys disappeared once they realized no physical harm would come to them. However, a few continued to feel agitated and anxious, and displayed panic as each new game was devised.

Jeff Tobin, the kid who slept naked, was the one that Vuch and Vinnie claimed to torture. Randy Miller was chosen by Meat and Massella. Randy was mostly silent during the hazing, keeping a distant attitude and his chin held high in performing all the degrading tasks. Vinnie was kind of impressed that Randy could stand on his own. Tobin, on the other hand, just seemed to get worse as the night progressed. He would break out in shaking spells and made the mistake of crying a few times as he was put through his paces. This was probably the worst thing he could do, as Vuch was merciless once he saw the kid was frightened of him. Vinnie proceeded with a fun-loving attitude. Vuch, as he continued to feel the beer set in, became somewhat ruthless in his control over Tobin.

Kirby made a quick trip back to the cabin to pick up a few more brews, and passed them out once most of the seniors had called it a night, drunken out of their minds. Some of the group tired quickly of the games, and headed out instead to the beach to go skinny-dipping, despite the rain. As a kind gesture, those going swimming brought along their captive sophomores, and allowed the younger boys to hang around with their older teammates as a reward for their success on Hell Night. Each of the participating sophomores was proud to accompany the upperclassmen and be considered, even for a while, a part of their group.

Meat, Massella, Vinnie and Vuch stayed in the cabin with Jeff Tobin and Randy Miller. Vuch and Meat had definitely not had their fill of the domination fun. The four seniors sprawled out on two of the beds and continued to make their captives perform for them, Vuch and Meat eagerly attacking the remaining beers. Meat still downed each can in one swift swallow.

"Vuchie, this is gettin' a little tiring," said Vinnie, laying his head down on his arm against the pillow. "I need somethin' to wake me up. How 'bout if we go swimmin'?"

Vuch was sitting on the end of the bed watching, as Miller and Tobin were wrestling. Massella appeared to have fallen asleep on the next bed. Meat was pacing in the cabin. "Yeah, later, okay. I wanna do some more of this." He looked up at Meat as he walked in circles, clasping and unclasping his hands. "Meatman, you look a little edgy."

Meat stopped and looked at Vuch. "Yeah." He continued to open and close his hands.

"Meatman, you're never at a loss for words. Okay boys, hold off your little competition here." The sophomores stopped the wrestling and stood looking at Vuch. "You guys might eventually get some size and muscle on those scrawny bodies, but ain't nothin' gonna give you no size in your dicks." Vuch laughed and took another gulp of his beer. "You don't got nothin' in the meat department." He looked over at Meat who was rocking side to side on his feet nervously. "Speaking of meat, why don't you show 'em what a real dick looks like, eh, Meatman." Without a word, Meat slowly walked over to where the two sophomores stood, pulling his large hog out of the slit in his shorts as he moved. The eyes of Jeff Tobin grew wide as Meat got closer, his dick hanging halfway down his thigh. He began stroking it as he approached, the shaft growing in size with every pull from his hand.

"Jeffy, you ever seen anything like that before?" asked Vuch menacingly. His mouth drew back in a gleeful grin. The boy could only shake his head slowly. He swallowed nervously as Meat got closer.

"Come on, Vuch, leave the kid alone. He's had enough." Vinnie spoke slowly, half-asleep. His eyes kept closing as he talked.

Vuch ignored Vinnie's comments. He stood up slowly and yanked down his own shorts, his dick was half-hard. "See, even I gots more than you little shits, eh." He pulled lazily on his dick as he spoke. He looked at Meat and smiled. "You know, Meatman, maybe we should wrestle the little boys. What you think?"

Randy looked directly at Vuch. "I think we've had enough for one night, okay... sir?" He didn't blink as he continued to gaze at Vuch. "It's late."

Vuch hesitated for a moment. Randy started to move, reaching and picking up his shorts. He put his legs into the opening and pulled them on. Neither Vuch nor Meat moved or said a word. Jeff Tobin stood frozen. Randy continued to look in Vuch's eyes as he moved toward the cabin door. Vuch and Meat followed him across the room with their eyes, but did nothing to stop him. Randy reached the cabin door, opened it, and moved quickly outside. Vuch looked back at Meat, then over to Tobin. Meat continued to stroke his dick — it had grown to full proportions.

Vuch smiled at Tobin. "Well, my little one... shall we have a go at a wrestle?"

Tobin looked nervously around. Both Vinnie and Massella were asleep and could offer no support. He started to shake again. "Come on, Tobin. Wrestle me!" Vuch pulled his shorts down the rest of the way, and yanked off his tee-shirt. He stepped up to the shaking boy, signaling for Tobin to get down on the floor in starting position. Tobin slowly got down on his hands and knees. Meat took a few steps away to give them some room. Vuch got down and put his arm around the kid's bare waist, in opening position for the match. He counted off. "Ready, one... two... three!"

The match began. Tobin tried to struggle as best he could, but his efforts did not last long — he was shaking so badly. Within a few seconds Vuch had him flipped over on his back and pinned to the wooden floor. Tobin looked up into Vuch's eyes. He panicked and started crying.

Vuch did not move, but held the boy firmly in place. "Come on, Jeffy... whatsamatter? Don't you like your puny little body pinned down like this?" His eyes gleamed in triumph. "Or perhaps you just don't like my body pushed so close to yours." He smiled again, showing all his teeth. He belched. "This too much for your little faggot mind to take?" Vuch ground his bare hips into the boy's naked stomach. Tears continued to silently flow down Tobin's cheeks. Vuch shifted his weight, so he could move his hips up the boy's torso. He held Tobin's arms pinned down over his head and sat back onto his chest, his semi-hard dick waving a few inches from Tobin's face. Meat let out a low laugh. He stopped pulling on his own hog and stood watching Vuch's antics.

Vuch bucked his hips slightly. "Come on, Jeffy... lick it!" Meat laughed again. Jeff Tobin looked up into Vuch's eyes, astonished. He shook his head slowly, his eyes still wetting up. Vuch pushed his hips closer to the boy's face. "Yeah. Come on, my little friend. Just stick ya little tongue out and touch it. That's all... just touch it."

Tobin moved his head side-to-side frantically, his whole body shaking uncontrollably. His face had turned pale. Meat got down on his knees and placed his hands under the back of Tobin's head. He laughed, then started to lift the kid's head up to meet Vuch's dick. Tobin tried to shake his head free from the lock that Meat had on it, but his strength was no comparison to the hulk that held him. Meat squeezed the sides of Tobin's head, so he involuntarily opened his mouth. "Come on, stick that tongue out... come on, Jeffy," Vuch taunted. Meat's fingers started getting wet from the boy's tears.

Finally Tobin had no choice. He slid his tongue out slightly. The tip of his tongue just brushed the end of Vuch's dickhead. Suddenly Vuch and Meat jumped up, releasing him. They laughed, as they walked back to where they had placed their clothing. All Tobin could do was raise his head slightly to see what they were doing, his energy wasted out. He brushed the tears away from his eyes. He didn't understand.

Vuch grabbed Vinnie's leg and shook him, as he buttoned up his shorts. "Let's go, Vinnie. Night's over."

Vinnie stirred and slowly got to his feet. Meat woke up Massella. As the four seniors started out the cabin door, Vuch turned back and looked at Jeff Tobin. He still sat in the same position on the floor. He was expressionless. Vuch took a few steps back toward Tobin. He smiled slightly and winked at him. "Don't worry about it kid, I didn't want you to suck it." He smiled his broad smile and nodded his head. "You did okay, Jeff. You're one of the team now." He turned and walked back toward the door. Just as he was about to step outside, he turned back. "You're an okay football player, too. Don't think we don't notice these things." He winked again.

Jeff Tobin smiled wide and wiped away the last of his tears.

* * *

Vuch and Vinnie walked back to the cabin by way of the beach. Some of the squad was still in the water, performing dunking rituals for the newly accepted sophomores. The rain had let up some, but even a downpour wouldn't have changed the playful mood everyone seemed to be in. Vinnie was still somewhat groggy and was glad that Vuch showed no interest in extending the antics of the evening. They watched the swimming for a minute, then continued on the path back toward the cabin. Vinnie watched his footing on the path, as the rain had begun to wash away some of the more solid areas. Small rivers of water cascaded down the embankments toward the lake.

"Hey, Vuchie, how comes Meat took off in such a hurry?"

Vuch turned and shook his head. He wiped a hand over his eyes and started laughing. "You don't want to know, my friend." He laughed harder. "You don't want to know."

Vinnie looked at him. He had no idea what this big mystery was about Meat. They went up the last of the hills to the crest of the embankment and turned down the short walkway to where the seniors' cabins were located. Meat was sitting at the desk as they walked into the cabin. He had the melon on his lap, held firmly between his legs, and was carving a large section out of it with a penknife.

"Hey, Meat. What's up?" Vinnie asked as he walked over and flopped onto the bottom bunk.

Meat merely looked over at him. He did not reply.

"So we gonna have a midnight snack goin' here, or what?" Vinnie asked, still trying to be friendly.

Meat again looked briefly at him and then continued his carving. Vuch walked over to his bed without making any comments. He pulled his tee-shirt over his head and pulled off his shorts. He lay down on his bed in just his underwear, smiling as he watched Meat. Vinnie looked at Vuch and again got a questioning look on his face. Vuch just continued to watch Meat, all the while smiling like a cat that had swallowed a canary. Vinnie lay back and let his eyes close. He could drift off again into sleep so easily. He kept catching himself beginning to drop, several times jumping awake as he heard some movement in the room. He opened his eyes to find he must have dozed a few minutes, the overhead light had been turned off and only the small desk lamp remained on. He looked over at Vuch. He had gotten partially under the bed covers, laying on his stomach with his head turned toward the open window. His face was buried into the pillow and he was snoring rather loudly. *The beer must have taken its final toll on him,* Vinnie thought. He did not wish to be Vuch in the morning when he had to deal with his pounding head.

Realizing he was still fully clothed, Vinnie crawled up off the bunk and walked over to the corner to drop his clothes onto the dresser. He peeled his shirt off and kicked his training shoes halfway under his bunk. At that moment, his attention was drawn to Meat's upper bunk. Meat had lifted himself up onto his arms, but remained laying face down against the mattress. As usual, he was completely naked, but now it appeared his hairy butt was pounding up and down against the bedding. Vinnie smiled to himself, as he figured out that maybe Meat had gotten himself a little over-excited tonight; now he was wacking off to relieve the tension. Vinnie reached down and unbuttoned his shorts and lowered the zipper. His eyes suddenly shot back up to Meat again, finally realizing what it was he was doing. Meat had positioned the large melon under his torso and was wildly fucking the hole he had cut in the fruit.

Vinnie stood frozen, watching Meat savagely pound into the melon, his large hog slamming again and again into the squishy middle. A loud slurping noise could be heard with each thrust. Vinnie's eyes grew wide with disbelief. Meat was actually fucking a piece of fruit! Meat pulled his huge member out completely with each backward thrust, paused a second, then plowed the head furiously back into the gaping hole. He clenched his teeth tightly together and raised his head up high, looking up at the ceiling. His thrusting grew in intensity — the melon beginning to crush under his immense weight. He began to let out a primitive cry as his hips pounded rhythmically into the hole. His hips bucked at a rapid tempo, as sweat dripped off his face. He let out a deep groan and withdrew his hog fully out from the depths of the melon. Suddenly his dick began to pulsate and shoot large gobs of white jism out over the top of the watermelon. He braced himself firmly up on his hands and looked down to watch the hot juice continue to spray across the green-colored skin of the fruit. After a long minute, his hog slowed its quiver and dipped against the side of the melon, the head retracting partway back into the foreskin. He pulled on the tip of his hog a few times, to release all the extra jism.

Vinnie shook his head, as if to wake himself up. He slowly began to pull his shorts down, moving as if in a dream. Meat turned and hopped down off the bunk quickly. He stood on the floor and shook his dick again, more white globs flying off and spraying the floor in little droplets. He turned back to the bed and pulled down the mangled melon from his mattress. He carried it over to the front door of the cabin. Opening the door, Meat lifted the large fruit up over his head and thrust it out into the darkness. He closed the door and pounded across the wooden floor back to the edge of the bunk. He again shook the shaft of his dick, retracting the foreskin back and letting a bit more cum drip off from the inside. He looked up blankly at Vinnie standing at the end of the bunks. Simply nodding to Vinnie in a greeting, Meat hoisted himself back up onto the top bunk and lay face down. Within seconds he was snoring away.

8

By Tuesday afternoon, even the coaches were beginning to smile once in a while. A lot of the tension and ill feelings that were first noticeable on the field, and that seemed to be interfering with playing like an actual team, had disappeared. The sophomores were much more widely accepted and it was not uncommon to see some of the upperclassmen spending free time giving pointers to some of the more talented younger players. The players from the Revere High camp came to scrimmage early Tuesday, and for the first time Northridge was able to play some actual game moves against opponents who were not familiar with the Northridge playbook. The starters were strong and even the attempts on the part of some of the second and third string players showed promise. The weather had only improved slightly. Although no major rain had hit the area, it continued to be overcast with mild drizzle. They had not seen sun since early Saturday afternoon. Since attention was totally on football and the team effort being demonstrated so enticing, nobody seemed to mind the ill-weather conditions they played in.

When the scrimmage action broke for dinner on Tuesday afternoon, Vinnie decided to use the time to grab a quick shower. The mornings had been easier to handle, but personal hygiene had definitely been at an all-time low this whole camp. He knew he could drastically use some time to clean up. As most were hitting the chow hall immediately, Vinnie knew that he would not have to wait for free showers, as had been the case on a few of the evenings lately. He was not surprised to hear the showers running as he entered the building, but sincerely hoped they would not be all in use. He quickly discarded his uniform, leaving it bunched up on the tile floor outside the shower room. His spirits were high, but his energy was a little drained from all his field time during the scrimmage. He dragged his sorry ass under a shower nozzle as quickly as he could. He needed the hot water to massage his muscles, and he needed it now.

Vinnie spun himself around under the shower to wet himself totally. He was surprised when he re-opened his eyes and saw Jeff Tobin under a shower across the room. He thought a moment about the fateful Saturday night of hazing. The last he could really focus on with Tobin had been some wrestling between him and another sophomore. Vinnie knew he had fallen asleep and missed some of the action. Whatever had transpired, he sincerely hoped Tobin had gotten over his crying and shaking spells. He would never make it as one of the team if he kept that pussy attitude. He simply had to be a man about it and take things as they were thrown at him. Vinnie thought a moment about Tobin's field action, it did seem he had a better attitude about playing, almost seeming less intimidated, but since he was third string at best, he didn't get much actual field time.

"Hi, ya, sir! How ya doing?" Tobin had left his place under the shower spray and came over to Vinnie offering his hand. Vinnie nodded and shook his hand quickly. He spun around under the stream of water to wet his hair.

"You looked great out there today! Man, I was wicked impressed. I know you probably don't give a shit about what some of us sophs think about your playing, but everyone's commenting on how fast you take everybody down. You are one solid hitting machine!" Tobin smiled and walked back to his own shower.

"Tobin, you okay?" Vinnie asked somewhat puzzled. Tobin did not seem like the same kid as the other night.

"Yes, sir, I am. Thank you." Tobin rinsed some soap out of his hair.

Vinnie continued to watch him carefully. His actions seemed so different from just a couple of days ago. "So ya actually survived the other night, eh, Tobin?"

"Yes, sir. No problem." He smiled brightly.

"You can skip the 'sir' shit, Tobin. Just call me Vinnie, okay?" Vinnie picked up his bar of soap and started to lather himself up.

"Oh, yes. Okay. Thanks." He smiled again.

"You know Tobin, you seem to have calmed down since the other night. Ya don't seem so fuckin' nervous." Vinnie started to scrub his underarm. He could smell the stench of day-old dry sweat.

"Oh, yeah. Thanks. I'm not, I guess. You know what Vuch said the other night?" He stopped rinsing and advanced a few steps back toward Vinnie. "He actually said I was an okay football player. Can you believe that? He said he's been watching me and stuff. Said he noticed my playing. I couldn't believe it! It made the whole thing that happened Saturday night all worthwhile, you know what I mean?" He took a few steps back, almost jumping in place as he talked. He was genuinely excited. "I mean, he's been helping me on my playing, too. He talks to me like I'm one of the guys, like I'm almost a friend. I can't believe it. It made Saturday all worthwhile. It really did!"

Vinnie dumped some shampoo onto his hand and started to rub it briskly into his hair. "Yeah, whatever, that's great Tobin. I'm glad you feel better." He rinsed his head. Whatever Vuch had said about his playing had certainly got the kid into a good mood. Vinnie quickly finished and walked out to get his towel. Tobin was still taking his time, happily content in his new-found camaraderie.

Tuesday night the downpours of rain really started. Sleep was unusually difficult, due to the noise of the rain pounding down on the cabin roof. The guys discovered that the cabin was not exactly watertight. They had to place several containers around the room to catch the rain as it seeped in through the beams in the ceiling. One of the largest drips came in directly onto Meat's upper bunk, but in typical fashion for Meat he ignored the water and slept as if nothing had changed.

Both Vuch and Vinnie got up slightly earlier than five on Wednesday morning, having had only a few hours of shut-eye. Meat continued his snoring, deep asleep despite the fact that rain dripped directly down onto his exposed butt. Vinnie dressed without much comment. He never did very well when he was deprived of sleep, and the thought of going out and scrimmaging that afternoon in the pelting rain did not sit well with him. Football was always the first thing he would want to do — anywhere, anytime, but Christ, hardly any sleep and sliding around on a muddy field was not the enjoyable part.

Even Vuch was not his typical cheery self as he dressed. He only smiled slightly and didn't said more than "hi". *Yeah, this is gonna be one hell of a day,* Vinnie thought to himself. The first drill session of the day was almost like watching a slapstick movie. All the guys tried their best, but in the deep, wet mud everyone was sliding into each other. Within minutes of starting drills, all uniforms were totally coated and wet. Vinnie could just imagine how full-uniform scrimmage would be after breakfast. Final selections had been made for the first offense and first defense, and the coordinators broke them off to work separately by 6:30 am. This would be the last scrimmage day with Revere. The rival camp game against them would be in just three days. It was finally coming down to show what they could really do as a team.

The formations, pass plays and running plays were endlessly repeated during the rest of the morning session. Coach Morrison made several repeats of the Strong Side Flood, having Vuch take a seven-step drop. Vuch was especially effective in deep floods, taking the drop and having the receivers faking a pattern and going deep. Vinnie worked strongly on the coach's orders to hook the tackle and stay up, never going down onto his knees. He stayed on his feet and blocked hard, remaining as high as possible and pushing with all his strength. If the defensive man slanted to the inside, Vinnie was instructed to go on to the linebacker. The line proved effective in its work. Vinnie was confident in their abilities, his only question was the amount of dependence he could expect from Taglienti. Due to the obvious abilities that Taglienti demonstrated, he was to be the guard next to Vinnie — the coach wanted the stong players on the right side. Taglienti was good, but his attitude toward Vinnie could very easily get in the way. Vinnie worked to keep his mind on the plays and not on his dislike of Taglienti working next to him.

* * *

The dining hall filled almost immediately, once the squad broke for breakfast. Massella and Kirby secured the usual table for their group. The food line moved slowly, as it always did once the onset of players hit the hall. The sophomores now surrendered their positions in line freely, throwing a few playful words back at the domineering seniors. Vuch leaned lazily up against Vinnie, as they stood in line with their trays. Vuch's hair was totally wet and matted down, it dripped onto Vinnie's shoulder as he rested against him. Vinnie pushed Vuch's head back off his shoulder. It immediately flopped back down again. "Come on, Vuch. Straighten up, will yas. I'm tired, too, you know." Vinnie pushed his head up again.

"Aw, lemme just sleep a coupla minutes. Come on, roomie. I'm so fuckin' tired!" He groaned and stood back up straight. "I need sleep." He turned toward the crowd in the dining hall. "I need fuckin' sleep!" he yelled. No one responded. "Thanks for the sympathy, fuckheads!" He turned back in line.

"Well, Meat got sleep anyways," Vinnie yawned. He took a few steps ahead, as the line moved.

"Meat could sleep through a nuclear bombing. The man sleeps dead to the world." Vuch advanced in line. The two passed by the layout of food. Vinnie scooped up three milks. "Gimme extra pancakes, will ya pal?" He half smiled at the guy dishing out the food. He was handed back a plate piled high. "Yes! Energy, please!" He nodded to the server and walked off toward the table.

Vuch smiled at the server. "I'll have sleep, please."

"Huh?" The guy looked curiously at him.

"Nothing, man. Gimme the same thing. Food, yeah, just gimme food." Vuch nodded and took the plate over to the table. He threw a leg over his chair and dropped into it with a thud. "Do me a favor, when I fall asleep down into my flapjacks here, just pick my head up so I don't drown in my fuckin' syrup." He poured a large amount of maple syrup over the stack on his plate.

"Wassamatta, Vuchie? Are we a little grumpy today?" Massella opened his mouth and displayed half-eaten pancakes.

"Our cabin fuckin' leaks!" Vinnie stabbed his fork into the top pancake on his plate. "So we ain't had hardly any sleep. I wouldn't piss me off, if I were you." He shoveled a forkful of pancake into his mouth, giving a 'Don't mess with me' look to Massella.

Kirby looked across the table at Meat, who sat with his head down near the plate and was shoveling in the food quickly. He didn't even seem to take the time to chew before the next forkful was up to his mouth. "Meat, how'd you sleep?" Kirby called down the table. Meat paused. A hunk of pancake fell out of the side of his stuffed mouth. He nodded.

"Yeah, Meatman slept." Vuch chugged down a swallow of milk. "The only one."

Vinnie put down an empty container of milk. He belched loudly. "The fuckin' rain came right down on him, and he sleeps like a fuckin' baby!" Vinnie picked up another container of milk and started ripping at the carton lid. All the guys looked down at Meat. He merely shrugged and kept stabbing at his food. "Well anyways."

Kirby reached his fork over and stabbed at part of a pancake on Massella's plate. Massella lifted his plate and tried to pull it out of Kirby's reach. The piece of pancake slid off the plate and landed on the table. Kirby scooped it up with his fingers and stuffed it into his mouth quickly. "Vuchie, what are the plans for the island? Tomorrow night, or what?" Kirby reached his fork back out toward

Massella's plate. Massella got up and moved over one chair, out of his reach. He triumphantly waved a pancake at Kirby and shoved it into his mouth whole.

"Yeah." Vuch sat up and dropped his fists down onto the table loudly.

Vinnie jumped, having been caught off-guard. "Jesus! I'm half-asleep here, do you mind!" He glared at Vuch.

Vuch smiled broadly. "Yes, gentlemen. Tomorrow night. Remember though, we will still need to have our victory over that pussy-ridden Revere High. Party, we shall, but a team we must remain! Mikey, make a note for me to remind our little sophomore friends to begin to take our gear over right after the scrimmage, will ya?" Vuch patted Massella on the back.

Massella gave him a look. "Yeah, right Vuch! I'll just notate it right here on my fuckin' steno pad!" He gave him the finger.

"Good. Good. But, please, not in shorthand." Vuch winked at him.

Kirby and Massella got up and carried their empty plates over to the dish bin. Meat continued to fork in mouthfuls of food, not paying any attention to what anyone else was doing.

Vuch leaned back in his chair. "Well, Vin, ya wanna head out into the rain again, or what? We can leave the human garbage disposal here to finish by himself." Vuch got up and waited, as Vinnie picked up his tray. They dropped them in the dish bin and went back out through the main hall door. The rain had let up and only a mist was in the sky. They carefully picked their way along the washed-out paths back toward their cabin.

"So where is this Revere High camp, anyways?" asked Vinnie. Vuch stopped a second to secure his footing as they started to ascend the incline toward the seniors' cabins.

"Well, come here." He went off to the side a bit and climbed up a steeper enbankment in the direction of the football field. Vinnie had to bend over and pull his way up the incline, using his hands to help in the ascent. He reached the top, where Vuch stood looking out over the lake. Vuch pointed out to the shore that was visible across the lake. "See that there? That's the island."

Vinnie looked at the shore, which was about half a mile out from their own beach. "That's the island?"

"Yeah. I told ya we swim out to it, didn't I? Yeah, I know I did. Anyways" — he waved his arm down to the left — "it extends down like, I don't know, about four or five miles that ways." He waved

his arm back to the right. "And I guess about a mile or so that way."
He pointed straight across. "Their camp is actually right across from
us, but the island is in the middle. It's further from the island's
shore to their beach than it is from our's here. It must be at least
three times as far. It's too far for them to swim, I know that. When
they bus over here for the game though, it's like a twenty-mile drive
to get here all around the shoreline."

Vuch started back down the steep incline to the path. Vinnie
slid part way back down the hill, his cleats getting buried in mud as
he hit the bottom of the hill. "Shit!" he yelled, as he shook his foot
free from the muddy hole. "This rain sucks, man."

Vuch laughed and grabbed him by the shoulders from behind,
giving him a hard shove. "Come on, peckerhead, let's get some rest
before the scrimmage."

*   *   *

The cabin floor was getting pretty caked with mud from the last
couple of days. Vuch pulled off his cleats and stood on a fairly clean
spot of floor, as he peeled his football pants down his legs. "Jesus,
look at this, will ya?" He sat down on the floor and had to use
several pulls to get the wet pants down and off his ankles. Vinnie sat
on the edge of his bunk, still fully dressed, and watched his room-
mate working to get his clothes off. Vuch managed to get one of his
socks down his calf and yanked it free from his foot. He fell back
against the wall behind him, as the leg came free. "Shit!" He righted
himself and started to tug on the other sock. His bare foot was all
muddy, and even his jock had gotten wet and stained through the
pants. "We might as well just play fuckin' bare-assed! A lot of good
these fuckin' clothes are doing us in this kind of rain." He threw the
second sock over against the dresser, it hit and hung limply from
one of the drawer handles.

"The rain's let up, Vuchie. Maybe we'll get some sun."

"Yeah, and maybe I'm gonna get laid while we're up here, too."
Vuch flung the wet pants over the back of the desk chair. He stepped
across the mud spots on the floor and tumbled onto his bed.

"Hey, let's not expect miracles, huh?" Vinnie laughed. "I don't
think there's a chance in hell of any of us gettin' laid while we's up
here!" Vinnie stood and began the same process Vuch just completed. Vuch pulled his shirt over his head and dropped it on the
floor beside the bed. He laid on top of the mattress in only his jock

and cup. Dirt stains went entirely up his leg and made a pattern across his chest. Vuch picked at the mud clumps around his nipples.

"Hey ya, Vinnie, when was the last time you got laid, anyway?" Vuch turned on his side, so he faced Vinnie as he undressed.

"I dunno." Vinnie pulled his shirt off and turned to lay it over the bedpost. "Hey, it's time we do your back again, man."

Vuch lifted his head up on one elbow. "No, seriously, man, when was the last time you actually got any pussy?"

Vinnie sat on the edge of his bunk and pulled his pants off the end of his feet. He propped one foot up onto the blanket and examined his healing progress. "Hey, this is just about healed totally. That shit you put on my feet the other night really did the trick." He wiggled his toes. "It don't hurt none at all." He looked up at Vuch and grinned. Vuch was still silently looking at him. Vinnie sat back against the wall. "Hell, I don't know! I guess it's been over a year if ya really want to know the truth. But keep that to yourself or I rip ya fuckin' head off. I told ya how that girl went screamin' about me an her slut of a sister." Vinnie extended his legs out across the bed. "And you? The big quarterback star? You must get the hog drained all the fuckin' time, eh?"

"Yeah." Vuch smiled widely and held up his right arm. "With this!" They both laughed. "I guess it's been quite a long time for me, too. I don't know, it's kinda weird, I'm like wicked comfortable just hangin' with the guys on the team and shit. And everyone that hangs with the team treats me like some fuckin' god or somethin'." He leaned forward in Vinnie's direction and lowered his voice. "But, like I'm really shy around girls, you know? I sometimes just don't know what to say. A lot of times I'd rather just hang with my friends on a Saturday night, than bother trying to get up the nerve to get a date." He paused. "Hey, please, Vinnie, this is just between us, okay?"

"Don't worry, Vuchie, I don't want my private life spread all around to anybody, either. It's cool. Just between us."

Vuch sat up on his bed and reached over to open the window. "The rain's stopped, let's get some air in here, okay?" He dropped back flat onto the bed and laid his arm across his eyes. The team was to hit the field and be lined up in full uniform at ten a.m. sharp. They were to run their final scrimmage with Revere, break for lunch and then work on whatever needed serious attention the rest of the day.

The rain had stopped, but there was still a thick cloud cover overhead. Vuch and Vinnie arrived at the makeshift training room at 9:15 for taping. Billy Ruggiero was just finishing up with Tony Marino as they came inside. Pete Taglienti sat over on a side bench with a couple of his friends. He was already taped up and appeared to be just hanging around. "Okay, Manta, let's get you over with." Billy motioned to the table. Vuch spotted Jeff Tobin outside, standing around under a tree with a few other sophomores. He tapped Vinnie on the shoulder as he slid up onto the table. "Hey, man, I'm gonna go arrange with a few of our soph disciples to clean up the mess in our cabin. Tobin and his buddies would lick my butt hole if I told them to. We might as well get some work outta them before we head to the island." He opened the door and started outside. "Hey, Billy, I'll be right back, man." He closed the screen door behind him.

"Okay, Vinnie, pull off those shoes and socks, I wanna tape up those toes again." Billy reached down and grabbed a roll of athletic tape, while Vinnie did as he was told. Taglienti stopped talking with his friends and sat just watching what Billy was doing to Vinnie. He got a smirk on his face as he saw how carefully Billy taped up Vinnie's feet.

"Piggies hurt?" called Taglienti, from where he sat on the bench. His friends laughed. Vinnie turned slowly and looked at Taglienti. He made no reply. Taglienti wiped the back of his hand across his lips. "I'll try not to step on your little toes, Manta." He got up and walked to the screen door, opened it, and spit outside. He leaned against the doorframe and smiled back at Vinnie. "Don't wanna wreck your pedicure!" He spit again and went out the door.

"Okay, Vinnie, you're set." Billy clapped him on the back. Vinnie was just staring at the closed screen door, a deep sneer forming as he clenched his teeth.

"Manta! Today, huh!" Vinnie jumped down off the table. He walked straight ahead and kicked the screen open with his cleat.

The scrimmage moved along quickly. Vuch was demonstrating excellent pass technique, starting out with several completions, but finding that Revere was strong in defense and was beginning to find open men to intercept his plays. Guy Mitchell and Tom Walter called the line over for some orders. Helmets were removed and the squad got down on one knee to listen up.

"Okay, we're showing weakness in blocking!" Tom Walter rubbed his hands together as he spoke. "I want to see blocking action out there! Manta! Nismont! Tag! Let's get those completions! Get their guys outta Carvuccio's way!"

As the team returned to the line of scrimmage, the rains came again in forceful downpours. Northridge was able to begin gaining decent yardage, the tackles and guards pulling together to allow Vuch to do his thing. It was in the final plays, after being rained on solidly for over an hour, that the tension ran too high. The line was in position, waiting for Vuch's count. As the ball was snapped, Taglienti moved one count too fast. He stepped to his left and took out Vinnie's man. The turn of his body enabled him to take down his intended target as well. Vinnie, as viewed from the sideline, was left just standing there looking stupid.

Once the break was called, the team headed immediately down for lunch — everyone wanted to just get the hell out of the downpour. Nismont and Alasambra ran past Vinnie as they took off in the direction of the dining hall. Alasambra turned and called back over his shoulder. "Manta, why'd you just stand there on that play?" He turned back straight as he continued to run. Vinnie felt the throb in his forehead. Taglienti was a fuckin' prick. He rubbed his knuckles into his closed eyes. Vuch clapped a hand onto his shoulder. "Hey, you okay, bro?"

Vinnie yanked his shoulder away from Vuch's grasp. He spun around, glaring at Vuch. He spit as he yelled: "Did you see that prick Taglienti? Did you?" He threw his helmet into the mud. "Did you see what that fuckin' pussy did? He cut me off! He took out my guy and made me look like a fuckin' idiot!" Vinnie eyes bulged in anger.

"Hey, easy, man. It's okay." Vuch put his hand against Vinnie's chest to steady him. Vinnie stepped back from Vuch's touch, nearly losing his balance in the mud, which angered him even more. He stood for a second, the rain pelting down over his face, and looked around the field. He spotted Taglienti over by the foot of the embankment near the path, his back to Vinnie. It was obvious he was standing there joking with his friends, he kept bending over slightly as he laughed. Vinnie took off toward Taglienti, running as quickly as the muddy terrain would allow.

Vuch watched as he sped off across the field, then bent down and picked up Vinnie's helmet. A pool of muddy water had partially filled up the inside. He dumped out the water, then started walking over toward them. As soon as Vinnie got to Taglienti, he reached out and spun him around. Before Taglienti could register who or what was happening, he felt a fist pound down against his teeth. Taglienti stumbled back and landed on his ass in the mud. He quickly jumped up and tackled Vinnie around the knees, sending them both backward down the slope and onto the edge of the field. Taglienti raised up his fist, but before he could strike, another blow came down squarely on the side of his jaw. He head twisted and plowed into a pool of water. For a moment he lay stunned, then lifted his face out of the puddle. Another slam came immediately down across his face, this time sending a string of blood out the side of his mouth. Vinnie pulled his arm back taking aim again, but Vuch ran over and caught his arm mid-air. He pulled Vinnie's arm back firmly, keeping him from sending another blow into Taglienti.

Two of Taglienti's friends jumped in and pinned Pete down also. "Alright, Vinnie! Enough!" Vuch screamed in his ear. He kept pulling at his arm which was still poised over Taglienti's face. Taglienti scurried backward and was helped up to a crouching position by his buddies.

"Jesus!" Blood flowed from the side of Taglienti's mouth as he spoke. "What the fuck are you doin', you psycho! Christ! He just came flyin' at me!" He wiped his mouth with his hand. Blood coated two of his fingers as he withdrew it from his lips. Vinnie tried to pull away from Vuch's grasp, but kept sliding in the mud. He couldn't get enough leverage to free himself, or his strength would have been no match for Vuch. Vinnie's eyes burned hatred. "If you ever fuckin' try to screw me up again, Taglienti... I'll fuckin' take you down so fuckin' hard!"

Vinnie managed to free his arm from Vuch, who immediately grasped him around the waist with both arms so Vinnie could not advance toward Taglienti. Vinnie poked the finger of his free hand out into the air at Taglienti. "Do you understand me, you motherfucker?" Vinnie spit as he yelled. "Do you!"

Taglienti recoiled. His eyes bulged at the intensity of the threat in Vinnie's voice. "Yeah, man. I heard you." His voice trailed off. "Yeah." Taglienti yanked himself free from the grasp of his friends. He stood straight and looked around. A small amount of blood still oozed out of the cut on his lip. His eyes darted side to side. "Yeah, man, no problem. No problem." Taglienti looked around nervously, glad that Vuch still had his lock around Vinnie's waist. He walked slowly up the hill. Taglienti's two friends nodded at Vuch and then followed behind Pete. Vuch squeezed Vinnie around the waist tighter. He leaned into his ear and spoke loudly. "You done?" He squeezed Vinnie's waist again. "You done, you stupid fuck?" Vinnie just nodded. Vuch released him. He stood there just looking at Vinnie watch Taglienti go up the hill. The sneer was still on Vinnie's face.

"Good one, bro." Vuch smiled his white toothed grin, then walked on up the embankment. After the chalk talk in the auditorium that night, Vinnie decided to go right back to the cabin and catch up on some sleep. Meat, as usual, had the same idea. They left Vuch in the auditorium talking with some of the guys, and walked out into the night together.

Meat surprised Vinnie when he patted him on his back as they started out on the path. "Heard you and Taglienti duked it out, eh?" Vinnie felt a sneer coming across his face. He didn't really want to go over this again, especially with someone like Meat. He had already had to recount the story to several guys during the afternoon and evening drills.

"Yeah. No big deal." Vinnie kept walking silently hoping that was the end of the subject. They reached the cabin and went in.

"I can't stand Taglienti," voiced Meat, as he pulled his clothing off in his typical brisk fashion. He climbed up onto his bunk and dangled his legs over the side again, watching Vinnie. Vinnie was just at the point of removing his shoes, in the time it took Meat to fully undress and get up on his bunk.

Vinnie paused, as he sat down to pull off his socks. "I thought you couldn't really stand anybody." He leaned his back against the metal frame of Vuch's bed for balance.

Meat scratched himself under his arms. "I like you. I like Vuch. Some of the other guys are okay."

"You like me?" Vinnie looked at him increduously. "Come on, Meat, you can't exactly say we're friends."

"Yeah, we're friends." He folded one leg up under the other and rubbed the top of his foot. "You're a friend of mine."

"Meat, I don't even fuckin' know you." Vinnie stood and unbuckled his pants and dropped them to the floor. "I never thought you even liked me. I thought you disliked me."

Meat looked up blankly. "No, Vinnie, you'd know it if I didn't like you. I consider you a friend. I just don't say a lot." He turned and laid on his back on the mattress, his hog flopping to one side as he moved. He was obviously going to sleep, and had said all that he intended to. Vinnie pulled his underwear off and dropped them in their usual place beside his bunk. He noticed the floor was perfectly clean, all traces of mud were gone. He guessed Vuch's sophomores had done their cleaning job.

"Maybe you should say more, Meat," said Vinnie as he slid in under his covers.

"What's that, Vinnie?" came the voice from above.

"Say more. Maybe you should say more. Especially to your friends."

Meat just grunted.

"Night, Meat." Vinnie turned on his side and was asleep in a matter of seconds.

* * *

Vinnie was awakened in the dark by a gentle nudge against his shoulder. He opened his eyes, trying to focus on what had happened. He drifted back into sleep. Again came the push... this time harder. "Whaaa?" He rubbed his eye with his fist. "What the fuck?"

"Slide over, Vin."

"What? What are you talkin' about?... Vuchie?" Vinnie sat halfway up in bed. "Vuchie?"

"Yeah, it's me. Slide over Vinnie, lemme in."

"What are you talkin' about?" Vinnie fell back down against the pillow. "Leave me alone, Vuch... it's the middle of the night. I need sleep." He pulled the pillow over part of his face.

"I do too. Slide over and lemme in with you." Vuch pushed against his side, and began to stick his legs under the bedcovers.

Vinnie pulled the pillow away from his face. His eyes were still sleepy and unfocused. "What are you doin', man? Get away. Go get in your own bed." He turned onto his side and faced the wall. Vuch slid in the rest of the way, his chest was against Vinnie's back.

"I can't get in my bed. I left the fuckin' window open. That last downpour soaked my whole mattress." Vuch waited a moment. No reply.

"Vinnie?" Vinnie had fallen back asleep. Vuch slid down a bit further, pressing his legs and whole upper body firmly against Vinnie's backside. He noticed Vinnie was sleeping bare-assed again. He pulled the covers closer to him, trying to keep the cool night air out. He buried his face into the back of Vinnie's neck. He felt warm and comfortable. Slowly Vuch drifted off to sleep.

9

Vinnie first stirred when he felt movement against his leg. He half-opened his eyes and then began to drift off again. He had almost dropped back into sleep when the movement came again against his left foot. Vinnie moved his torso slightly. He was on his side and facing the wall. He opened his eyes and looked down toward the foot of the bed. An arm was wrapped around his waist, the hand dangling in the air, but with the thumb pressed against Vinnie's stomach. His senses became more awake, and he could feel a body pressed closely against his back and butt. Vinnie lay perfectly still and tried to remember what the hell was going on. His thoughts suddenly focused on Vuch pushing him aside in the middle of the night. The body laying so tightly against him must be Vuch.

Movement came from directly behind his head. Vuch was shifting his face slightly, burying it against the back of Vinnie's neck. He could feel the warm breath on his skin. The arm tightened more around Vinnie's hips, the fingers moving slightly across his stomach. A feeling of excitement shot through Vinnie's body. He looked at the light on the wall in front of his face. It had only the very beginnings of a grey tint — the sun was still not nearly up yet. It was very early in the morning, he judged possibly around four.

The face behind him shifted again in sleep. Vinnie now could feel Vuch's lips slightly touching his neck. He closed his eyes and relaxed. Soon he drifted back into sleep. Movement again stirred Vinnie awake. Time had passed, because he now observed the room was filled with a reddish glow. Vinnie had also turned onto his other side in his sleep, he now lay facing back toward the center of the cabin, his eyes focusing directly in front of him. Vuch still lay asleep, his face only a couple of inches away from Vinnie's own. Vuch's arm remained draped over Vinnie's waist, though now the hand lay against Vinnie's butt. In turning onto his other side, Vinnie had pulled the blankets and sheet off from the back of his body. Vuch's hand lay on Vinnie's naked skin, the fingers gently cupping around his butt cheek. Vinnie focused closely on Vuch's face. He could see the rapid shifting of Vuch's eyes under his closed eyelids. Vinnie remembered that was called 'rapid eye movement'— it meant Vuch was in a state of deep sleep. His movements and shifting of his body were involuntary. He must not realize that he had been snuggling against Vinnie's neck earlier, nor was he aware his hand now lay against Vinnie's ass.

Vuch's breath felt warm as it hit Vinnie's face. It had a sweet smell to it, not the expected rancid odor. His lips were parted slightly, and even in this dull light his teeth gleamed brightly. A light coating of moisture was visible. Vinnie moved his lower body slowly, adjusting more comfortably on his side. Vuch responded in his sleep, pulling himself closer around Vinnie and wrapping one of his legs between Vinnie's calves. Vinnie suddenly realized he lay naked, as his dick began to respond to the movement against it. He instantly felt uncomfortable at the thought of the two of them lying so closely together. He tried to clear his mind, but his hard-on continued to grow. He could feel the shaft lifting off the bed sheet, the blood filling his dick and causing a warm sensation through his lower body. His dick rose and came to rest against Vuch's hip. Fortunately, Vuch was wearing his jockey shorts and Vinnie's dick did not come into direct contact with his skin — that would have been way out of line.

Vinnie closed his eyes tightly, trying to think of a decent way to get out of this position, without having to try to explain why his hog was rock hard and rubbing against his buddy's body.

"Morning," said a raspy voice. Vinnie could feel the breath increase against him as Vuch spoke. He re-opened his eyes. Vuch was staring right into his eyes, the trademark smile beginning to cross his lips. He licked the moisture off his teeth, then smiled again.

"Er... hi," Vinnie said slowly. He had no idea how to respond to this situation.

Vuch did not move, as he came awake. He let his arm remain on Vinnie's butt and kept his leg entwined in Vinnie's. He licked his lips a few times to wake up his mouth. "You sleep okay?" he asked. His voice remained in low tones.

"Yeah. Er, yeah, I guess so." Vinnie took this opportunity to shift slightly to his left and onto more of his back. This, at least, put a few more inches between them, and got his hog away from rubbing up against Vuch's body.

Vuch shifted his arm a little, but let it remain on Vinnie. "I wasn't sure you'd even remember that I got into the sack here with you. I can just imagine your surprise when you opened your eyes." He chuckled a bit.

"No... no, I remembered you said your bed was wet," Vinnie stammered. "It was no surprise. I tried to keep adjusting so you could have enough room... I guess I didn't do so good... cause we got all tangled up a few times." Vinnie spoke in a nervous, rapid manner. He felt extremely uncomfortable. He didn't want his physical state, or his lying so close, to be misunderstood. "It's all my fault. I'm sorry... I guess I didn't give you enough room." Vinnie pulled back another inch, trying to show he was offering more space.

Still Vuch did not attempt to move his hand or his leg. He yawned. "Hey, no problem. I was perfectly comfortable. The bed is nice and warm." He placed his left arm up under his head, raising it off the pillow, but kept his right arm across Vinnie. "So what time is it anyway, bro?" He turned his head to look out into the middle of the cabin. Vinnie noticed the back of his hair stood up where he had been lying against it.

"Uh, I don't know. The alarm hasn't gone off yet. I don't know... somewhere around four-thirty."

"Ah, good. Still time to relax." Vuch closed his eyes. He finally lifted his arm off Vinnie and scratched his armpit, then let the arm drop back down to rest on Vinnie's thigh. The movement of the sheet from the hand coming down outlined Vinnie's still half-hard dick. "Did you dream last night?" Vuch turned more onto his side and put his face back down on the pillow, his chin now laying on Vinnie's shoulder.

"Nah."

"I did. I dreamed we kicked ass on the field against Revere." Vuch rubbed his leg up and down Vinnie's. Vinnie recoiled from the touch. "Feel those hairs? I was thinkin' about shavin' those off so my legs would look better, what do ya think?"

"I dunno. Yeah, I guess." Vuch pulled the sheet back from his legs and lifted his right leg up in the air. He ran his hand over the hair. "I don't know. Just a thought. This wicked big moose of a guy named Joey, who competes in bodybuilding, shaves his legs. I was just thinkin' about it, that's all." The movement of the sheet from across Vuch's legs shifted part of the blanket covering Vinnie. His crotch area became exposed as Vuch pulled his leg out.

"I dunno. I guess you could shave 'em. Lots of work though, eh?" Vinnie yanked part of the blanket back to cover himself.

"Yeah, I guess it would be a lot of work. Hey, Vinnie, you gotta go?"

"What? What are you talkin' about? Go where?"

"You know... go take a leak. You got a piss-hard."

Vinnie turned red, and shifted his position again. He was feeling uncomfortable and embarrassed. "Er, yeah, I gotta go. I'll wait, though." He turned slightly away.

"Oh, hey man, I didn't mean to embarrass ya or nothin'. I only noticed cause, well... there it was, ya know. No big deal." Vuch smiled again and nudged him on the shoulder. Vinnie moved another inch away and shrugged. He didn't know what to say. God, he wished this would all go away! "No really, man! It's just cause you sleep in the buff, ya know?" Vuch kicked the blankets off his waist area. He had his white jockey shorts on. "Look, man, I gots one too." He lifted his hips up and pointed to the outline of his hard-on in his underwear. "I get it every mornin'. Or whenever I sleep right close to somebody. Just body contact, ya know?"

Vinnie looked away. This was not getting any better or any more relaxed.

"Yeah, that's nice, Vuch. You got a hog too. Congratulations. Can we talk about somethin' else now? Please!"

Vuch shrugged and pulled the blankets back up around his chin. He still lay against Vinnie's shoulder. "Yeah, sure, Vin. Sorry. Didn't mean to make ya uncomfortable." Vuch moved his face down on the pillow, now his hair rested against Vinnie's cheek. "I guess I've just had to share a bed enough that these kinds of things are just no big deal."

Vinnie relaxed a bit and let his head fall partly against Vuch's hair. "Yeah, well it's no big deal for me either." He crossed his ankles. "Really. No big deal."

* * *

Once the guys were dressed, they set about their usual task of rousing Meat. Each morning it seemed more difficult. "Ya know," said Vuch, as he stepped back from the edge of the bunk, "he's sleepin' more soundly every fuckin' night. It's like the more he puts into playin', the more he puts into sleepin'." He moved back and leaned his butt against the edge of the desk. "Meat!" he yelled at the top of his voice. The snoring stopped. "Meat!" he yelled a second time. Suddenly the legs flew over the side of the bunk and Meat came jumping down. In two strides he was over to the dresser and digging through the drawers for clothes. Vuch stood with his mouth still open from yelling. He barely had time to inhale.

Vinnie walked by Vuch and patted him on the chin, physically closing Vuch's mouth in the process. "I think he's up!"

"We gots to lay out all the shit the sophs are to pick up, right, Vuch?" Meat snorted out, sleep still in his voice.

"What?" Vuch was still standing, trying to figure out how fast that had all happened. "Oh, yeah.... right."

"What are ya talkin' about?" Vinnie stood at the open cabin door, ready to step out.

"We have to pile all the stuff we're gonna take to the island in the middle of the cabin here. That way, the sophs will know what to load in the boats to take over to the island." Vuch walked over to their dresser, pulled open a drawer and started yanking out clothes. "You better do it now, Vin. They're gonna start takin' stuff probably before dinner. The coaches usually let 'em slack off in the afternoon, knowin' they got all that rowin' to do."

"What time do we go over?" Vinnie still leaned against the doorframe.

"Six. We always go right about six." Vuch smelled one of the shirts he picked up from the floor. Deciding it would still be wearable, he threw it into the pile collecting on his bed. "We're only gettin' one full night over there this year, I heard Billy talking to Morrison. They want us back here by ten tomorrow night, so we're rested for the final game on Saturday morning." He smelled another shirt, decided it was too ripe to take, and dropped it back into the dresser drawer. "They'll be making the announcements once we hit the field this morning."

Vinnie hesitated and stuck his head out the screen door. He grinned and turned his head back so Vuch and Meat could hear him. "We got sun, boys! We got pure A-fuckin' sunshine out here!"

Meat shoved past him out the door. He stood outside in just his jock and cup. "Yeee... Ha!" he yelled at the top of his lungs. He jumped down off the steps and danced around on the dry path. Sun shone brightly down through the trees. Meat stepped out into an area that was flooded in sunshine. He held his face up toward the sky, letting the light blanket his skin.

Vuch appeared at the doorway and stuck his head past Vinnie's shoulder. "Jesus, not a fuckin' cloud in the sky." He slapped Vinnie hard on the back. "It's gonna be a great day, bro." He pulled his head in and walked back to his bed, playfully throwing himself onto the clothes pile that was forming in the middle of the mattress. "What a fuckin' primo day to go over to the island! I am so fuckin' psyched!" He let out a yell of pleasure. Vinnie walked over to the dresser, pulled open the drawer under Vuch's, and began to pull out his clothes.

The morning and afternoon drill sessions were actually the most fun they had had all week. Everyone had a real festive attitude, partly because of the anticipation of the island, but also because of the growing relationship between all the levels of players. Offensively, the coaches concentrated on an attack based on multiple sets, using motion and shifting. Out of this came the two basic plays they drilled, the pitch and the blast. These were endlessly repeated all day. First offense would run them for several repetitions, then second would run, and finally, the third tried them. Vinnie and Vuch were both pleased to see Jeff Tobin being put into second offense, agreeing that there was more than just a change in his attitude and personality — it extended also into his playing abilities. He performed much more confidently. Vinnie knew this all had to do with his acceptance by Vuch. Vuch really could work magic with just his smile and a kind word.

After lunch, the announcement was made that the sophomores did not have to report to the field. The juniors and seniors would work on more drills, the first offense being made up entirely of the upperclassmen. The sophomores eagerly went about their delivery tasks. Two rowboats had been secured to use for the transport of the upperclass belongings.

Vuch had been right, their cheerful attitude stemmed from the fact they were able to get rid of their tormentors for an entire night and party amongst themselves. Although the past Saturday night was the only time of group hazing, many of the other seniors had utilized the sophomores for personal tasks and cabin cleaning. They probably needed the rest from the extra work — the football practices being more than enough of an energy drain.

After dinner, Vuch, Meat and Vinnie made one last trip back to the cabin before the trek to the island would begin. "Well, they gots all our stuff," said Vuch surveying the room. "Vinnie, if there is any clothes that you want to wear right when you get there, one final boat trip goes over during the swim."

"No, I sent everything I need in my duffle." He leaned against the desk watching Vuch and Meat check out their dressers for last-minute stuff.

"Well, then just the shirts on our backs and the shoes on our feet." Vuch walked to the door. "Gentlemen, we are off!"

Meat pushed his way past Vuch and bounded down the steps again. Vinnie and Vuch walked out and watched, as Meat ran down the pathway toward the beach area, howling at the top of his lungs. Vuch turned to Vinnie and shrugged. "Hey, the man's an animal... what can I say?"

The crowd of upperclassmen had gathered on the beach. The last items were being tossed into the boats as guys were pulling off shirts and shoes and sweats. "Hey, Vuchie, they could just stick this shit in one boat. Why bother having two go over?"

Vinnie dropped his sneakers into the bow of one of the rowboats. "'Cause, bro, we ain't gettin' stranded over there without no boat! Two sophs row over and leave us one of the boats." He slapped Vinnie on one of his ears. Vinnie pulled away, annoyed. "That'd be pretty fuckin' stupid to stick us over there without any safety net, don't ya think?" He pulled off his tee-shirt and dropped it on top of Vinnie's shoes.

"Yeah, okay." Vinnie walked over to the water's edge. Greg Alasambra sat silently in the middle of a seat of one of the boats. Vinnie walked up and leaned on the side, causing it to tip slightly. Alasambra reached out quickly and grabbed both edges of the boat to steady it. "Hi, ya, Gregie. All set for the big swim?" Vinnie seated himself on the frame, tipping the boat again.

"Hey, cut it out, will ya!" Alasambra reached out and returned it to a straight position. "No, I don't swim. I don't swim at all." He looked nervously side to side to make sure the boat was upright.

"You don't know how to swim?" Vinnie asked. He grinned.

"No, I don't! You got a fuckin' problem with that?" Alasambra's voice got high-pitched.

Vinnie stood up. "Hey man, no, not at all. Take it easy." Vinnie held up his hands in protest. "Just take it easy, Greg... Jeez!" The boat rocked again as Vinnie stood up, removing his weight from the one side. Alasambra flashed a look of panic again and tried to balance it.

Vuch walked up to Vinnie. "All set? Let's get goin'." He started to wade into the water, and Vinnie followed. Once they got knee deep in water, Vuch leaned into Vinnie. "Try to stay clear of Alasambra until we're securely on land. He's a bit highstrung around water." Vuch pushed off and started to swim.

"No shit!" yelled Vinnie, as he dove into the deeper water. The sun was still high enough in the sky to allow a perfect view of the land as they swam toward the opposite shore. All seventy-four upperclassmen were journeying over to the island. Alasambra was obviously the only one who could not swim. He sat in the center of the boat throughout the trip, a constant look of panic on his face. The swimming attire of the group varied from actual swim suits through jockstraps to buck-naked — the norm being loose gym shorts. Halfway across Vinnie caught up with Vuch and the swim became a race to the land. Although the half-mile was not a great distance, they had already been through a day of football practice. Many of the guys arrived on the beach quite out of breath.

* * *

Vuch beached just ahead of Vinnie, and took an immediate opportunity to lay flat on the sand and recover. He lifted his head and watched as Vinnie pulled himself up out of the water. "Come on, you pussy! Come on, Vin, all out! Get those legs movin'!" He lay back and laughed, closing his eyes and starting to soak up the rays.

Vinnie came up the beach breathing hard, water dripping from his torso, and dropped to the sand. "Jesus Christ! I can't catch my breath." He fell to his knees. "Shit, I got a kink in my neck, I can't breathe... gee, this was a fuckin' great idea to swim here!" He continued to gasp and sat back on his heels, trying to stabilize his breathing.

"Whatsamatta, Vinnie? Got a pain in your little neck?" Vuch mimicked sarcastically. "Poor baby."

"Suck me." Vinnie flopped down into the sand headfirst. He lay still on his stomach, letting the warm hot sun dry his back. Vuch propped himself up on one elbow, reached over and started massaging Vinnie's neck. Immediately, another uncomfortable feeling came over Vinnie. He tensed at the touch of Vuch's hand.

"Relax. Jesus!" Vinnie consciously tried to relax his muscles. All around them guys were emerging from the water and falling into the sand in immediate relaxation.

Vuch looked over to the edge of the water and saw the boat carrying Alasambra setting up on shore. "His highness Gregory just docked."

"I'll bet he's not out of breath. I should have taken the boat over."

"No, actually he might be more breathless than you, Vin ol' boy, he's got that look of fear all over him." Vuch intensified the pressure of his hand. "Looks kinda green to me."

Vinnie flipped over onto his back. The sun felt immediately warm against his chest. Sand stuck to the black hair covering his entire front side.

"Now how ya gonna get any color like that? You got enough hair and shit all over you, no rays are gonna get through that!" Vuch turned and slowly lay back, purposely displaying his well tanned and hairless body.

"Yeah. We know. Thanks, Vuch. Yeah, you have a golden tan. And we're all really happy for you." Vinnie adjusted himself so his head rose slightly to the angle of the sun. "You prick."

Vuch lifted his hips up and reached down and slipped his shorts off. He rolled up the wet shorts and tucked them behind his head like a pillow.

"Ya gonna burn ya hog off, ya stupid shit."

"Nah. I lay out without clothes all the time."

"No tan lines, eh? Girls like that, I suppose."

Vuch lifted himself back up on his arm and turned to Vinnie. "I don't really know. As I said, it's been so fuckin' long, I don't even remember how." He flicked a few grains of sand off Vinnie's side.

"Well, it's like riding a bicycle, Vuchie."

"No, I think it was a little more enjoyable than that!"

Vinnie opened one eye and grinned. All around them, activity had already begun. Guys were hooting and throwing each other into the water as fast as they were coming out. The two sophomores who had rowed the boats over were busy unloading all the last-minute gear they had transported. Vinnie lifted one leg up and planted his foot firmly into the sand, pointing his knee up toward the sun. He could feel the shifting of the loose, wet shorts. One of his nuts flopped against his thigh, exposing it to the hot rays. He made a mental note not to stay in this position very long. Unlike Vuch, he did not lay out without clothes during the summer. He did not want a fried testicle.

Meat lumbered up beside them and dropped to the sand right next to Vinnie. Vinnie raised his head for a moment to see who it was. "Hey, Meat! Survive that nice vigorous swim?"

"Yeah." Meat lay down on the beach, his body covering with sand as he adjusted himself. He responded with only the one word.

"Okay. Nice talkin' to ya, Meat." Vinnie turned and opened his eyes. Meat was actually smiling back.

Vuch suddenly sat upright. He spread his legs slightly to get his balance and looked around. Vinnie turned his head and looked at him. In the bright sunlight, he could see the line that Vuch had purposely created in shaving. The hair grew thick, all at once, in a straight line about three inches below his navel that ran downward toward his cock. He realized Vuch must shave his stomach hair carefully to create that look. He did not have any tan line at all — his golden skin the product of many hours lying naked in the sun. Vinnie etched the picture into his mind. Vuch's dick was longer than his own. Vinnie had often had jokes made about how short and fat his hog was, but it grew to far larger proportions when he got aroused — the length ending up not being anything too long, but the thickness growing to three times what it was when soft. Ever since he had been a child, to him it had always been his 'fat hog'.

Vuch turned and looked at Vinnie. "You know, we should go gather up our stuff and secure it with the other bags that came over earlier." He got to his feet and started putting on his shorts.

"Yeah. Okay. Whatever." Vinnie stood up and brushed sand off his stomach.

Vuch led the way toward the boats. "Meatman, you comin' or what?"

"Fuck it, man. We only got another few minutes of rays comin' down. Just grab my bag. The leather one. You know it." Meat closed his eyes.

Vinnie and Vuch gathered up their stuff and Meat's bag. "So like... where do we stow this stuff? Where do we sleep?" asked Vinnie.

Vuch pointed his chin in the direction of a path that led into the woods. He boosted one of the bags up around his shoulder and held his shoes and shirt in his hands. "Follow me. This way." He led off onto the path.

Once away from the beach, the light dimmed considerably. Dusk was approaching in an hour or so, and the filtered sunlight coming through the trees was minimal. Voices could be heard ahead, but due to tree branches bending down over the sandy path, no one could be seen. Pine branches scratched against Vinnie's bare chest and arms, as they pushed their way through the brush. "Shit!" Vinnie stopped a moment and pulled a burr from the hair on his arm. "Vuchie, this sucks. We shoulda put our shirts back on before we came through this shit."

"Just up here, Manta. We just gotta go a bit more." Vuch pushed on ahead and turned so his back would push away a large pine branch. He stood and held it out of the way for Vinnie to pass. Once past the grove of dense pines, they came to a clearing that opened up like a large courtyard. Brick fireplaces were staggered around the edge of the circle that made up the border of the clearing. Pine needles blanketed the forest floor like a carpet. Sunlight flooded part of the circle, the setting sun making its way down over the tops of the giant trees. Vuch dropped the gear on the ground.

"This is it?" asked Vinnie. "This is where we stay? You're shittin' me, right?"

Vuch smiled. "Not here, dipshit. There." He pointed off to the far edge of the clearing, opposite where they stood. The shadows somewhat obscured the view, but Vinnie was able to make out some sort of wooden building structure — a height of at least three floors. The wood was painted a dark red, making it difficult to comprehend just how large the building actually was. A white wooden railing seemed to wrap around each floor creating a porch effect all around the building. "What the fuck is that?"

"It's an old deserted boys' camp. You know... like a summer retreat kinda place." Vuch picked up the gear again and started walking to the building. "It's where we stash our stuff and sleep sometimes. Some of the guys sleep inside here, some like to sleep down on the beach." He turned and grinned. "Cause we gots ourselves quite a supply of brew with us, some of the guys just pass out... wherever."

"Cool," Vinnie nodded. "I need a good night of partying right about now." They approached the bottom of the building. It was quite large. The structure looked like it had been deserted for quite some time. The boards were rotting and much of the paint had chipped off. The roof itself sagged down on one side, giving the appearance that it might not stand all that much longer. "Is this place even safe?" Vinnie looked in through one of the doorways. The doors themselves were missing.

"Yeah. It's okay. Some of it, especially up on the top floor, ya should kinda steer clear of, but we've all been in here the last few years and nothing has come down on us yet." Vuch walked into the first floor lobby. The room had high ceilings and was huge. His voice echoed off the old bare walls as he spoke. "Course I slept down on the beach last year, but Meat and a lot of the guys bunked in here. Might have mice and shit, though." He kicked some old boards that were laying on the cement floor.

Kirby and Massella came running in. Kirby was leading and carrying two gymbags. Massella was chasing him and obviously trying to get one of them back. "Give me the fuckin' thing, you prick!" Massella caught up to him and yanked one of the bags out of his hand. Kirby stood laughing and trying to catch his balance. "Hey, men." Massella swung the bag over his shoulder and spun in a circle, checking out the room. "Jesus, this place, like... falls down more every year, huh? I guess it's the beach for sleepin' this year." He dropped his bag on the floor, got down on one knee and started digging through the contents. He immediately got back up off his knee, remaining in a stooping position as he looked through the bag. "Jesus, stay off this floor. It's got all kindsa nails and shit." He pulled out a pair of dry shorts. Keeping his shoes on, he pulled off the wet pair he had swam in and started to get into the dry ones. One of his shoes caught in the leg opening and he stumbled against Kirby. "Shit!"

Kirby braced him until he could get his foot in the shorts. He then stepped back and pulled the shorts up over his hips. Massella placed the wet shorts in his bag, stood back up and walked around the perimeter of the lobby. Vinnie noticed that he had forgotten to zip up the new pair of shorts he had put on. Reddish pubic hair jutted out the fly as he walked.

Vuch looked at his watch. "Okay, it's 7:30. It'll be totally dark in about forty-five minutes. Let's find where they stuck all the food, get a fire going and eat." He headed back out the open doorway to the clearing outside where everyone was gathering. "It's party time!"

The food that had been sent over was minimal at best. It consisted mostly of sandwiches and pre-cooked chicken. Fires were lit in several of the stone fireplaces that were scattered around the edge of the clearing. The pre-cooked food was placed in aluminum foil and heated over the flames. Vinnie noticed that the seniors took charge of getting the meal cooked and distributed. This being their second year on the island, they knew how to go about feeding all the guys. It was no small task, but everyone pretty much antici-pated getting wrecked on the beer and couldn't really give a shit about the quality or amount of food. After the meal, it was decided that everyone would just go wherever they wanted. The island was big and many of the guys wanted to go exploring. It was decided that all would meet on the beach at 10:30. Coolers of beer were located inside the boys' camp lobby and down at the beach. Every-one took what they wanted with them.

* * *

Vuch, Vinnie, Kirby, Massella and Meat hung together, as usual. "Okay, let's get a coupla six-packs and head over to the rocks on the far side of the island." Vuch tipped his head in the direction of an-other path that led off into the woods. Meat pulled the packs out of one of the coolers and followed Vuch's lead into the darkness. The guys stayed closely together, with Vuch in the lead. There was only the light coming down from the moon, and even that would be-come obscured by the trees every few feet. The guys were constantly stumbling into each other as they made their way down the wind-ing path.

"Vuch, do you have any fuckin' idea where you're goin'?" Massella playfully shoved Kirby, who in turn fell into Vinnie.

"Hey, cut it out." Vinnie turned and shoved back. Massella fell back against Meat who was taking up the rear of the line.

"Oh, sorry Meat. I just meant to get these two fucks," Vinnie chuckled, although he knew Meat could not even see him in the darkness.

Vuch stopped and turned back to the group. "Yeah, Mikey, you remember this beach over here? It's just a little ways more. You know... the one that looks over onto the other camp." They emerged a minute later onto another, smaller beach. It was mostly rocks, the sand not being the fine granular type over on the other side of the island. Vuch climbed up on top of a large boulder that stuck out into the water. The guys spread themselves out, some on rocks and some on the coarse sand. Beers were immediately opened.

"Where is this?" Vinnie chugged down the first half of a can in one gulp. Kirby pointed out across the water.

"See those lights? That's the Revere camp." Vinnie looked out. The lights appeared small across the expanse of the lake.

"It's only about three times as far as we swam. It just looks further cause it's dark," added Massella. Meat got up from his seat on a small rock, climbed up onto the boulder and sat next to Vuch. He popped his second beer and started chugging it down. He let out a large belch as he finished off the can.

"Easy, Meatman... we only got two six's with us," said Vuch.

"No way, Vuchie." Kirby patted the jacket that was rolled up next to him. "I figured when we travel with Meat, we have to travel with more. I got two more six's in here."

Vinnie reached out a hand to Kirby for another brew. "Good man. You got some brains, eh, Kirb?"

"No, I know Meat!" Everyone started laughing. Meat looked up and waved the finger at them all. Vinnie stood up and kicked off his training shoes and waded into the water. He still wore the shorts he had swam over in, but they had dried by now. He considered going in for a dip, but figured he'd chug a few more brews first.

"Anybody feel like swimmin' later?" He waded in up to the bottom of his shorts and then came back onto the shore.

"Yeah. Let's get ripped and then go in." Kirby stood up and took another beer. He shucked his shoes and walked along the water's edge. "We ain't gone swimmin' this year like we did the last couple. We was always goin' in, just about every night."

Massella looked up at Vuch. "You didn't even go in the night of the hazin', Vuchie."

"Yeah, I know. I got kinda shit-faced." He cupped his hands and held them out to Massella. Mike threw a can through the air into his hands. "Besides, it was rainin', you dumb fuck!"

Meat held out his hand and was tossed his fourth. Over the next hour, the guys finished off most of the remaining beers. Meat and Vuch again drank more than anyone else, this time though, Vinnie did his fair share of consumption. By the time they were ready to swim, Meat and Vuch were having a hard time controlling their actions. Meat remained on his perch at the top of the rock. Vuch decided to come down off it, as the other guys were about ready to go into the water. He slid down the face of the boulder and tumbled into the sand as he hit the bottom.

"Ow! Shit... I guess I'm feelin' this a bit."

"Yeah, no shit, Vuchie. You look pretty wasted!" Kirby stuck out his hand and helped him to his feet. Vuch rocked on his legs as he tried to get his balance. Vinnie came in from the water, where he had been wading again. Kirby and Massella started pulling off their clothes to go in.

"Vuch?" Vinnie walked up to him. Vuch just stood wobbling on his feet, his eyes not focusing on anything. "Vuch... you okay?"

"Yeah, man. No problem." He leaned an arm around Vinnie's shoulder and started pulling down his shorts with one hand. The motion of him moving unexpectedly, threw weight against Vinnie's body. Having had many beers himself, Vinnie lost his balance as Vuch yanked on his shorts. Both of them started falling. Vuch's shorts were down around his calves when they lost their footing. He reached out, but only managed to hang onto the waistband of Vinnie's shorts as they fell — both landed a few inches deep in water, Vuch mostly on top of Vinnie.

"Get the fuck off me!" Vinnie pushed Vuch back with one arm. Vuch started laughing and tumbled off Vinnie's body. Vinnie looked behind him and saw Vuch laying partway in the water, his shoes still on and his shorts and underwear tangled around his ankles. Vinnie burst into laughter. "Swift, Vuchie... real swift." He got to his feet and removed his own clothing. Tossing them up onto the dry sand, he turned his attention to Vuch who continued to lay in the water, paralyzed with laughter.

Kirby and Massella were already up to their chests out in the lake. "What the fuck are you queer boys doin' over there?" Massella dropped under the water and quickly came back up. "Are you comin' in, or you gonna lay around laughin' all freakin' night?" Massella pushed Kirby unexpectedly. Kirby fell back and his head went under the water. He came immediately back up and started a wrestling match with Massella, dunking each other. Vinnie reached down with both arms to steady Vuch and tried to lift him to his feet. Vuch could only continue to laugh and could not offer much assistance. Halfway up, Vinnie lost his grip and Vuch fell back down, his head going under the surface of the water. He managed to stop giggling.

"Vin... maybe if you get these fuckin' shorts off from around my feet! I can't stand up like this." He again lost his balance and his head dunked under the water slightly. He started laughing again. Vinnie swayed a bit from the beer. He stood straight up and tried to clear his head. He bent over and grasped both of Vuch's feet at the same time. He pulled, removing Vuch's sneakers and clothing all at once. As the clothing came free from around Vuch's legs, Vinnie fell back onto the shoreline, ending up in a sitting position at the water's edge. His dickhead hung down and was lapped by the small waves as they came aground on the sand. Both guys broke into simultaneous drunken laughter. Meat still sat high up on the boulder and watched the antics down on the ground. The beer was overtaking him — he had to take a leak badly. He looked around, trying to decide whether to venture down off the rock, or just take a whizz from where he sat. Putting down his beer for a moment, he stuck his hand down and pulled aside the leg opening of his gym shorts. Before he could even manage to remove his huge hose from the confinement of the material, he started to spray out his water. A portion began to soak the shorts. He pulled harder and quicker, and finally managed to free the flowing shaft from its entrapment. He aimed his dick as best he could, the foreskin remained covering the head and caused the direction of the powerful piss spray to arch up in the air and splatter down onto the sand a few feet from where Vinnie and Vuch sat.

"Holy shit! Check it out, Meat got a fuckin' fountain goin' up there." Vuch climbed up onto his knees and then managed to stand up. "Don't you spray me, you fuck!"

Vinnie also got to his feet and quickly started to wade into the deeper water. "Come on, Vuch. Let's get in, huh?"

Vuch waved his hand at him. "Yeah, I'm comin'. I'm comin'." He staggered over to the bottom of the rock. Meat had finished pissing out and picked his beer back up for another slug. His limp hog still remained out and hung along his thigh. Vuch climbed carefully up a few feet of the boulder: "Hey Meatman, you comin' in swimmin'?"

Meat looked down at him. He shook his head and answered in a quiet voice. "No. Thanks, anyway."

Vuch turned and leaned his bare butt up against the side of rock. He balanced carefully on a ridge. "Are ya sure? Why not?" He spoke, matching the low tone.

"Naw, Tony... you go ahead in. I'm just gonna sit here. I'm fine... really." He squashed the empty beer can with his fingers. "Go ahead, Tony. You go have fun... just be careful." He belched loudly. Vuch nodded and climbed back down onto the wet sand. He smiled up at Meat, then turned and ran into the water, his dick bouncing in the air with every step.

The swimming didn't last very long. Massella and Kirby both felt they'd had too much to drink, even though they hadn't had nearly as much as Vinnie, Vuch and Meat. Within twenty minutes of going into the water, the guys were sitting back in the sand and talking. Meat had come down off his boulder and sat alongside Vuch.

A loud whistle blew off in the distance from across the water. "What was that?" Vinnie turned and looked at Vuch.

"The Revere camp. They blow that whistle for a light's-out signal." He leaned forward and looked over at Massella. "Mikey, what time is it? That can't be their light's out!"

Massella looked at his watch. "Yeah, shit it is! It's fuckin' midnight!" He jumped to his feet. "Man, we were supposed to meet the other guys on our beach an hour and a half ago." He started gathering up his clothes.

"No big deal. Take it easy, Mikey. We had quite the party here ourselves. Besides, you know there'll be guys partyin' all fuckin' night long. We didn't miss anything." Vuch lay back in the sand and pulled on the hair of his nuts. "You know somethin'? You guys wanna have a little fun?" He sat back up grinning.

"Like?" Vinnie could hear the mischief in his voice.

"You guys all game to take a little trip?" He got up on his knees. "A little... boatride, maybe?" He chuckled.

Vinnie looked to Massella and Kirby. Both were nodding a 'yes'. Meat was looking across at the lights on the opposite shore. Vinnie followed his line of sight. Across the water, the lights were beginning to go out. A sneer began to spread across Vinnie's mouth in pleasant anticipation. "Let's go," he said softly.

10

Vuch had been right, many of the guys were still scattered around the beach partying when they arrived back to pick up the boat. Meat piled another two six-packs into the bow of the large rowboat. There was more than enough room for the five of them, but Vuch had to turn down the other guys who would have done anything to be able to participate in a hazing of the Revere players. The guys had to work the boat out around the point of the island that extended down about a half-mile. Navigation proved a complicated task, as each of the guys was quickly approaching a drunken level. Once around the point, the lake opened up and appeared larger than they had anticipated. Meat, who had volunteered to do the rowing, aimed the boat toward the few points of light that remained on at the Revere camp. He rowed steadily, keeping the boat balanced and moving along at a good speed. Kirby and Massella playfully wrestled in their seats.

"Remember men, when we get closer to the shore, we're gonna have to quiet down. We don't know if any of them are still gonna be up, and we want this to be a surprise attack," whispered Vuch. They sat silently, listening to the sound of the oars lapping into the water. Vuch reached down and grabbed another brew. He signaled and tossed one to Vinnie's waiting hand.

"So what we gonna do, Vuchie?" Kirby asked, his voice loudly breaking the silence.

"Will you shut the fuck up, you stupid shit!" Massella remarked. "They're gonna hear us!"

Kirby cupped a hand over his mouth. He released it and spoke in a hushed voice. "Oh, yeah, sorry."

Vuch leaned off his seat and got closer to them, kneeling down on the metal floor of the boat. "Yeah, I had an idea." He sat down cross-legged on the floor and took a long gulp of his beer. "We could just do some of the same shit we did to our soph pals the other night, but we already did that and they probably do some of the same shit over there anyways." He took another chug, some of the beer spilling down the front of his shirt. He wiped it partially off with his hand. "But, I figured we should do somethin' original, ya know. Somethin' that will make our mark. Somethin' that will make them always remember the camp this year, and our senior class, right?" The guys all nodded. "So anyways, I was thinkin', what we gonna do? What can majorly fuck 'em up?" He smiled wide. "Well, we got the game the day after tomorrow. It's like the last thing we're gonna do before we leave. Well, think about it. Their playin' pretty much sucked this week, right? So, like the coaches are gonna ride 'em all day tomorrow to get ready for this game." All the guys were quiet, listening to Vuch's every word. "Well, I say let's keep them from being able to practice tomorrow."

Still silence. Vinnie looked at Kirby and Massella. Mike shrugged. "Can't practice without footballs." Vuch finished off his beer, held the can up in the air and crushed it. He turned his head and spit over the side. "Nope. Can't play without footballs." He smiled to himself.

Vuch navigated the boat so it would hit shore a few hundred yards down from the actual beach. Meat pulled the bow up onto the land and waited while the guys stumbled out. Using as much strength as he could muster, given his inebriated state, he hoisted the full front of the rowboat securely onto the grass.

Within a few seconds, all were once again relieving themselves. The boat ride over had taken considerable time. Vinnie had needed to whizz so badly that he'd considered letting it go over the side of the boat. He only stopped himself when he remembered that Kirby and Massella had witnessed the soda can incident on the bus, and decided he would manage to hold it rather than risk the embarrassing comments they would certainly make. Once the guys had finished their watering chore, Vuch signaled them to huddle.

"Okay, the deal is... there's a storage hut somewhere out on the edge of their field. Just like ours. I remember it from when we played the game over here two years ago." He belched, as he gathered his thoughts. "Okay, we have no idea what's goin' to be goin' on here. Guys might still be up. Guys could be out on the field. Who the fuck knows?" He consciously lowered his voice and pulled the huddle in closer. "So we gotta stay low to the ground. We gotta keep our eyes peeled." He glanced around. "I don't know any way to the field without going by the cabins that are right along the water's edge. So stay cool. No unnecessary sounds." He looked around again. "Got it?"

Everyone nodded. Another belch was heard. They slowly made their way, staying parallel with the shoreline as they approached the camp. Vuch and Vinnie, who were feeling their brews more than the others, stumbled against each other several times. Vinnie wiped out face-first, as he climbed over a fallen tree. Vuch quietly laughed as he worked to get Vinnie back on his feet. Once up near the cabins, the guys got down on their hands and knees. The only way they could guarantee getting by without being seen was to crawl past the front of the cabins right at the shoreline. Unlike the housing over at the Northridge camp, these were more exposed to the outside. The walls consisted mainly of just screens, and the warm weather encouraged the campers to leave the shutters in their upright positions. This made the visibility to the outside very easy.

They carefully and quietly made their way past the cabins, passing directly under the windows. The mud was wet, as it was within a few feet of the water's edge. Although the interior lights of the cabins were out, voices could be heard in conversation. Vuch signaled for the guys to be especially quiet as they stayed as low to the ground as was possible. Once past the final cabin, Vuch got to his feet and pressed his back up against the side wall of an outbuilding. His chest heaved in breathless excitement.

Vinnie came up to the wall next. "Jesus," he spoke in a whisper. "I hope there's another way we can get back."

Kirby came around the corner of the building. "I got fuckin' mud coverin' my knees and hands, Vuchie!" His voice raised slightly. Vuch put his finger up against his lips to signal to be quiet. Kirby and Meat finally came around to the wall. Meat had managed to cover himself with the wet mud. His face was streaked, giving him the appearance of a soldier prepared for combat.

They paused while everyone caught their breath. Vuch pointed off in the direction behind the outbuilding. "We gotta go over there. I think the field is just on the other side of that group of buildings. We're lookin' for a storage shed." He began to lead off. "Remember, keep your voices down and stay low to the ground." He spun around to lead the way and walked directly into a low-hanging roof beam. He stopped and rubbed his forehead.

"Yeah, our great leader, here.," chuckled Vinnie. He pushed Vuch's shoulders so he started off in the right direction. The guys worked their way slowly across the expanse of lawn between the buildings. Voices could be heard coming from various parts of the camp, but they did not see anyone out walking around. Vuch had led them way off to the far side of the camp by taking them along the water and past the cabins.

Once over near the group of buildings that bordered the field, Vuch signaled for another huddle. "Okay, this is the edge of the field." He looked around, trying to see in the darkness. Everything beyond just a few feet was invisible. "I know the equipment shed was next to the trainer's shed and also was a coupla buildings away from their showerhouse." He paused and crouched down and pushed his back against the wall of the building. The other guys got into a stooping position so they could continue to hear his whisper. "Look, since I don't really know which direction we should be headin' in... I'm gonna go over this way and check out what's over there. Kirb, you head that way and scout around. The rest of ya, just hang here... Okay?"

He signaled with his arm for Kirby to move. Vuch nodded to the guys remaining and slid off alongside the wall, feeling with his hands as he made his way. Meat stood back up and leaned firmly against the wall, his eyes closed. Mike Massella stayed down on the ground, his head darting back and forth as he watched each of the guys make their way off into the darkness.

"Meat... you okay?" Vinnie got up and stood alongside him against the wall.

"Yeah. Thanks." Meat opened his eyes and smiled. Vinnie purposely lowered his voice even more, so that Massella could not hear him. "How comes ya didn't go swimmin' with the rest of us?"

Meat shrugged. "I dunno. Maybe I just drank too much, ya know?"

Vinnie looked at him and nodded. "Go with us next time. Tomorrow, okay?"

Meat looked at him for a few seconds before replying. "Thanks. Yeah, okay." He turned his head for a moment to check out what was going on.

Mike still crouched, watching for either Vuch or Kirby. Neither had returned. Meat turned back to Vinnie. "So you and Vuchie gettin' along pretty good, huh?"

Vinnie shrugged. "Yeah, I guess so. Vuch is a cool guy."

Meat looked down at the ground and nodded his head slowly. "Yeah, he is." He kicked at the ground with his foot. "Some people take a while ta get ta know him. He's so fuckin' popular, ya know? He being the QB and all. He's lucky though, everybody seems to like him... once they get ta know him." Meat looked up and straightened his back. "He's all fun and games, though."

Vinnie nodded again. "It takes some of us a while ta get ta know you, too."

"Yeah, well... there's not much to know."

Meat got back down on his hands and knees and worked his way up beside Massella. They caught sight of Vuch coming back along the wall slowly, keeping himself pressed tightly against the wood on the side of the building. When Vuch reached them, he waved his arm so they would stand up. He leaned in tightly, swaying right in Vinnie's face as he spoke.

"Yeah, it's this way. I saw it down there just a ways. We gotta go past their showerhouse, and I heard some guys in there. But, we'll be okay if we go around the backside of that building. Then it's just... like two more buildings down. No problem. " He looked around. "So where's Kirb?"

"He ain't come back yet," said Massella.

"Well, we can't wait around. He'll find us. Come on." Vuch started to move them back along the wall.

Vinnie suddenly had to stop for a second — he got a wicked rush of dizziness from the beer. "Hold it a sec, guys." He leaned his head back on the building.

Vuch leaned up against him. "Vin, you gonna lose it, or what?" His breath stunk of beer in Vinnie's face.

Vinnie shook his head. "No... just hold it." He blinked his eyes a few times. "I got a rush goin' here, but I ain't gonna puke." He nodded his head. "Okay, let's move."

Kirby came up alongside them from back where they had waited. "Hey, thanks for waitin' for me, slugs." Vuch cocked his head, signaling to continue. They silently made their way to the end of the building. Taking turns, they got low to the ground and ran across a section of lawn that was fairly lit up from a combination of some floodlights angled toward the shower house, and the bright moon overhead. Once on the other side, Vuch led them in a detour around the back of the shower building. Loud voices could be heard inside, and at least one of the showers was running. Just as Vuch stuck his body out to make a run for the next building, two of the Revere players came around the corner talking and carrying towels. Vuch immediately threw himself back into the darkness, knocking himself hard into Vinnie. Stunned, Vinnie fell back into the wall, Vuch's elbow coming full force into his left eye. All the guys froze and remained perfectly still until the Revere guys passed, remaining unnoticed in the shadows.

Once they heard them inside the showerhouse, Vuch moved up to check on Vinnie. "Hey, man, I'm really sorry. You okay?"

Vinnie stood holding a hand against his throbbing eye. "That fuckin' hur, you dickhead!" He spoke in an angry low tone.

Vuch reached and pulled Vinnie's hand away from his eye. "Lemme see."

Vuch leaned in to get a look. He could see nothing because it was so dark. "Can ya see okay?" He reached his hand up and gently placed his fingers on Vinnie's temple.

Vinnie swatted his hand away. "I'm fine. You ain't gonna see anything in the fuckin' dark, you moron. Check it out when we get back to the island." He pushed on Vuch's shoulder. "Can we get this over?"

Vuch stepped back out into the light and made the run across the lawn. Each of the guys followed one at a time. Once over this last expanse of lawn, they only had to pass two smaller sheds before they came up to where Vuch stood. He already had his hand in place looking at the padlock on the door. "Meatman, what you think about this?" He cocked his head again to summon Meat up next to him.

"This ain't no problem. The latch is rusted and just hangin' on by a few screws." He placed his powerful hands on the latch — one securing the lock itself, the other pressing against the worn wood of the frame. He pulled. One screw came immediately out. Now only one other screw held the lock in place. Again he applied hard pressure. Nothing moved. "Find a thick stick or a rock or somethin', so I can use it to pry this fucker out."

Meat looked at Vuch and waited. Vinnie bent down and picked up a stick laying at his feet. "Meat, a stick ain't gonna do it. Ya can't pry a lock open with somethin' so flimsy." He tossed the stick out into the darkness.

"Meatman, you're wearin' boots. Kick the shit outta it." Vuch pointed down at Meat's work boots. Meat moved back a few steps. Bracing himself by holding one arm against the shed, he kicked up at the lock with all his power. His foot slipped hard against the wood, missing its mark and sending Meat falling down onto the ground.

"Well... not quite that hard." Vuch grinned.

Meat angrily got to his feet. "This fucker is comin' open!" He aimed again and slammed the toe of his boot into the latch. The latch and the padlock went flying and landed on the ground at least five feet away.

"Alright, Meat!" voiced Vinnie. He patted Meat on the back.

Vuch smiled. "Okay, Let's see what we got ourselves here. Kirb, you stay out here and watch for any Revere pussies wanderin' around." Vuch opened the shed door and stuck his head inside. "Jeez, it's dark."

"Duh!" said Vinnie, as he leaned in behind him. "Well, there's gotta be a light switch, right?"

Vuch fumbled his hand along the wall just inside the door. His hand found the wall switch, and he flicked it up. One single dim lightbulb in the center of the shed came on.

"Well, we don't gotta worry about anybody seeing the bright lights go on." Vinnie pushed on Vuch's back so he would move into the shed. Taking a step inside, Vinnie looked around. "You sure ya only wanna take the footballs, Vuchie? We got a lotta shit in here we could rip off." Vinnie pointed around the room at the many pads and helmets. "They even got tackling bags and stuff. We could leave 'em without nothin'."

Vuch stopped and walked over close to Vinnie. He reached up and pinched his cheek. "And what movin' truck are we using to cart all this away?"

Vinnie shrugged. "Never mind," he said in a low voice.

"Duh!" Vuch whispered back. He smiled and looked around at the boxes piled along the walls. "They'd be in some of the boxes."

"Don't have to go far lookin'." Meat pointed to a couple of boxes just inside the doorway where he stood. "They got 'em right here."

Vuch walked back and quickly scanned them. "Okay, we got only two boxes. Must be seventy-five to a hundred footballs in here." He stuck his head out the doorway and called Kirby and Massella in. "They're in two boxes. They won't be heavy. Meatman, can you manage one? Vin, you and I on the other here. Kirb and Mikey can do watch, as we make our way back." He reached down and grabbed one side of a box. "Come on, Vin."

Vinnie bent down and took hold of the other side of the box. "Vuchie, we can't take these suckers back past the cabins! Do you know any other way back to the boat?"

"We're gonna have to cut part way across the field here. Then I know what direction we have to go in, but I don't got no idea what we got to go past to get back down to the water." Vuch and Vinnie picked up the box and moved it out of the shed. "Kirb, you and Mikey keep about twenty yards ahead of us. See if you can tell the best way to go, once we're back off the field."

The group started their trek across the center of the football field. Since the field was in total darkness except for moonlight, carrying the boxes proved difficult and they had to slow down considerably. Halfway across the field, Vinnie stopped and put down his side of the box. "Vuch, I can get this better if I just carry it myself. You go scout with the other guys."

"You sure?"

Vinnie nodded. He bent down and hoisted the large box up into his arms. "No problem." he said. Vuch moved on ahead and caught up with Kirby and Massella. They had spotted a road which led back down to the beach.

"Looks like it's used for boat launchin'. It must go right down to the dock area, about fifty yards off from where we landed. You think we can get down past the main part of the camp unseen?" Massella whispered to Vuch.

"We don't got much choice, do we?" Vuch shrugged. He waited a few minutes for Meat and Vinnie to catch up with the boxes. "Vinnie, we're gonna have to do this two men to each box. We're gonna need that extra ability to run or duck out of the light fast. With two to a box, we can at least have a bit more speed if we have ta run."

"Whatever." Vinnie put the box down and waited for Vuch to get back on the other side. Vuch picked up his side and the group quickly made their way down the service road. Kirby kept watch ahead, signaling them to continue each time he scouted an area. Shortly, they came up against the last building before the beach. "We only gotta clear this last lit area, then we're home free, boys." Vuch smiled in excitement.

"Vuchie, lemme take this myself. Really, I get better leverage if I don't gotta worry about you balancing the other side."

Vuch nodded. "Okay, Vinnie."

Kirby led out into the light with Meat right on his heels. Once they had cleared, Massella got low to the ground and passed quickly through the beam of the spotlight. Vuch waited, while Vinnie took his turn. Once Massella arrived on the other side, Vinnie shot out with the box securely in his arms. Just as Vinnie reached the center of the road, the two guys who had been up at the showerhouse came around one of the outbuildings on their way back to their cabin. "Hey, you!" A shout echoed in the darkness.

Vinnie froze for a split second, then realizing he had been spotted, decided he had to make a dash for the darkness. Hoisting up the box for a bit more security, he ran all out for the bushes where the others waited. The sudden increase in speed caused him to falter on his feet. He tipped the box too much to the right as he dashed for safety. Two footballs toppled out of the top of the box and rolled down the road toward the water. By the time Vinnie got off the road, the other guys had made a run for the boat. He kept his speed, the box bouncing in his arms. Behind him, he could hear the shouts increasing. The two guys had caused enough ruckus to begin to alert some of the other campers.

Vinnie arrived at the boat just as Meat and Kirby were pushing it back off the land. "Move it! Come on, Vinnie!" Massella grabbed hold of the other side of the box from Vinnie's arms and helped throw it into the bow of the boat. "We gotta get outta here. Hurry!" Massella jumped into the boat as the bow came free.

Vinnie stood in the water, his shoes flooding. "Where the fuck is Vuch?" He looked around. "He was behind me. Where is he?" Vinnie's voice rose in panic. The level of voices was increasing. Shouts could be heard as a few of the campers began to search for them. "They think we went to the boat launch area. We got a minute maybe... if we're lucky." Meat got the oars into place, ready to pull out in a hurry. Suddenly two footballs flew into the boat from the air. Each loudly thumped against the metal bottom, one bouncing back up and ricocheting off Meat's arm.

"They're comin' this way. Let's go!" Vuch jumped past Vinnie and tumbled into the boat. Vinnie pushed off from the shallow water and the boat drifted out. Meat used the oars and spun the boat, pointing it out into the lake. "Meatman, stay close to the shore and take us down to the left there. If they think we got into a boat, they're gonna expect us to be goin' out across the lake. Just row slowly down the shoreline here." Meat directed the boat as he was told. They moved slowly along, staying within a few yards of the land. The voices began to sound further away. The Revere campers were now shouting for the search to direct up toward the parking lots. "They don't know we got out in a boat. We're home free."

Vuch reached back and picked up one of the footballs. He tossed it back to Vinnie. "Gentlemen, our mission was a success."

They tossed the ball back and forth as Meat began to head the rowboat back in the direction of the island. "Hey, Kirb?"

"Yeah, Vuch?"

"Kirb... what don't I have in my hand?"

"A brew, Vuch."

"Don't ya think we should do somethin' about that?"

11

It was 3:30 when they finally pulled the boat back up onto the beach area of the island. Despite the late hour, the sand was still dotted with several groups of partying guys. The ones who were still able to stand helped empty the boxes and loose footballs out of the boat. Vuch decided it would be best to hide the evidence as quickly and securely as possible. Kirby and Massella went off with the other guys to place the looted footballs deep into the rubble of the boys' camp. Meat, Vinnie and Vuch walked back and sat around the campfires that were still burning in the fireplaces surrounding the clearing. They held on to two remaining beers each, laughing and trying their best to find their mouths as they continued to drink.

"I'm feelin' this. I'm tellin' ya... I'm feelin' this!" Vuch fell back against the stone side of a fireplace. "I wasn't so fucked up... until we got back here on the island."

Vinnie finished off the beer in his hand and tossed the can aside. He reached and picked up the last of his allotment. "I don't even know how much I've had." He popped the top. "Not that I care!" He laughed and held onto his side as he tumbled into Vuch's shoulder.

"Hey, Meatman... what you doin'?"

Vuch pushed back against Vinnie and leaned slightly over toward Meat, who lay silently on his side staring at the fire. Meat did not reply. "Meat?... Meat! Earth callin' Meat!" Vuch yelled, his words slurring.

"I ain't doin' nothin'. I'm just layin' here." Meat's dazed eyes looked back at Vuch.

"I thought maybe you had fallen asleep. Or passed out!" Vuch drunkedly waved his hand at Meat.

"I'm gettin' there. I might just crash right here." Meat lifted an arm up under his head. "Meat, you're gonna get cold." Vinnie lightly pushed on his head.

"Meat, you're gonna get cold," he repeated, having a hard time forming the words.

Vuch thumped hard on Vinnie's leg. "No, man, you forget who you're talkin' to. He sleeps in the buff in the cabin. He's fine that way. Besides, it's fuckin' hot tonight!" Vuch struggled to pull his tee-shirt off. He got it stuck up over his head, his arms tangled in the material. "Aaah! It's got me! It's got me!" he yelled. He started laughing uncontrollably.

"You freakin' idiot!" Vinnie reached over and pulled the shirt off with one arm. Once the shirt came free, Vuch fell down into Vinnie's lap. "You are so shit-faced!"

Vuch turned on his back, his head laying on top of Vinnie's crotch. "Think so?" He belched. "Yeah, maybe just a little."

"Well, what'cha wanna do?" Vinnie leaned in Vuch's direction, swaying as he tried to focus on Vuch's face. "Ya wanna go to bed? Should we get some shut-eye?" His words came out slurred.

Vuch leaned one arm against Vinnie's shoulder. He reached out with his other arm and grasped the edge of the stone fireplace. With a great deal of effort, he pulled himself to his feet. "No, I wanna walk around." He started to stagger away from the campsite. He paused and waved his arm drunkenly back at Vinnie. "Come on, Vin, ol' buddy." He tripped on a root of an unseen tree. "Fuck!... come on, Vinnie,... no really... let's go for a walk... here." He turned and continued into the darkness.

Vinnie looked down at Meat. His eyes were closed, and his mouth was hanging open to the side. No sound came out of Meat's mouth, but it was apparent he was dead to the world. Slowly Vinnie pulled himself up and followed the path that Vuch had taken. "Vuchie..." Vinnie whispered as he picked his way slowly along in the darkness. "Vuchie..." He then realized he was whispering for no reason. "Hey... fuckhead!" he yelled.

"Yo!" came the response. Vinnie estimated Vuch must be twenty yards or so ahead of him. He was on the right path, though. "Vuchie... where the fuck are you?" The trail suddenly opened up at the water. He had reached a small area of shoreline. It wasn't any kind of beach, but rather a small rocky area jutting out into a point of land. "Vuchie... what the fuck? Where the hell are you?" he spoke in a normal tone.

"Over here, man."

Vinnie squinted his eyes. He could barely make out Vuch's shape standing at the edge of the water out on the point.

"Come on out, Vinnie," he called.

Vinnie carefully picked his way along the rocks and made his way out to the small peninsula. "What are ya doin' out here?" He kicked off his sneakers and walked barefoot through the shallow waves.

"Just gettin' some air, man. I kinda was feelin' pretty fucked up." Vuch jumped a few times, taking deep breaths into his lungs. "I just didn't wanna get sick later. I kinda want this night to keep goin' on, that's all."

"Yeah... well, whatever. Don't get fuckin' sick on me here... hey, take it easy, Vuchie... don't be jumpin' around like a fuckin' lunatic. That's how ya gonna make yaself get sick, man." Vinnie squatted down on his heels. He playfully darted his hands around in the water, watching the rippling effect.

"Hey, man... wasn't that football raid the fuckin' balls, or what?" Vuch laughed loudly.

"Yeah, man... the fuckin' balls, alright." Vinnie grinned.

"Hey, I made a joke and didn't even know it. Get it, the fuckin' balls! Get it, we stole the fuckin' balls." Vuch roared at his own humor.

Vinnie grinned and shook his head. "Yeah, Vuch, I get it. Funny." They walked around in the shallow water silently. Vinnie paused and gazed out across the water. "Hey, ya Vuchie..."

"What, bro'?" Vuch tripped on a submerged rock. "Fuck!" he hissed. Vinnie squinted his eyes in thought, still looking far off in the distance. "Hey!" Vuch yelled, startling Vinnie.

"What?" he snapped.

"What were you gonna say?" Vuch asked meekly.

"Oh, yeah... sorry. I didn't mean to bark at ya." Silence fell again.

"What were ya gonna say?" Vuch asked a second time, now slightly impatient. He tripped again, this time falling face down into the shallow water. He flung out his arms to catch himself, the drunkenness causing his reflex action to come after he began to sink under the surface.

Vinnie continued to look out across the lake, not even acknowledging Vuch's plight. "Vuchie... I guess what I want to ask is... well... I was like wonderin', ya know? About, like... what you said about Marino before. When you was talkin' to me about... like, like how he likes... ya know, how he like gets it on when he's horny, and all... ya know?"

Vuch shook his head violently trying to get the water out of his hair. His fall had drenched him totally. He lifted himself up onto all fours, and remained on his hands and knees as he looked at Vinnie. Water dripped down his face and off the end of his chin. "Oh, yeah?" he answered only half-listening, as he pushed off from the lake's sandy bottom and rocked back onto his heels. He braced himself to try to get to his feet.

"Like, I don't know... it's just been in my mind since ya said it, that's all. Like... I look at him, and listen to him and all... and like he just doesn't seem the type, ya know what I mean?" Vinnie looked down and watched the waves.

Vuch got to his feet. He walked over toward Vinnie, leaning one arm clumsily on his shoulder. "So, like, what are ya tryin' to say?" He gave Vinnie his full attention now. Vinnie turned and looked into Vuch's eyes. He saw the effects of the beer in the glassy stare of his pupils. The focus in Vuch's eyes kept shifting, verifying his intoxication.

"I don't know, man. I don't know why I keep on thinkin' about it." Vinnie paused. He looked away, unable now to look Vuch directly in the eye; drunk or not. Vuch lifted his arm off Vinnie's shoulder and took a couple of steps to the side. He looked out across the expanse of the water himself, now.

"Oh, yeah. You mean like... he don't come across like a fag." His voice was very quiet.

Vinnie nodded silently. He bit his lip, then shrugged his shoulders. "Yeah, I guess that's what I meant," he said softly. "He don't seem queer-ass, ya know?"

"Yeah... okay, I know whatcha mean." Vuch half smiled, his voice spoke with a hint of sadness. "Yeah, I know exactly what you're sayin' here." His voice became almost a whisper. Vuch stomped his feet on the rocks, trying to get the last of the water out of his sneakers. He started to walk back toward the path. Vinnie grabbed his sneakers and ran to catch up. Vuch was already part way up the path when Vinnie caught up to him.

"Hey... wait up... let me get my fuckin' sneakers back on." Vinnie bent down and hopped on one foot and then the other, as he tried to pull on his shoes. He fell against Vuch's back. "Hey, Vuchie... you're all wet, man."

Vuch stopped and turned to him. "No shit, Sherlock. Gee, you're swift... you catch on fast!" he hissed.

"What?" Vinnie looked puzzled. He stood up straight, his footwear in place.

"Nothin'." Vuch smiled. He turned and continued into the woods.

"Hey ya, Vuchman!" a voice was calling out from the darkness ahead. "Vuchie!" Vinnie stumbled into Vuch, who had stopped in his tracks and was listening to the shouts of his name.

"Who's callin'?"

"I dunno. Must be Kirb or somebody." Vuch lifted his arms overhead and let out a shrill hoot.

"Vuchie? Where the fuck are ya?" The shouting was getting closer.

"Over here, dumbfuck!" Vuch pushed on through the dense branches, Vinnie following him closely behind. "Hey, ya Kirby!" he cheerfully greeted his teammate as they came upon each other, the moonlight providing illumination.

"Hey, bro'. Jeez, man, you're all fuckin' wet. What the fuck happened?" Kirby patted the wet shirt that was plastered to Vuch's chest.

"Yeah, well... I kinda fell in." Vuch smiled wide, rocking slightly as another wave of nausea passed over him.

"Hey, listen man... we's gettin' together some cards. What you think? You guys want in, or what?" Kirby pulled his tee-shirt off and slung it over his shoulder.

Vuch turned slowly to face Vinnie, being careful not to move too quickly. He waited a moment for his eyes to re-focus. "Hey Vin, what'cha think?" He leaned in close to Vinnie's face, his breath warm against Vinnie's skin.

Vinnie shrugged. Vuch turned back to Kirby. "Yeah, okay guy... we're in!" he chirped, waving his arm clumsily in the direction of the camp. He started to pick his steps slowly, relying on Vinnie directly behind him to steer, as they began to make their way back to the campsite. As the three came through the last of the brush into the clearing, they were greeted by Meat, standing up on top of one of the stone fireplaces. He was dressed only in his boxer shorts, and was dancing to soundless music. "Ride me, baby! Ride me... Ride me all night long!" he sang in a loud flat tone. He pounded his chest in gorilla fashion, the sweat dripping down the dense matted hair covering his entire torso.

"Uh... I think that's 'Rock me, baby', Meat." Kirby was pulling his tee-shirt back on over his head. He continued to walk, his view blocked as he tangled the cotton around his face. He tripped on the edge of the fireplace and went down flat, skinning his knee on the rough stone as he fell. "Mother!" he gritted his teeth as he turned and sat cross-legged to examine his bruise.

"Rock me?" Meat stopped his dancing movement and looked down at Kirby. "You sure?"

Kirby was wincing as he looked up at Meat's hulk overhead. He hissed in pain as he replied, "Yeah. I'm sure." He lightly touched the scrape, flinching from the sting.

Meat shrugged. He started dancing slowly again. "Rock me, baby! Rock me... Rock me all night long," he continued. He gyrated his hips in a bucking fashion, lifting his arms in time to a non-existent beat.

"Kirb... ya okay?" Vuch kicked at his side lightly as he stood over him. Kirby winced again, but nodded. He silently got to his feet. "Okay, then!" Vuch clapped his hands. "Who's up for losin' at cards?" He flashed his white teeth and glanced around the campsite, a look of anticipation on his face.

Meat stopped his movements and looked down at Vuch. "I'm in." With that said he returned to his imaginary music. Although it appeared that most everyone was beyond the capacity to even see the cards coherently, much less play the game, the usual cohort got together. Vinnie was a bit taken aback that Sal Cardone and Tony Marino were being included; his mind still in confusion trying to separate the Tony that he knew was a decent guy, and the Tony that was rumored about.

The guys entered the lobby area of the building. It was piled high with knapsacks and bedrolls, a massive storage area of the team's stuff. "Massella's got the cards and chips... but, well, we ain't got no money, Vuchie," Kirby commented as he rummaged through his personal gear.

Vuch sat down on the stone steps that went up to the second level. He adjusted his butt, the thin cloth of his damp shorts rubbing hard against the concrete. "Ain't no problem. We'll just play strip, that's all." He leaned back against the iron handrail, pausing as he let his mind clear.

"Vuchie... you okay, man?" Vinnie bent down and looked into his eyes. "Ya don't look so good."

Vuch nodded. "Yeah... actually I feel pretty good." He sat up straight. "Vin, grab some extra clothes and shit for us... let's pad ourselves up... so we's don't get starkers too fast in the game." He winked at Vinnie, then pulled himself to his feet. The group spent the next few minutes clothing themselves with extra layers, the result being a peculiar fashion assortment. An old wooden cable spool was located and set up as the playing table. Makeshift chairs were assembled from various crates and boards. Fortunately, camping lanterns had been brought over from the football camp, so lighting was sufficient.

* * *

Vuch was the first to seat himself. He looked around impatiently as the rest of the group took their places. "C'mon guys... let's move it, huh?" He reached and grabbed the deck of cards and began shuffling. "The night's gettin' away from us here." He began to deal out the first hand. "This is straight five-card stud, men... none of this wild card shit. My brain ain't gonna handle complicated shit, ya know?" He looked around the group, flashing his white smile again. Vinnie began to pick up the cards dealt in front of him on the table. He looked around at each of the faces, the lantern giving them a ghoulish appearance.

Tony Marino had located a knitted winter hat and pulled it tightly down over his nearly shaved head. His face looked even more like a boxer now, a mean appearance glaring out from his two beady eyes. Sal Cardone sat with several sweatshirts on over each other. His forehead was beading up sweat immediately, as the heat of the night was too excessive for that amount of clothing. Vinnie figured he would probably welcome losing fast, just to rid himself of some of the layers. Kirby and Massella had added a few items, but appeared fairly confident in their playing abilities, so they didn't throw on anything extreme. Meat, in his usual manner, had only pulled on an extra pair of boxer shorts, which he proudly wore over his head as a kind of chef's hat. Meat, out of everyone, certainly didn't care if he ended up sitting around naked. In fact, he would probably prefer it. Vinnie and Vuch had each added a couple of layers of shorts and tee-shirts, Vuch shucking his damp items for drier, yet oddly combined gear.

Tony sucked in loudly through his nose, then sent a large glob of spit and snot cascading out onto the wall nearby.

"Good one, Marino!" Massella piped up. He returned his attention to his hand, trying to evaluate which to discard. The play moved along slowly, each guy having his own problem with seeing and reasoning. The first hand ended up coming down to Vinnie and Kirby.

"Okay, Manta, ol' pal... whatcha got?" Vinnie slowly laid out each card, finishing with two pairs of queens.

"Loser!" Kirby laughed. He fanned out his hand onto the spool, proudly displaying a full house. "Take it off, Vin!" he smiled widely.

Vinnie stood and pulled off one of his extra pair of shorts, almost losing his balance as he tried to get his sneakers out of the leg holes. Everyone cheered and hooted as he sat down again and the next hand was dealt out. Marino lost the next play. He stood and pulled his tee-shirt off, taking care to leave his knit hat in place over his head. He sat back down, the muscles in his shoulders showing their pump beautifully in the flickering light of the camping lantern.

"Jeez, Marino... can ya get any more muscular, or what?" Massella joked.

Marino shrugged. "Yeah, probably..." he flexed his chest "...and I will, too." He flexed a second time. His biceps flooded with power, as he snapped into a double-bicep pose.

"Fuckin' awesome, Tony."

"In-fuckin'-credible."

The game resumed, Vinnie periodically looking over at Marino, carefully evaluating his size and appearance. He was one hell of a specimen, a bodybuilder's dream. Kirby and Massella ended up going head-to-head on the next few hands, each losing several pieces of clothing. Since they had not added too many extra items, they both came down to sitting only in their jockey shorts by the time their turns passed.

"Read 'em an weep." laughed Vuch, laying down four kings to beat Sal Cardone's three queens. "Ya ain't got much to lose there anymore." Vuch tapped out a quick drum roll with his hands on the edge of the wooden spool. He reached out his hand to Kirby, as he awaited Sal's move. "Toss another beer, bro."

Sal stood and kicked off a sneaker, leaving him only in his jockeys too. He squeezed the cotton crotch of his white shorts as he sent the sneaker flying into the wall on the far side of the lobby. "I gotta take a leak." He stepped slowly around the guys, making his way to the open side of the make-shift table.

"Good idea!" Marino got to his feet.

"Okay, piss-break!" Vuch announced. The guys began to make an effort to get to their feet, a few of them having to get assistance from others. Kirby and Massella leaned on each other as they made their way across the lobby and out the main doorway. Once they had stepped around the corner of the building, they all lined up in a row.

"Distance contest!" yelled Kirby. As they pulled out their hogs, each guy leaned back, trying to create ultimate distance in their shot of water. All seven of the teammates began to arc an upward stream of hot piss into the night air. "It's me, man!" shouted Kirby, "I gots the highest! I'm the man!" he hooted. He took a slight step back, trying to keep his balance, in the process catching the heel of his foot on a small stump sticking up in the dirt. He stumbled backward, going quickly down first on his ass, then falling completely over. He put out his left hand to catch himself, but his reflexes were too slowed from all the beer. He went down hard, his right hand continuing to hold his dick in its pissing position. The stream of hot urine continued to flow out, now running over his right hand and arm as he lay sprawled out on his back. "Oh, shit!" he cried helplessly.

Marino turned his head to the side and looked down at him. "Yeah, gee, Kirb... you're right..." he growled in a low voice, "I don't thinks I can shoot far enough ta cover myself with my own piss like that." He shook his hog dry, then stuffed it back in his shorts.

"Uh, yeah, Kirb... you sure are the man!" Massella broke out in laughter. As he finished his own need, he turned slightly and shot the last of his own drops on Kirby's already piss-soaked hand. He laughed even louder.

"Hey... you fuck!" Kirby shook his hand and wiped it on his dampened underwear. "Shit!" He dropped his head back on the cool ground and closed his eyes in embarrassment.

"Nice goin', dumbfuck!" Vuch offered his hand to help Kirby back up to his feet. Kirby looked up, then stuck out his right hand.

Vuch suddenly pulled his hand back quickly. "Ah, the other hand... if ya don't mind," he smiled, then burst out laughing. Kirby reddened in the face, withdrawing his wet hand and offering up his dry, left one. Vuch tugged him back to a standing position.

"Fuck," Kirby whispered to himself, as he slowly walked back around to the front of the building.

Back inside, the guys returned to their positions at the playing table. "Hey ya, Kirb, nothin' personal, but ya shorts reek a' piss now."

Kirby looked down at them, stepping forward into the light. The entire pouch area was damp and had a yellow tint to it. He scowled at the appearance. "Yeah... I guess so. Fuck." He shrugged, then inserted his two thumbs in the waistband of the jockeys and gave them a quick tug. They slid down his thighs and bunched on the floor in a pile around his ankles. He stepped one foot out, then used the leg hole still around the other ankle to lift it up enough so he could grab the shorts with his hand and pull them off. He raised them toward his nose and gave a deep sniff.

"Oh man! Don't whiff 'em!" yelled Massella. Kirby made a sour face and tossed them far across the length of the lobby. They splattered somewhere in a dark corner. "Well... somebody's gonna get a surprise in the mornin'." He shrugged again.

"Well Kirb, I guess ya outta luck for playin' anymore," Marino joked. Kirby looked down at himself. He stood completely naked. He ran his left hand down over his body, checking to make sure there wasn't any residue of piss coating him. Vinnie focused his eyes on Kirby, taking notice of his appearance really for the first time. Kirby stood about six feet tall. His frame wasn't extremely muscular, but it had good strong definition. Vinnie thought for a moment about when he had seen Kirby for the first time back in the weightroom at Northridge High. He had been doing a fair amount of weight on the leg extension machine when Vinnie had stopped to watch them. He now noticed that Kirby possessed a good deal of leg development for someone his size. He had to be about fifteen pounds lighter than Vuch. His entire torso was coated with a very fine, almost silky looking light brown hair. It extended down over his arms and legs as well. *Obviously he didn't participate in Vuch's shaving ritual*, Vinnie thought to himself. His chest was well defined, but nowhere near the musculature of himself or Marino. Vuch had him beat also, considering their similarity in weight.

The singular defining aspect that Vinnie took note of was Kirby's development of his abdominals. Kirby being light and fast, he had obviously spent a great deal of time on flexibility exercises. He had certainly been paying his dues on working his stomach area, as well. He had a deep cut of the six-pack abdominal look that many bodybuilders strive for, but can't obtain due to wanting to keep massive size on their frames. Kirby might be on the smaller side, but he was one of the most cut and defined guys Vinnie had ever seen. Confident that he did not have any unwanted odors still coming from him, Kirby decided to sit back down. He turned his back as he looked to make sure his bare butt was not going to sit on anything unpleasant. As he bent over, Vinnie noticed a small tatoo on the back of his shoulder.

"Hey, what's that tatoo ya gots?"

Kirby turned back and faced Vinnie. "Oh, ya never notice that before?" He spun around again so his shoulder pointed down at Vinnie. "It's a four-leaf clover." He pulled the skin down slightly, displaying it for Vinnie's appraisal. "It's an Irish thing, ya know?"

Vinnie nodded, raising up off his seat slightly so he could take a closer look. "Hey yeah, that's cool." He touched the green ink lightly with his fingers.

Kirby turned and faced front again, dropping loudly down onto his bench seat. "Yeah, it is, ain't it? I got it on my sixteenth birthday." He smiled brightly.

"I been thinkin' 'bout gettin' somethin' on my leg." Vinnie nodded as he spoke. "My calf actually. I was thinkin' 'bout maybe a barbell, or somethin'."

"Yeah? Cool." Kirby glanced back at his shoulder, cramming his neck to get a good view. He patted it lovingly with his hand. "Yeah, man. Do it."

Vuch finished dealing another hand. All the guys picked up their cards. "Jesus, man. This sucks. I ain't had no decent hands the whole game," Massella whined.

"It's just how you play, Mikey," voiced Vuch. He chuckled under his breath. "You suck."

"Hey, what was that?"

"He said 'you suck'," responded Sal. "And you do."

"Hey, I ain't that bad." Mike discarded, then picked up his new cards. "Well..." he surveyed his new hand, "then again... maybe I am." He shook his head and folded his hand. "I'm out again. Jesus!" He stood up and yanked down his shorts, placing them carefully near him. "I want these babies back as soon as the game is over."

"They're safe, Mike. Who's gonna steal your smelly cum-stained shorts, anyhow?"

Tony Marino upped the ante against Vinnie, and Vinnie called, confident in his current hand. "Well?" he looked intently at Marino.

"I gotcha on this one, Manta." Marino stuck out his tongue and wagged it playfully at Vinnie, leaning in towards his ear. "Beat this." He layed out his cards with assurance.

"Strip, a-hole," chided Vinnie, laying out three kings to beat his three queens.

Marino threw his arms up over his head. "God! Oh, shit... I was so fuckin' positive... so fuckin' happy with that hand! Aargh!" He stood up and spun in a circle in place, clapping his hands together in frustration. "I don't believe it! I don't believe it!" He stood still shaking his head and looking down at his cards as they lay revealed. "My best hand! My best hand all fuckin' game!"

Vinnie had crossed his arms across his chest and been watching him with glee. "C'mon fucker... off with 'em." Marino looked down at his shorts. Vinnie hadn't noticed before, but Marino was wearing those lycra gym shorts that hugged your body tightly while you lifted. His legs and crotch bulged in the elastic fabric. The immense size of his legs put the delicate material under tremendous strain. Marino shook his head again, then peeled the taut shorts down his muscular thighs. He had to sit back down to get them all the way down and off, the heavily worked definition in his leg muscles preventing an easy removal. He fell backward as his feet came free of the leg holes, sending him off his seat and knocking him part way into some duffles that had been piled behind where he sat. His bare feet shot up in the air, sending his big balls and dick into everyone's view. Applause came from around the table.

"Okay, now I don't feel so bad," smiled Kirby, as he watched Marino pull himself back up. "Thanks for the show, guy."

Marino just shrugged nonchalantly, unfazed by his display.

"More brews, men. Let's take five," commanded Vuch. Once again beers were distributed. The guys remained at the table, looking around at each other as they chugged on the drinks. "Well, we's gots three guys here that are starkers. I still got one pair of shorts and one tee-shirt left. Vinnie, you got what? One tee-shirt and shorts... same thing. Sal?" Vuch looked across the table.

Sal looked down into his lap. "Just my underwear, Vuchie," he replied.

"Meatman? Jesus, Meat... you still gots your skivvies on, huh?" Vuch leaned over toward Meat and glanced down under the table at him.

"And his way cool hat," added Vinnie.

"Yeah. My hat," answered Meat.

"And your hat," echoed Vuch.

* * *

"Let's just kick back and shoot the breeze, Vuchie." Marino tugged on his dickhead. It scraped slightly against the bare wood as he adjusted his seating.

"Yeah." "I'm tired a' playin'."

"Okay by me," Vuch shrugged. He stuck out his hand to request another beer from Massella.

"Ah, sorry Vuchie... the well's run dry." Massella shook his head indicating "no".

Vuch shrugged again. "Okay," he repeated. "Hey, Sal... what was the deal... the real deal... with you and that cheerleader on the bus last year? You know, the one on the bus on the way home from the Hyde Park game?"

Kirby leaned his forearms on the spool, tilting in toward where Cardone sat.

Sal smiled wide and shrugged.

"Hey, yeah. C'mon, Sal... fess up. What the fuck really went on. C'mon man... we've been wonderin' since last year," Massella added. "What's the scoop?"

Sal winked at Vuch. "Well, should I? Should I ruin the suspense after all this time? What'cha think, Vuchie?"

"Yeah. Sure, why not. Hey, for Vinnie's sake here, start it at the beginnin', Sal." Vuch nodded. His eyes sparkled with enthusiasm.

"Okay." Sal leaned back against a stack of knapsacks that were piled along the wall behind him. He tilted back on his bench, lifted his legs up onto the wooden spool, and playfully crossed his bare feet. "Okay, since yas always wanted ta know." He reached his arms up and clasped his hands behind his head. He rocked slowly back and forth.

"Hold it a sec, Sal." Kirby pushed his torso back against the stack of personal gear, just a few feet down from where Sal sat. He reached behind and plumped up a few bags, making a better pillow to support his shoulders. Massella did likewise, settling in against the gear like a large overstuffed chair. Kirby and Massella each placed their bare feet up onto the table, starting a game of big-toe wrestling as they molded the duffles into a comfortable shape.

"Okay. All set." Massella directed.

"Okay. Anyways, Vinnie... see I was seein' this girl all last summer and the beginnin' of the school year. Through the fall and all, ya know? Her name was Sheri Dooley, right? Anyways, we's was goin' together and everything, you know, like not seein' anybody else or nothin'... ya know sorta steady an' shit. That's what she called it anyways. Okay, so like we had been goin' out all summer... goin' to movies, the beach... all that shit, right? An' well, she was pretty hot for me, right? I mean who wouldn't be, ya know?"

Kirby hooked the big toe of his right foot hard against the toes of Massella's left foot. He applied as much pressure as he could, trying to make Massella give in. His attention snapped back to Sal.

"What you mean, 'who wouldn't?'" he grinned. "Like how 'bout every other girl in school for starters?"

"Fuck you," Sal replied. "Now, let me finish. Anyways so like she was all hot for me... we would like, you know, make out all the fuckin' time, and she'd let me feel her up and shit. But like... every time I'd go poppin' a boner, right... she wouldn't even like, feel it up, ya know? I mean I was gettin' all hot and shit... and she wouldn't do nothin' for me. I was goin' home and poundin' it myself every night, ya know?"

"Well, so far, nothin' new." Massella winked at Vuch. "Only just like every fuckin' broad out there." He freed his toe from Kirby's assault, now placing his foot in the offensive position. He began to jab at Kirby.

"Yeah. I know." Sal shifted his shoulders. "So like it was really frustrating. I mean I liked her and all, but jeez, a guy can only take so much. I mean shit! So anyways there was this other chick, Debby Clydes, her best friend. She was pretty unattractive, wicked overweight, smoked cigs a lot. A real mess. Anyways, I think Debby pretty much always had a thing for me, right? She used ta always come around and hang around with me an' Sheri. You know, go places with us like a fuckin' third wheel and shit. I used ta complain ta Sheri and stuff. I mean, who'd want this fat girl, all this cheap dyed blond hair and freckles and stuff, you know... hangin' around with ya. I mean we used ta go places and I would like, tell everybody we was just bein' nice ta her cause theys was friends an' stuff. She was like, really pathetic. So she hanged with us all summer long. The three of us... everywhere. And when I could get Sheri alone, once in a great while, I'd end up fistin' myself in my bed at night. Not a great situation. So's me an' Sheri started like, really havin' a wicked lotta fights, right? I mean I was fuckin' horny all the time, and I had to put up with this Debby-fat-ass in my face everytime we went out. Jeez, it was hell."

"Sounds it." Vinnie nodded.

"Yeah, man. And this Debby chick was a load, all right." Massella flexed his toes and turned his foot to get better aim at Kirby's. "

So the game just before the Thanksgiving game last year... you know, the weekend before? Well anyways, it was at Hyde Park." Sal turned and looked directly at Vinnie. "I don't know if ya know where Hyde Park is... but it's 'bout twenty-five miles or so from Northridge." He began to address the whole group again. "So like some parents drove ta see the game. In fact, most parents. So any of the guys who wanted to go home with them, rather than the team bus, well they could, ya know? Sheri and Debby, as usual, drove together ta see the game. After the game we three was just standin' around, hangin' out as usual before we headed back in Sheri's car. Well, the stupid-ass broad gets ticked off at me again. She starts screamin' at me an shit. Then I gets pissed off at her and I told the bitch I was gonna take the team bus back. Screw her, ya know? So I gets on the bus and start waitin' for the rest of the guys. We weren't leavin' for a little while."

Sal turned and spit on the floor, then cleared his throat. "So I'm just sittin' there, and suddenly fat-ass comes up in the door of the bus. She says to me that Sheri was pissed at her and left her there in Hyde Park. I find out later that Debby actually told Sheri she was gonna go home with some relative that lived in Hyde Park. Just screwin' around with her, ya know? Just sayin' that ta get her ta leave. Well... I didn't know that. Not then. So I feel kinda bad for her. This fat chick being stuck there in Hyde Park and all. And I knew that most of the team wouldn't be comin' back on the bus. So I thought I'd be nice. What the fuck. I tell her she can come back on the bus with the team."

Kirby turned his gaze away from Sal and continued his attack of Massella's foot. He curled his toes with all his strength and snapped Massella's big toe.

"Ow! Fuck!" Massella shot upright, pulling his foot off the table. He reached forward and massaged his bruise. In the light of the lantern, Vinnie was able to notice his powerful calves. It looked like he trained his leg and foot muscles regularly, sharpening their strength and increasing their size to support his heavy frame. Massella had quite large and heavily muscled feet also. Dark hair sprouted from each toe and across the top of his foot, intersecting a series of veins that raised slightly from the body of the foot, showing the power he possessed. He bent his leg, pulling his bare foot up into his lap, and pulled it across his right thigh. He then lifted his right thigh up slightly, forcing his left foot to rise up so that he could inspect his injured toe more closely. The change in his position sent his left knee slipping down over Kirby's leg and into his lap. He didn't take any notice of his intrusion, as he was eyeing his toe with intense concentration.

"Hey, Mikey... watch it. You're about a half-inch from kneeing me in the right nut," Kirby complained. Massella did not reply, but continued to move his big toe back and forth, trying to restore feeling.

"What the fuck are you two pussies doin'?" demanded Sal. Kirby looked up at Sal and shrugged.

"Never mind them. Continue Sal... this is where it's gonna get good." Vuch directed the attention back toward Cardone, who folded his arms across his chest and took a deep breath.

"So like... we got underway in the bus, ya know? An' it turned out only like, four other guys were even botherin' to take the bus, which was fine by me, cause I wasn't too pleased that this fat chick was travelin' with me anyways, you know? I certainly didn't want most of the team guys to even know. I mean, like... I was just doin' her a favor anyways... cause she didn't have a ride back, right? So I was sittin' in the back of the bus, ya know, like I always do... and well, she was sittin' back there with me too. What the fuck, you know? So... it was dark by then, and I was just tryin' ta catch some z's, cause like, I didn't want ta talk ta the bitch. Jeez. I mean sittin' back there was bad enough. So I was sittin' with my eyes closed, not sayin' anythin', right? And suddenly I feel this hand on my crotch. Rubbin' the front of my football pants. So I like, freaked inside, you know? I mean, I knew who the hell it was. I mean, shit! It was this Debby broad grabbin' my gator! I like, kept my eyes closed... tryin' ta figure out what the fuck I was gonna do. I mean... how the hell do ya tell a broad ta get her hand off ya gator? Shit!"

Tony Marino started laughing. "Yeah. Who the hell ever says that? Mosta my time, I'm tryin' to get a chick to touch it."

Sal smiled in acknowledgment. "Right. So... I'm just sittin' there tryin' to decide what ta do... an' she starts pullin' the lacings, like she really knew how ta undo 'em, ya know? Really quick and shit. Then she slides her hand right in and down into my cup. I swear! She is this wicked pro. In like, a second, she had the whole fuckin' cup and jock pulled free... and she starts slidin' her hand up and down real slow on my gator. I couldn't fuckin' believe it! So's I of course... just keep my eyes glued closed... I mean, shit... it was startin' ta feel real good. I like lift my hips up just a bit, ya know, real little... but she gots the clue and starts pullin' my pants down my legs."

"No shit?" said Kirby, a wide smile crossing his face. He glanced nervously down at his lap, Massella's knee still dangerously close to his jewels. He shot Massella a dirty look, but he was still engrossed in massaging his toe.

"So, I'm sittin' there... and she's pullin' my pants and jock down my thighs. I figure by now... what the fuck?... I may as well just sit back and let the slut do her thing... you know? I mean... it sure looks like she wants it, right? So the bus is pretty dark. We just had a coupla lights on, but the whole bus is almost dark. All I could see, if I open my eyes a little bit, is the flashin' of car lights goin' by, an' shit. So it's really pretty fuckin' easy for me to imagine it wasn't this fat-ass broad, but really my girlfriend. So that's what I was doin'. So... my gator was startin' to pop up and spring ta life as she's pumpin' on it, right?"

Sal paused and looked around the group. He had all of their attention now. Meat had put his head down on the table, leaning on his arm. The boxer shorts he wore as a hat flopped down and hung over the right side of his face. Only one eye peered intently at Sal. Massella had let his foot alone, but kept his leg crossed over his thigh. His knee was still invading Kirby's lap, but Kirby had forgotten about it and now only listened to Cardone's story. Vinnie and Vuch were leaning back, slumped against all the backpacks. Tony Marino's shoulder had fallen against Vuch's, his eyes alert and wide as he took in all that Sal had to say.

"So now my gator and balls were hangin' free, and this chick's got her hand wrapped tightly around my shaft. An' she's pumpin' an' pumpin'..." Sal paused again and smiled. "It kinda surprised me cause I got an uncut dick, right? An' like some other broads have given me shit about it. It pisses me off, too. I mean... I got this big dick just waitin' an' wantin' pussy, ya know? An' these bitches are complainin' just cause I got a hood over my gator. Pisses me off!"

Sal turned to face Meat. "Hey, you get that same kinda problem, Meat? The chicks not want ta touch yours?" Meat continued to look Sal with his one exposed eye, showing no expression and not replying.

"Well... thanks for that answer, Meat." He turned back to the group. "But this fat broad... she don't care none. No siree. Not her. She just takes my big ol' cock and is wailin' on it with her tight fist. And let me tell ya, men, she was no slouch at it. So's I've got my eyes closed, enjoyin' her thing, right... next thing I know... she's bendin' down an' lappin' at my cockhead like a fuckin' ice-cream cone. Lick, lick, lick. Man, she's actin' like it's the tastiest thing she ever got her tongue on."

"No shit," Kirby whispered under his breath. Massella adjusted his sitting position slightly, sending his knee down further into Kirby's lap. The contact was enough to begin to stir Kirby's balls, and his dick started perceptibly to rise. "She was really lappin' at ya?" Kirby's voice was becoming almost inaudible.

"Goin' ta town on it, bro'."

"Cool."

"So, I'm just tryin' to keep from shootin' my load, cause this bitch is chowin' on the foreskin an' all... like she is never gonna let up, ya know?" Kirby adjusted his position, pushing himself further back against the stowed gear. He pushed his hips slightly forward, driving his balls harder against Massella's knee, as his dick began to snake down along his hairy thigh. He continued to listen intently to Cardone's story. "But... like, I get to a point, you know... where I just can't hold my spunk any longer. She's dartin' her tongue all along the skin, an' gettin' it real fuckin' wet... jeez, it was like this fuckin' vacuum suckin' machine... only she was real wet and kept it slidin' all around, ya know? Not like some chicks that get their teeth dug into ya gator. No, she slides all nice and easy, gettin' the juice all stirred up from my nuts, know what I mean? So's I, of course, start pumpin' my load into the bitch's mouth, right? I mean I'm shootin', like, gallons of jizz into her fat little mouth, and she don't gag none. Naw... she starts lappin' it all up, takin' the full load down her throat. Shit, man...that was like the best fuckin' head I'd ever had. No shit." Sal shook his head, as he remembered the feeling.

"Did ya fuck her then?" asked Massella.

"No way, man. She was too fuckin' fat an' ugly. An' I ain't sinkin' my gator into somethin' that looks like that. No way I'm lettin' her ride the baloney pony, man." He shrugged. "It can't fantasize that much, ya know?"

"Yeah. Makes sense," responded Massella.

Vuch looked around at the group. "Well, it looks like we're all pretty wiped here. And shit, the brews are all gone."

"Yeah. I'm callin' it a night." Massella pulled his leg away from Kirby's lap and dropped his feet back onto the floor. He stood up, pausing a moment while he flexed his toes, making sure they had not really brusied from Kirby's foot wrestling. He stepped out from around the table. "Hey, you comin', Kirb... or what?"

Kirby looked up from his seat. "Yeah. Sure. Just give me a minute." He remained in his place.

"I think Kirb's gonna have to spank the monkey tonight." Vuch pointed at Kirby's growing problem and began to laugh. Kirby turned red. He adjusted his leg to cover his half-hard dick. He bent down toward the floor and scooped up his shorts, starting to put his legs into their openings.

"Gettin' pretty excited there, huh?" teased Sal. Kirby turned a deeper shade of crimson. He pulled the shorts on as quickly as he could, adjusting his hog in the shorts to try to conceal his erection. He quickly moved out from behind the table and walked off toward the door to the outside, without saying a word.

* * *

"Hey, Meat," said Vuch. Meat remained with his head down on his arm on the table. The boxer shorts he wore as his hat now fell down over most of his face. The one eye that had been exposed, now was closed. His breathing was deep. Vuch got up and moved over to Meat. He lightly shook his shoulder. "Hey, man. Get up." Meat still did not respond. "Okay Vin, what ya say we go out an' sit outside. I'm feelin' wicked drunk. I guess it's good we're outta brews. I think I'd just puke anything else up. Walk me outside will ya?" Vuch stumbled against Vinnie as they made their way back out to the fireplaces. "Shit. Wait." Vuch paused and leaned harder against Vinnie's shoulder. "I'm gettin' this wave a' sick comin' over me. The whole freakin' world is spinnin', ya know what I mean?"

"C'mon Vuch, let's just sit down here against the fireplace. You just need air that's all." Vinnie lowered him down against the stone, then sat down against his side, anchoring them in place.

"Thanks, Vinnie. No shit, I think I had way too much. I'm really glad you're here." Vuch tried to smile, the corner of his mouth grotesquely turning up. His eyes began to unfocus. He slumped down tightly against Vinnie's arm. "Ya know Vinnie... you're like a really, really, really... good friend to me." Vuch belched. He tried to push himself up into a sitting position, but then slid back down against Vinnie's arm. "No... really!" he laughed. "A really, really good friend." His breath smelled foul.

Vinnie doubled over in laughter, waving his middle finger at Vuch. "A really good friend, huh?" he smiled.

"Honest, Vinnie... a really, really..."

"Vuch! I got it!" he laughed again and playfully punched Vuch on the shoulder. "A really, really..." he waved his hand in a circular motion, indicating the phrase went on forever.

"That's it!" yelled Vuch at the top of his lungs. Their attention was suddenly turned back to the entrance of the building. Meat had come to the open doorway and stood leaning against the doorframe. He slid one hand down into his jock and tugged at his balls. He shook his head violently, causing the boxer shorts on his head to puff up like a chef's hat. He reached his other hand down into his cup also — and now stood unconsciously playing with his nuts, the jock pulled partway down his thighs. "Ride me," Meat spoke in a husky voice.

Vinnie arched one of his eyebrows and looked at Meat strangely. "What?"

"'Ride me'. It's 'ride me'." Meat stumbled on one of the small steps. He leaned his shoulder harder against the door jamb.

"What the fuck are you talkin' about?" asked Vinnie.

Meat placed the side of his face on the wooden frame. "The song. It's 'Ride me, baby'." He belched loudly. "Ride me." He closed his eyes, appearing to almost go to sleep standing up. "I'm sure of it," he mumbled.

"Come on, Vuchie." Vinnie bounced his legs to get Vuch more alert. "We gotta call it a night, okay?"

Vuch looked up at Vinnie's face and tried to focus. "Okay. Okay. I wanna sleep up there." He waved his arm toward the building, giving it too much effort so his arm came down hard against his leg.

"Where?" Vinnie tried to follow with his eyes to where he had pointed.

"Up there." Vuch pushed himself off Vinnie and sat up, his body unsure of how to balance. With some effort he pointed his arm again at the railing around the porch of the second floor.

"You wanna sleep up on the porch? Up there?" Vinnie shook his head. "No way. It's probably dangerous. It'll cave in on us. We'll be too heavy."

Vuch pushed himself up and got to his feet. He staggered in place, looking up at the porch. "Come on... you pussy! We can do it." He weaved over toward the doorway of the building, stepping around Meat as he entered. Vinnie sat a moment watching him stagger, then slowly pull himself to his feet, using the fireplace as support. As he walked into the lobby of the building, he saw Vuch over on the side digging through some of their gear.

"What the fuck are ya lookin' for... find it in the mornin', okay?" Vinnie walked over and pulled him back up to a standing position. Vuch was holding some gear in his arms. "You gonna change your clothes?" Vinnie swayed as he talked.

"No, man." Vuch started for the stairwell. "This is my sleepin' bag." He pulled himself by one arm up the cement staircase. Several times he almost tripped over boards and debris that were laying all over the steps.

Vinnie came up behind him. "What do you mean sleepin' bag? We were supposed to bring a sleepin' bag?" He stumbled on a step and cursed. "Vuch, no one told me to bring along a sleepin' bag to camp. They said we had blankets and sheets provided!" He emerged up on the wooden porch that wrapped around the building. Vuch was already up at the very front of the building. He had dropped the bag onto the deck and was leaning out over the railing. Vinnie reached and grabbed him by both shoulders, pulling him back away from the railing. "You're gonna kill yourself. Stay away from the edge, okay?"

"Okay." Vuch tried to smile, his mouth curved into a drunken grin. He tipped forward into Vinnie's chest.

"Vuchie, did you hear me? I don't got no sleepin' bag. Maybe Meat can sleep in just his clothes... but that ain't gonna work for me." He reached his arms out so Vuch steadied. "Can you sleep in your clothes, cause I can't. Lemme have the sleepin' bag."

"Screw you!" Vuch tried to hold himself up. "No, I can't sleep in my clothes! I got wet when I had to chase the footballs, and I fell in out on the point. I'm all mud and shit. I put on dry clothes, but I still got all this fuckin' dirt all over me." He started to yank down his shorts. "Just sleep in the bag with me. It's big enough."

Vinnie looked down at the rolled-up bag. "You sure?"

Vuch waved his arm at Vinnie. "Yeah. Yeah, I'm sure." He fell to his knees as he tried to pull the shorts off his ankles. He sat back and pulled them free. He dropped them beside him, then kicked off his sneakers. "Vin, I gotta whizz. Help me up, will ya?" Vinnie pulled him to his feet. "Where do I go?" Vuch spun around, almost falling back down. Vinnie grabbed him around the shoulders from behind, and walked him up to the edge of the railing. "Just let it go here."

Vuch leaned back against Vinnie's chest and arched his hips up. A stream of hot piss began to shoot in a curve out over the edge of the clearing. Vuch sighed and relaxed, pushing himself further into Vinnie's arms. He reached down and grabbed his dickhead to shake the remaining drops out as the flow subsided. He roughly pulled his nuts as he pushed away from Vinnie and turned around.

Vinnie walked away from him and spread out the sleeping bag. He turned the top down and pointed at the opening. "In," he commanded. Vuch staggered forward and fell down onto the cloth bottom. It took some effort for him to slide his legs down into the bag and turn onto his back. His head fell back and hit the floorboards with a thud.

Vinnie quickly undressed, dropping his shorts beside him for easy reach in the morning. He slid down into the bag bare-assed alongside Vuch. Vuch immediately turned his head to Vinnie. They were so close, Vinnie's torso was raised and up against Vuch's side.

"Vinnie, I don't think I can go right to sleep. I'm too up, you know?... Can we talk awhile?"

"Sure." He looked at Vuch out of the corner of his eye. "What do you want to talk about?" Vuch's breath smelled of stale beer. He turned on his side so he could see Vinnie as they talked. He lifted his arm up and let it fall back down on Vinnie's stomach. Vinnie tensed slightly, but relaxed quickly as the liquor began to wave over him.

"What's your family like? Are you close?"

"Yeah, pretty much. About normal, I guess. It's just me and my Mom and Dad." Vinnie lifted one of his arms and propped it behind his head. "But, we're close, I guess."

Vuch moved his head a little toward Vinnie. His hair rubbed against Vinnie's ear. "Mine isn't. We're not really close. It's just me and my Dad. He tries... but I don't think he really knows what to do or say sometimes, you know." Vuch reached and played with the zipper of the bag with his hand. "I don't think he knows how to raise me alone. He really follows my football, though. He's there at every game. Never misses one."

Vinnie chuckled. "Yeah, that sounds like my Mom. She's always at my games. Usually tells me what we did wrong, too. She's funny. She's cool, you know?"

"That's kinda weird... your mother being into the games, huh?"

"Yeah, but it's kinda okay... nice, ya know... that she's always there. My father tries to be there too, but he works a lot, so my Mom... she kinda represents the family at the games." Vinnie laid his hand over his eyes. "One time she actually went up to the coach and was giving her opinion of the weakness in the offense." He moved his hand and looked at Vuch. "And you know what? She was right! She actually pointed out things the coach agreed with. It was so fuckin' funny!" He looked intently at Vuch. "What happened to your Mom?"

Vuch looked out at the trees that rose up over the roof of the camp. "She died... a few years ago." He looked up silently at the darkened leaves of the trees.

"Oh... I'm sorry." Vinnie continued to watch Vuch's eyes. "So it's just you and your Dad? You don't got any brothers or sisters?"

"I got a brother," he said softly. "Well, a half-brother." He turned and looked at Vinnie. "We're gettin' closer. There were a few years when we didn't get along at all."

"Well, that's good I guess, huh?"

"Yeah. I guess so," said Vuch, his voice fading. "Vinnie, what do you like about football?"

"What do I like? I don't know... all kindsa things. I'm good at it, so I guess I like the fact it's somethin' I can really do, you know?"

"Do you like the friendships? You know... like, do you like hangin' around with the guys?"

"Yeah, I guess so."

"I think that's the best part for me." He reached up and covered his mouth as another belch overtook him. "I really like the way the guys all look up to me." He moved his head more against Vinnie. "Treat me like their best friend, you know?"

"And the girls look up to you, too, right? I mean... you're like the big football star to them." Vinnie grinned at him.

"Yeah. Yeah... kinda." His voice trailed off again. "I don't date much. I don't care that much about it."

Vinnie looked at him again. He began to feel his dick swell under the cover of the sleeping bag, and shifted uncomfortably. He felt nervous again that Vuch's hand was on his stomach, but before he could adjust position another wave of dizziness passed over him. He laid his arm over his eyes again, trying to keep the world from reeling before he re-opened them, then he felt Vuch's head move closer. He stayed still, keeping his eyes covered, as Vuch moved his lower body against him, his leg crossing over on top of Vinnie's own. As he settled, his head came to rest right in the small of Vinnie's neck.

A moment later, Vinnie could feel Vuch's hog hardening against him. Vuch's breathing changed, slowing down and growing louder. He began to slowly buck his hips into Vinnie in a slow rhythm. He moaned slightly, his breathing changing to a periodic snort. He was partway asleep.

Vinnie felt his own dick stiffen to full size, and start to pulsate up and down against his stomach, just an inch from where Vuch's hand lay twitching. He removed his arm from over his eyes, and turned his head slightly so he could look at Vuch's face. He lay there with his mouth part open, his breathing slowing more. A small stream of saliva was visible in his mouth, his tongue settled lightly over his bottom lip. The movement of his hips slowed down, but his dick was still hard against Vinnie's side. Vinnie concentrated on the feeling. He could focus his mind and actually feel the movement of Vuch's cockhead as it moved back and forth, the shaft having a different feel to it as it passed over the hair on Vinnie's massive thigh. Vinnie felt pre-cum begin to leak from his dick. His whole body was beginning to vibrate and come alive from the feeling of Vuch slowly fucking against his body. Vuch's breathing jarred, he licked his lips and twisted his head further into Vinnie's neck. His tongue remained loosely hanging out over his lips. After pausing, his hips began their slow grinding movement again, digging against Vinnie as his dick slid back and forth. Vinnie stared down at Vuch's partially open mouth. Another wave of drunkenness flowed over him, as he gave in to the call of the liquor. Leaning his head slightly forward, he parted his lips gently and allowed his tongue to brush against Vuch's soft mouth. Vuch's tongue clumsily responded, lightly tugging against Vinnie's lower lip. Vinnie felt his own dick bounce against his stomach as it pulsated in excitement, then the warm flow of cum as it shot out and up his chest. A moment later another intense wave of dizziness flowed over him. He drifted off into blackness.

12

Vinnie awoke to sun streaming into his eyes. He slowly lifted his head up — a rush of pain shot through his temples. He lowered his head back down and took a deep breath, laying with his eyes closed for a moment. He slowly opened them and let the light filter into his head a bit at a time, then rolled his head side to side trying to work the kink out of his neck. Gently he lifted himself up onto his elbows and focused his vision on his surroundings. A breeze blew through his hair; sunlight drifted through the dense leaves of the trees overhead. He raised his arm and looked at his wristwatch. It was 8:53.

"My God, I think I died," he whispered to himself. He raised his hand to his head and flattened his hair down his forehead. He felt his eye hurt and touched two fingers to the spot; it pulsated in pain. He squinted his eyes and remembered being elbowed when they were sneaking around the Revere camp the night before. He slowly sat up, rubbing his hands down his face. He let his mind focus on the night before. They had all gone swimming. Then they drank. Boy, did they drink. He reached beside him and picked up his shorts. Then they had gone on that stupid trip to swipe the footballs. And they had drank more. And more. He put his legs through the openings in the shorts and pulled them up as he got to his feet. He balanced himself, looking down at the activity around the clearing. Guys were moving around everywhere, and food was being prepared on the grills over the fireplaces. They had managed to get the footballs. But what did they do with them? He supposed they brought them back here. Somewhere. He remembered laying around the clearing drinking more... and the card game... and Sal Cardone's blow-job story... and Meat singing... and Vuchie wanting to sleep up here.

Vuchie. He looked down at the sleeping bag. He remembered he had been next to Vuch. And close to Vuch. He looked around. Vuch was not up on the porch area. He looked down at the guys in the clearing. He couldn't see Vuch anywhere. He looked back down at the sleeping bag. His shirt lay next to it, thrown on top of his shoes. He stumbled a little as he reached and retrieved the shirt, his head throbbing more as he bent down and slipped his training shoes on over his bare feet. The shoes were still almost totally covered in mud, a remembrance of the raid. He sat back down and made sure he had put the shoes on the proper feet. Soreness was creeping back into his toes. His head weaved a moment. He turned and spit over the side of the railing. His mouth felt dry and rancid — he needed to clean up badly.

Pulling himself up, he turned and walked along the border of the railing, then started down the stairwell. As he reached the bottom, he saw that most of the team were up and sorting through their belongings that were scattered around. He rubbed his head again as he walked over to the corner where they had stowed their gear.

"Mornin' Vin, ol' boy!" Mike Massella clapped him hard on the back. Vinnie slowly turned and looked at him. "Shit, you don't look so good, Vin."

"Yeah. That's how I feel."

"Well, breakfast is cookin' out there. A lot of the guys have eaten, but I know there's still some. Go get some food in ya." Massella walked to the other side of the room, and began talking with Kirby and Marino.

"Hey!" A shot of pain went through Vinnie as he raised his voice to call across the room. He put a hand back up to his temple. "Any of you guys seen Vuch?"

"Nope. Not all mornin'," replied Kirby. The three of them went out the doorway. Vinnie bent down slowly and dug through the pile of his stuff. He found his gymbag and slowly slung it over his shoulder. He reached inside his duffle and pulled out a clean tee-shirt and pair of shorts. Rubbing his hand down his forehead again, he straightened up and walked out into the clearing.

"Hey, Vinnie, what's up?" Sal Cardone came walking over, a bright smile on his face.

"Not much."

"Gee, you don't look so good, Vinnie. You didn't seem to be that fucked up at the card game last night." Sal bent down and looked at Vinnie's face closely. "Wow, you got a shiner startin', too! You guys get in a brawl over at the other camp?"

Vinnie blinked his eyes a few times to adjust them to the bright sunlight. "Sorry to disappoint you, my eye had a run-in with Vuch's elbow." Vinnie began to walk off.

"Where ya goin'?"

"I need to go down to the beach and clean up. I think I'm a little on the grungy side."

"No, don't go to the beach." Sal raised an arm and pointed down a side path. "Go down there. A stream runs through the center of the island. It's better... the water flows. Clean up down there. Everyone does."

Vinnie nodded slowly and turned in that direction. He took a few steps, then turned back to Sal. "Hey, you haven't seen Vuchie today, have you?"

"No. But I've only been here a few minutes, I slept down on the beach."

Vinnie waved and continued down the path that led to the stream. As he walked along, a feeling of confusion began to overtake him. He imagined it was a combination of the after-effects of the liquor, together with his not understanding what had truly gone on the night before. Maybe his memory had been clouded. Maybe what he had believed had occurred was really just a dream on his part... or a drunken misinterpretation. Maybe nothing had really happened at all. Maybe.

He weaved his way along the path, carefully pushing aside stray branches that kept whipping into his face. This area was more difficult to travel, as the tree and weed growth had just about taken over what might have originally been a fairly wide pathway. Within a few minutes, Vinnie began to hear the sound of voices talking and laughing somewhere ahead. The loud echo of cascading water could be clearly identified, as he got nearer to where the stream was located. Suddenly the path opened up into a wide area. Vinnie was amazed for a moment at the degree of activity. There were some forty or so guys spread out around the stream and rocks. The water cut through a high rocky area above, and came crashing down over moss-covered boulders. The effect was almost like a waterfall. The guys had made good use of the opportunity to horse around and get clean in the process. Clothes had been discarded along the banks of the stream — piles of shirts and shoes were all carelessly thrown together. Closer to the edge of the water, a line of jockstraps was abandoned, where the team had pulled off their remaining restrictions before plunging freely into the water.

Vinnie looked up at the top of the waterfall. Several guys were lined up waiting for their turn to throw themselves into the flow. He recognized Tony Marino on the edge, preparing to shoot down into the stream. "Hey, ya...Vinnie!" Marino called from above. "Check this out, man!" He bent his knees down, balancing carefully on the brink of one of the rocks. He looked down, checking his clearance, then jumped out. He flew through the air, his dick slapping up hard against his stomach from the force of pushing away from the rocky perch. He just had time to grab his nostrils closed as he plumeted into the rush of the water. Vinnie smiled and watched silently for a second until Marino came bobbing back up to the surface. He had been carried several yards understream — he waved his arm in triumph as he came up. "Fuckin' A, Manta! Come on, ya gotta try this shit! Ya wouldn't fuckin' believe the rush of throwin' ya'self off those mother rocks!" He swam over to the edge of the embankment and pulled himself up onto his knees. He shook his head wildly, water showering out from around his head. He stood up, shaking the remaining water droplets from his body.

"Nice one, Marino!" Vinnie smiled widely.

"Aw, it's the fuckin' balls!" Marino walked over and stood beside Vinnie. He pointed back up at the top of the rocks. "Watch this, man... Tollini's gonna ride the motherfucker right down. Watch this!" Chip Tollini picked his way carefully up to the top of the boulder. He paused and surveyed his point of descent.

Cheers and catcalls came out from all the guys along the sides of the stream. "Come on, you pussy!" "Hey, Chipper.... kiss your fuckin' jewels good-bye!" "What fuckin' jewels... he don't got them to lose!" "We'll know if you get a fuckin' rock up your ass... by the fuckin' smile on ya face!" "Come on, Chip.... slide that ass down!" Chip looked down at the crowd and waved. He steadied himself, then jumped out a little, purposely sliding his butt along the moss-covered area. He came shooting down along the slippery rocks, his arms waving widely in the air to try to gain some balance. His body spun and went down into the water headfirst. He immediately rose back up out of the stream. "Yeeee... haaaa!" He smiled and dove back under the frothy brook.

"The man's fuckin' nuts!" Tony Marino reached down and squeezed his balls. "That water's fuckin' like ice, man."

"Yeah, well, I gotta clean up in that. I smell, man. I gotta get some of this sweat off." Vinnie pulled his shirt off over his head.

"Yeah, well... take it from me, Vinnie, lay in the sun for a few minutes before ya go jumpin' into that water, man." Marino sat down on the grass and spread his legs out wide. He pulled on his nuts as he continued to look up at Vinnie. "My balls... they're all fuckin' shrunk from the cold... ya know? They fuckin' hurt. That water's real icey, man." Marino bent his head down and examined his shriveled sack.

Vinnie tugged down his shorts and dropped them on top of a dry rock. He flopped himself down on the grass next to Marino. "Sun feels good, huh?"

Marino looked up from his examination. "No shit. I fuckin' love the summer. Me and Vuch used to go to the beach all fuckin' last year, man. No shit... we used to go almost every day. We ain't got there even once this year. This is about as much fuckin' sun as this bod's gonna see this season." He returned his eyes and fingers to his attempt to stretch out the skin of his testicles. Vinnie reclined his body fully out in the rays. He lay down onto his back and rested his head on one of his training shoes. He let his legs open and placed one hand behind his head, lazily turning his head to the side. The warmth of the sun felt awesome on his face.

"Manta... look at this will ya?" Tony nudged him with his foot.

Vinnie slowly re-opened his eyes. "What?"

Marino slid further over near him. He lifted one of his legs up, giving Vinnie a clearer view of his nuts. "See how these are all shrunken and shit?"

"Yeah, Marino... I see. But what the fuck do you want me to do about it? I ain't no doctor, or nothin'." Vinnie squinted in the sunlight, trying to see what Marino was making such a big deal about. "Yeah... your nuts got tight. Big fuckin' deal. So do mine when I get cold. Now get your sacks outta my face, huh?"

"So ya thinks it's normal, huh?"

"Yeah, Tony... I think it's normal. They just gotta warm up. That's all." Vinnie closed his eyes again.

"I hope so. These are like my life, you know?" Tony spit into his hands and rubbed the warm saliva into his sack. "Without these baby's... and Tony ain't nothin'." He laughed and spit into his hands again.

Vinnie raised his head and looked Marino in the eyes. "Yeah... so I heard." He spoke with a slight tremor in his voice. He closed his eyes tightly, Vuch's half-serious warning about Marino replaying in his mind. He opened his eyes again to find Marino staring at him intently, a shit-eating grin pasted on his face.

"So, you hear about my exploits, huh?" he chuckled quietly, massaging his tight balls while he talked. "Yeah, man, I got quite the reputation." He twisted his neck, the action causing a cracking sound in his spine. He sighed in relief, shrugging his shoulders to relax the kinks. "Hey, man, I hadda work hard to live up to some of those stories," he winked at Vinnie.

Vinnie sneered, his upper lip curling across his front teeth. "Yeah, well... I think you do a pretty good job of gettin' stories spread around." Vinnie's eye began to twitch slightly, he could feel his blood pressure rising.

"What's that supposed to mean?" snapped Marino. His hand had stopped rubbing his nut as he stared at Vinnie.

"Nothin', man." Vinnie's voice trailed off.

"No, Manta... finish. What the fuck does that mean?"

Vinnie squinted in the bright light. He sat up, pulling one leg underneath his ass to form a slight padding against the hard ground. He held onto the bare toes of his crossed leg, pinching them as he continued. "It's just that I heard some stuff around, that all," he answered.

Marino shrugged. "I guess you mean the talk goin' around about me bein' led by my dick, huh?" He resumed his massage.

Vinnie felt his anger build. He was ready for a confrontation. Just let the fucker try to explain it. Vuch wouldn't lie. It wasn't just guy shit goin' around. "You tryin' to deny it?" Vinnie prepared to jump down his throat.

"No, man... I don't deny nothin'. In fact, I'm the one who starts mosta what you hear. What, you think anybody cares what the fuck I do? Mosta the guys are jealous that I'm gettin' my pud sucked all the time. They wish they got their nut as often as I do. Big f'in deal." Marino smiled at Vinnie again. Vinnie was silent. Why the fuck had he admitted it? Even worse, why the fuck did he tell everyone about it? He should have hid in shame, hoping that no one would ever find out.

Vinnie looked blankly at Tony. "Marino, why the hell do you admit it to the guys? I mean it's bad enough you'd do somethin' like that... but to brag about it?" he looked in disbelief at his teammate.

"I don't fuckin' brag about nothin'. Sometimes me an' the guys shoot the shit about how long it's been since we all shot a load. Not that it's any of your fuckin' business, but that's how the stories come out. But, what the fuck do you mean 'bad enough that I'd do somethin' like that'?" Marino lost his smile.

"Well, Christ, Marino... what the fuck is a big guy jock like you doin' queer shit for?" Vinnie tried to lose the sneer he could feel on his lips. He wanted to be civil to Marino. After all, Marino had never done anything against him personally.

"Man, it ain't no big f'in deal. Jesus, Manta, you'd think I murdered someone or somethin'. I just get my nut off... so what?" he shook his head. "An' it ain't like I'm fuckin' humpin' every chick and guy around. Just sometimes, when I'm wicked horny... well, I gotta cream. Big deal."

"What about how all the guys are gonna think about you?" Vinnie had calmed down. He was trying to make Marino see how bad this could look for him. "I mean, ya don't want all the other guys thinkin' you're some kinda dumb-ass fag... do ya?"

"The guys don't think that, Vinnie. Jeez, get over it, will ya? I been doin' chicks and guys for a long time... and the team all knows that. They think it's kinda funny... that I get so much ass. Anyways... even if they didn't, I wouldn't care what they thought about me." He smiled again, his shaved head glistening from sweat in the sunlight. "I'm just who I am, Vinnie, I can't change that. I think mosta the guys respect that. I don't try to hide nothin' from nobody." He shrugged.

"You really don't care what they think about you?" Vinnie's voice lowered, his mind in deep thought.

"Naw. Not really. Fuck 'em if they can't just like me for being me. You know?" he flashed a wide grin. "Besides, if they says anythin' bad... I'd beat the shit outta 'em!"

"Ya know... ya don't come across like a guy that does other guys."

"Hey, hold on, pal... I don't just do guys. I like ta get my nut. Sometimes, it just don't matter to me who sticks their lips around my hog. If it's the right person... well shit, I'll shoot my load down their throat." Marino nodded. "An' I know I don't look like I'd let a guy suck me off... but what's someone like that supposed to look like?"

Vinnie shrugged. "I don't know. Some kinda limp-wristed little shit, I guess." He shrugged again.

Marino shook his head. "You're the dumb-fuck, Vinnie. You'd be surprised ta see the kinda guys that have done me. I wouldn't let

no pansy suck my hog, man. These guys were big fuckin' bruisers."
Marino tugged on his nuts. "Most guys are the type you'd never
think are fags." Marino drummed his fingers against his stomach as
he talked in an excited state. "I wouldn't tolerate it if any of the
guys started talkin' about me being a fag or nothin'. I'm a guy. An'
what my hog here does, doesn't change that. An' just cause I like to
get off... don't mean I have any less respect. I know that, believe me.
It ain't no big deal."

Vinnie nodded. Somehow he thought this was true. Marino was
an alright guy, he decided. Maybe it didn't matter that he balled
guys, too. He winked back at Marino, indicating things were cool.
"Hey, Marino... you seen Vuchie today?" Vinnie turned his head
slightly and watched Tony massage his balls.

"Nope." He pulled one nut down and continued to rub it. "I
don't know where the fuck he went."

Vinnie sat up and looked around the banks of the brook.

"Eeeeaaah!"

Vinnie turned his eyes back up to the top of the rocks. Taglienti
came over the edge, waving his arms in the air as he fell down into
the stream.

"Vinnie, ya gotta go try it." Marino jumped up to his feet and
started off in the direction of the rocks.

"Hey... what happened ta ya delicate little nuts?" Vinnie called
after him.

Marino started climbing up the rocks, his hands pulling him up
as he got his footing. "Fuck that! As long as my hog still gets hard...
what the fuck do I care!" He reached the top and waited in line for
his turn at the edge. He yanked on his balls a few more times to
loosen them up.

Vinnie took his time lounging in the sun. There was something
exciting about lying in the sun buck-naked, having all the guys clown-
ing around, and knowing he didn't have to even think about anything else. He had the whole day. Several times the guys tantalized
him to go up on the rocks and try his turn at jumping. The water
felt so incredible against his sweating skin, as he plowed into the
cold from the top of the boulders.

*   *   *

It was around noon when Vinnie could finally tear himself away
from the antics and return his thoughts to bathing. Some of the

other guys had the same thoughts in mind and had started a pile of half-used bars of soap and watered-down shampoo over by the flat rocks at the edge of the stream. Most of the guys were lounging in the hot sun by midday, so Vinnie knew he could take his time cleaning up before everyone would be roused again to go in the water. He carefully picked his way along the rocks, the bottoms of his feet burning. He dropped his clothes down onto a log that was sticking up, reached his hand down and scooped up a handful of soap. The hot sun had practically melted the bars together. A mixture of blended soap colors formed a coating in his palm. "Oh this is just pissa!" he groaned. He walked a few steps down into the stream. Using his clean hand, Vinnie splashed the cold water up over his chest and shoulders, then began to rub the lather into his skin. He felt his nuts begin to tighten from the immediate temperature change. "Well, Marino, ol' buddy... now I know how ya feel," he said to himself.

Vinnie was startled suddenly by a huge splash into the water directly next to him. He ducked down as a wall of water came up and over on top of him. He looked around in confusion, waiting for the perpetrator to surface from under the water. A second later, Meat lifted up out of the stream. "Hi, ya, Vin!" he exclaimed with a wide smile on his face. He pushed his arms under the water and sent another shower down on Vinnie.

"Shit, Meat... that's so fuckin' cold!" Vinnie shook the excess water off his upper body. "Cut it out... Jesus!" He quickly rubbed soap into his hair and rinsed, shaking his head briskly side to side.

"Yeah. It is a bit cold, eh?" Meat walked back up out of the brook and dropped down onto the large flat rock where Vinnie had left his stuff. Vinnie dropped briefly all the way under the water, then jumped back up. He pushed water droplets off his chest as he walked up onto the rock and sat down next to Meat.

"My fuckin' balls are blue, man." Vinnie squeezed them, performing the same ritual that Tony Marino had done.

"No shit. My dick retracted way into its skin," complained Meat.

Vinnie smiled and leaned forward a bit, eyeing Meat's crotch. "Hey, Meatman... if that's retracted and small... we should all have to suffer with such a small tool!" He laughed and leaned back to get some sun on his face.

Meat shrugged. "Hey, ya got it, then ya got it." He followed Vinnie's lead and reclined out in the warm rays.

Vinnie turned his head toward Meat. "Hey, Meat... ya haven't seen Vuchie today... have ya?" He shifted his eyes nervously as he watched for Meat's expression.

"Yeah, I seen him." Meat said quietly.

"You have?" Vinnie sat upright quickly. "Well where the fuck is he? I haven't seen him all morning." Vinnie rubbed his hands together, as his voice became more animated. "He slept up on the porch area of the camp last night... but I ain't seen him since I got up. Where the fuck did he go?"

Meat got up and started walking back down into the water. "He went back to the camp." He waded out further into the flow of the water, then stopped and stood waist deep, the brook swirling around him.

Vinnie leaned forward and raised his voice slightly so Meat could hear him. "But I checked all around the camp when I got up. You mean he went back there after I came down here to the stream?" He got to his feet.

Meat looked briefly over at Vinnie standing at the water's edge. "No... I mean he went back to camp." He turned his back and splashed more water over his head. "The football camp." He dunked under and re-surfaced.

Vinnie plowed out into the water and stood next to Meat. "What do ya mean, he went back to the football camp?" His voice was raising in pitch.

Meat turned to him, his face taking on a glaring look. "Are you deaf... or just stupid? I just said he went back... okay?" Meat walked a few paces down in the direction the stream was flowing. Vinnie followed right behind him.

"But why? Why did he go back? He didn't even say anything to me about it?" Vinnie shook his head in disbelief and confusion.

Meat turned his eyes briefly back to Vinnie. "He didn't know what to say." He looked away quickly. Vinnie stood just staring down into the water, watching the patterns that were forming as the water swirled around his legs. Meat walked back up onto the rock and sat down, facing back toward the waterfall. He watched as a few of the guys began to climb again up to the jumping perch.

Vinnie slowly walked up next to Meat and crouched down. He spoke in a soft tone. "Meat... I don't understand. What happened?"

Meat turned to face Vinnie. He stared at Vinnie's face for a moment before answering. "Hey, man... it's none of my business... okay? Whatever you an' Tony got goin' is your concern, not mine."

His eyes shifted back to the rocks, as Chip Tollini once again yelled and threw himself over the edge.

Vinnie wrinkled his forehead in further confusion. "Wait a minute. What the fuck are you talkin' about... Tony... Marino? What's fuckin' Marino got to do with this?" He pushed against Meat's leg to get a response.

Meat turned and glared again. "No," he sighed. "Tony... Vuch's name is Tony."

"Oh... yeah. Okay... so I forgot. I never call him that. Nobody does. I just didn't know... okay?"

"Yeah, well... there's a lot that you don't seem to know." Meat looked down at his hands as he spoke.

"What's that supposed to mean?"

"Nothin'. Okay... just fuckin' nothin'." He looked back again at Vinnie's eyes. "Just don't hurt him, okay. Just be careful and think before you do stupid shit, okay?" He looked away.

Vinnie rubbed his hands over his eyes. He looked off at the cliff as he spoke. "Did Vuch tell you about last night?"

"Yeah." Meat kept his gaze on the guys jumping off the rocks.

"I swear, man..." Vinnie stammered, "I swear... I don't know what the fuck happened." He rubbed his hands nervously together again. "I just don't know what happened. We was drunk... you know? That's all. We was both drunk." He put his hands over his eyes. "Drunk and confused."

Meat spun his body around so he faced Vinnie directly. "Yeah, well the thing is... is that Tony wasn't confused. I think maybe you weren't either... but that's your business. I only care about Tony. I only wanna look out for Tony, okay?"

Vinnie nodded silently. He continued to watch Meat, not knowing what to say.

"Look, Vinnie. I don't wanna get into your business. But there's alot you don't know. I watch out for Tony. He watches out for me. We take care of each other, you know? And I don't know... I don't understand alot... you know how everyone thinks I'm just this missing link of a stupid shit... but, I know Tony. I know what's goin' on with him. I think I know what's goin' on with you. But all I care about is that he is okay in this... you know what I mean?"

"Yeah. Yeah... I do." Vinnie smiled a little. "He told me when we first got here how you two would do anything for each other. I was kinda surprised... but I guess you're really lookin' out for him."

Meat sighed again. "Look, Vinnie... maybe I shouldn't say anything... but maybe I should. I don't know. I wanna help him. I wanna help you." He paused, looking closely at Vinnie's face. "Look... has he said anything about his family? Anything about life at home?"

Vinnie shrugged. "I don't know. Not much... really. I know his Dad makes that shit he put on my feet. And he told me last night that it's just him and his Dad. His mother died a few years ago."

Meat's voice softened even more. "Yeah... she died a few years ago." He squinted his eyes. "She was my mother, too." His voice trailed off.

Vinnie's eyes widened. "Shit. You mean you and Vuch are brothers?"

Meat shrugged. "Half-brothers." He looked down and picked at the rock with his strong fingers. "See she and Tony's father were married and shit. They had Tony. But then Mr Carvuccio... Sam's his name... well Sam was drinkin' and shit. Not abusive or nothin', he's a okay guy... he really is... but drinkin' cause of work pressures and shit. Well anyways... our Mom felt kinda rejected and lonely, you know? Well... I can understand that. I mean he was workin' all the time and stuff." Meat paused and drew in a deep breath. "Well anyways, she started havin' an affair with my father. He was single... and well, it just happened." He shrugged again. "Well, she became pregnant... with me. Just four months after havin' Tony. She told her husband. Tony's father knew... but well it was hard. When she had me, she gave me to my Dad to raise. Tony's father could forgive her, but... well, he didn't want me around to remind him. Not all the time anyways." Meat rubbed his eyes. "So me and Tony, we grew up separately. We didn't even really know about each other. We knew each other in school, but we saw our Mom separately. She lived with him... and then would come visit me and my Dad when she could. Anyways, I guess the guilt kept eatin' at her. She never forgave herself, you know? We all fuckin' loved her... and she never forgave... herself. About four years ago she killed herself. Sat in the fuckin' garage and carbon-monoxided herself to fuckin' death."

Vinnie's mouth dropped open as he listened. His voice came out in a raspy whisper. "Jesus, Meat... I'm so sorry."

Meat shrugged again. "Anyways... it all came out after she died, you know. Tony and I found out about each other. Our dads were finally able to talk. Can you believe that shit? Our Mom dies... and then they can finally talk! Jesus Christ!" He glanced back up at

Vinnie, a strong look coming into his eyes. "So me an' Vuchie... we just decides that he and I are gonna fuckin' take care of each other, you know. Be there for each other." He half-shrugged one last time and stared down at the sun shining on the rock.

Vinnie looked off into the distance. "Yeah. I know. I understand. Fuck... this is a mess."

"Vuch cares for you. I don't understand this shit. But he tries to talk to me. I try to understand and listen to him. We try to be there for each other. I ain't no stupid fuckin' cave man, Vinnie... I seen what has been goin' on. You two need to talk. You need to be honest. Don't play stupid fuckin' games with each other."

"Hey, I ain't playin' no games. I don't understand this shit either, man."

"Yeah, well... do you care about him? You know what I mean?"

"Yeah, I know what you mean... I don't know. I guess. Fuck, I don't know!" Vinnie got to his feet. He shifted his weight back and forth nervously. "Hey, maybe you're just readin' alot into this. Maybe too much. Hell, man..." he lowered his voice to an angry whisper, "hell... we ain't no fuckin' fags!"

Meat stood up and dropped his arm onto Vinnie's shoulder. Vinnie instinctively pulled back a little. "Shit, man..." Meat grinned, "and you guys think I'm the fuckin' Neanderthal!" He shook his head in disbelief. "We're all just the fuck who we are, Manta. That's all... just who we are." He bent down and picked up his own shoes that he had tossed next to Vinnie's when he first surprised him in the water.

"You know, Meat... as I said... you could just be readin' too much into this."

"Oh yeah. Maybe. Like how a couple of nights ago Tony slept in your bed with you. Back at the cabin?" Meat smiled. "Hey, I don't sleep that dead to the world, you know?"

"See... you got this thing all wrong, Meat."

"His bed was wet."

"Yeah... exactly... see there is an explanation. That's all it was."

"Ah, okay... if you say so." He turned and started to walk away from Vinnie, then paused and turned back. "Except I was takin' this nap that afternoon... see?... an, well, I was there when that pussy Tobin and his buddies were there cleanin' up the cabin. Yeah... it's kinda funny, cause it started rainin' real heavy, you know... and well Tobin, he closed the window over Tony's bed." He smiled back at Vinnie. "So ya see, ol' Vuchie's bed couldn'ta been wet, huh?" He smiled again and winked at Vinnie. "Give him the day to think. You too, I guess. But if I were you, man... I'd fuckin' do some serious talkin' with him tonight." Meat nodded and smiled genuinely. He turned and walked off down the path.

* * *

Vinnie spent the rest of the day walking around in a daze. He retreated from the antics going on at the stream, and opted instead to go back over to the quiet side of the island and sit on the rocks that he and the guys had swam around the night before. The sun still beat down a full summer heat as he sat looking out over the lake from the top perch Meat had used while they had all been in the water. He had put his loose gym shorts on since he was walking back through the island, but kept his shirt tucked into the waist-band of the shorts — the shirt bundled together like a rag hanging down his leg. He reached down and pulled the shirt out of its confines and dropped it on the rock next to him. He kicked his shoes off, sending them falling down the side of the rock. They landed in a tumbled pile on the sand below. He squinted his eyes and looked out at the shimmering sun reflected off the lake. One hand dropped against his leg and he began absentmindedly to rub the hair from his nut that hung out the leg opening of his shorts. His face grew tense as he thought about Vuch. "I can't fuckin' deal with this shit," he whispered to himself.

He let the past few days begin to run through his mind. The camp had been fantastic. He really liked the guys on the team, and valued their abilities. Northridge seemed to have some of the most talented guys he had ever seen in high school. He had had a pissa time getting to know the guys on a personal level. He could already regard Kirby and Massella as friends. Tony Marino seemed like a decent shit. Meat also had more than surprised him, showing a rough exterior, but definitely having a big heart inside. And then there was Vuch. As incredible as everything seemed, there definitely was Vuch. He stood up and scanned the horizon. "I can't deal with this fuckin' shit!" he yelled out at the top of his lungs. His voice echoed across the water. Vinnie bent down and picked up his shirt. He climbed down the edge of the rock and walked into the shallow water, beginning to wade slowly through the small waves that lapped the beach. "I gotta find Vuch," he whispered to himself.

It was just before dinner time that the first boat went back over to the football camp. Chip Tollini took a few of the guys over, piling the boat high with personal belongings. They sent back both of the boats that had been used to row over the island supplies. It had been a tiring couple of days, and due to some remaining hangovers and additional partying at the waterfall, most of the guys were opting to go back over to the main camp in the boats rather than swim again. This slowed the whole process down considerably. Both of the rowboats were again piloted by sophomores, but each could only carry a handful of the guys once a fair amount of personal belongings had been loaded.

Vinnie waited patiently for most of the guys to go back across. He had a deepening need to see and talk to Vuch, but he was really nervous about what to say. He had intense feelings for Vuch — that he knew, but he didn't want his feelings misinterpreted. But then again... how do you misinterpret feelings you can't understand? It was almost eight by the time Vinnie beached over at the camp. He grabbed his duffle and went directly back up to the cabin. As he came in through the door, only silence greeted him. He stood in the middle of the room, his duffle still hanging over his shoulder, and scanned the small cabin. Vuch's bed was empty, although Vinnie saw the stuff that he had brought to the island piled in the middle of his bed. He walked to the edge of the bunks and looked over to the corner near the dressers. Nothing. He took a few steps back so he could see up onto Meat's mattress. As usual, Meat was laying face down, naked to the world. Vinnie dropped his bag on his bed and turned to go back outside.

"He ain't here," said Meat's muffled voice.

"Meat?"

Meat lifted his face up off his pillow and directed his voice to Vinnie. "I ain't seen him since I got back. And I was in one of the first boats back over."

"Well, where is he? His stuff's all here, right?" Vinnie approached the bunks.

Meat lifted himself up on to one elbow. "Everything but his sleeping bag. He must be plannin' on sleepin' somewhere else. He must be pretty upset, Manta." Meat rubbed his eye roughly with his finger. "He wasn't in the dinin' hall, cause I asked some of the guys who were here for dinner. They seen him around earlier, but he disappeared before we all started headin' back over here from the island."

Vinnie folded his arms and leaned against the wall. "Meat, I gotta find him. I gotta talk to him. This whole fuckin' thing is drivin' me fuckin' crazy."

"Yeah, well... what ya gonna say?"

"I don't know. I really don't know." Vinnie turned and started back toward the door. "But, I gotta find him. Listen, do me a favor, Meat? If he comes back here, will ya tell him I'm lookin' for him?"

"Yeah, sure Manta. No problem." Meat dropped his head back down into the pillow. Vinnie opened the cabin door. "Hey, Vinnie," Meat lifted his head back up, "whenever he used to wanna go and talk with me... about our Mom and shit, you know? We used to go down to the campgrounds by the lake in West Northridge. Sometimes we used ta stay there all night and sit and wait for the sun to come up. You might wanna keep checkin' down by the lake. It's a possibility, you know?"

"Hey thanks, Meat. I'll do that." Vinnie took a step out the door and then stuck his head back in. "And hey, George?" Meat lifted his head back up and looked at him.

"What?"

"I consider you a friend too. Thanks for talkin' to me."

"Manta, get the fuck outta here, will ya?" Meat turned his back as he rolled on his side.

"Later, George." Vinnie closed the door behind him.

A few seconds later, Meat replied, "It's Meat. Meat." He closed his eyes and started drifting back into sleep. "Just look between my legs. It's Meat." His voiced trailed off.

Vinnie searched all the areas of the camp for over two hours, passing back across the beach each time he went to a different section. Vuch was nowhere to be found. A lot of the guys said they had seen him at various times that evening, at various parts of the camp — but it appeared that Vuch did not want to be found. Most of the camp was already turning in for the night, as Vinnie again headed down to the beach area. The game with Revere was scheduled for the next day, so most guys wanted their sleep. Vinnie walked along the sand, thinking about the game. They still had one of the biggest moments of camp to go — to show they were a team. To show their abilities against Revere. Revere... the team with no footballs. Vinnie smiled to himself. They would play their game, then go home. And it would be all over. Maybe a lot more would be over, too.

He looked at his watch. 11:15. It was late. He wasn't getting anywhere. His eyes scanned down the beach. Nothing. He stopped and walked to the water's edge, listening to the quiet lapping of the waves against the sand. He looked out across the water, and his eyes fixed on the lone figure sitting out on the far end of the docks. He started walking.

* * *

"Vuchie, I been lookin' all over for you all day." Vinnie's voice shook a little as he stood behind Vuch. Vuch's bare legs dangled silently off the edge of the dock, his feet moving slowly back and forth in the dark water. Vuch turned his head to Vinnie. He smiled, a sadness apparent.

"I been around."

Vinnie kicked off his shoes and dropped down beside Vuch. He was surprised at how cool the night water was already. He kicked his feet through the darkness. They sat silently for a few minutes. "I was surprised you left the island so early today."

Vuch shrugged. "Yeah, well I needed to get away, you know."

"From me?" Vinnie asked quietly.

"From everything, I guess." Vuch moved his feet more quickly through the water. "Not, not from you. Not really."

"Do ya wanna talk about it?" Vinnie turned to him and tried his best to smile.

Vuch shrugged again. "Hey, Manta... I told ya... ya can't smile worth shit... especially when ya don't feel like it, ya know?" Vuch pulled one leg out of the water and placed his foot up on the dock. He rubbed his toes lightly. Suddenly his eyes grew wide and he leaned in slightly toward Vinnie's face. "Shit... lookie at that fuckin' eye! Guess my elbow is kinda hard, huh? It hurt much?"

"Nah."

Vuch looked back down, his eyes fixing on the reflection of moonlight in the water. "So talk... if ya want." His voice trailed off in a low whisper.

Silence again. Vinnie began to clench his right hand into a fist, then relaxed it, laying his palm flat against the hardness of his leg. "Vuchie... I don't know what to say."

"Say what you want... I don't care." Vuch's fingers played with the end of his toes. He slid his foot back into the water, abruptly turning to Vinnie, his smile gone. "Say what you feel. Say what's on your mind... it doesn't matter."

"Of course it matters... I don't even know what to say, ya know? I don't even know what to think. Hey, Vuchie, we were both drunk, you know? Things happen when guys get drunk. Things they don't mean to happen. Like things get just fuckin' confusin', you know?" He squinted his eyes as he looked at Vuch's face.

"Yeah, okay, Manta... we was drunk. Right." Vuch got to his feet. "Let's just forget the whole thing, okay. We won't get drunk no more together, okay?" Vuch stomped his feet lightly to get the water off. He turned and started walking off the dock.

"Hey, wait up." Vinnie scurried to his feet and hurried after him, leaving his shoes on the end of the dock. Vinnie caught up to him as he stepped onto the cool sand. "Vuchie, hold on, will ya?" Vuch stopped and turned silently to Vinnie. "Hey, I'm not sayin' we can't get drunk together. Hey... that's what guys do, right? Hell, we can still do all kinds of shit. We're friends, Vuch. We can still get drunk together."

"Right. Still get drunk together... right. Just as long as things don't get outta hand, right? Just as long as we do things guys do... right?" Vuch widened his eyes.

"Yeah. Well, no... that's not what I meant. I just meant that we just gotta realize that we can't get all bent outta shape when stupid shit happens just because we gots drunk, that's all." Vinnie went to put a hand on Vuch's shoulder, then grew very self-conscious and slowly pulled it back.

"It didn't happen cause I got drunk, Vinnie!" He started to walk along in the sand. Vinnie followed.

"It didn't?"

"No."

"So what's up?" Vuch stopped and turned to face him.

"I don't know... I like you... I like being near you." Vinnie looked at his face. He smiled nervously.

"Yeah... well... I like you too, Vuchie."

"Forget it, Manta... this conversation ain't goin' nowhere. We're walkin' all around the real issues here. Just fuckin' forget it, okay?"

"Vuchie, wait a minute. Jesus... just give me a fuckin' minute here, okay. Fuck." He looked down at the sand. "Look, how comes you ain't gots your sleepin' bag up in the cabin?"

Vuch sighed. "I ain't sleepin' up there tonight. I need to think. I wanna sleep down here on the beach." He started walking slowly again. "I just need to be away for a little while."

"Away from me?" Vinnie stood back a few paces. Vuch stopped and turned back to him.

"No, not you."

"Then let me sleep down here with ya, okay? Just me and you."

"You'd wanna do that?"

"Well, we gots talkin' to do... and well, I gots thinkin' ta do myself."

Vuch walked back over to him. "You'll freeze. You don't have a sleepin' bag."

"What... suddenly I can't sleep with you no more? What I smell or somethin'?" Vinnie smiled wide.

"Well, yeah... ya do smell... but that's got nothin' to do with it." Vuch returned the smile.

"So, let's camp out, bro'." The guys spread Vuch's sleeping bag out under an overhang of trees at the far end of the beach. "You know Vuchie, we're gonna have to get up pretty fuckin' early in the mornin'." Vinnie paused a moment, his hand on the waistband of his shorts, deciding if he felt comfortable sleeping bare-assed with Vuch again. "What the hell." he mumbled. He pulled them off and climbed into the bag naked.

Vuch purposely left his underwear on and slid in tightly against Vinnie. "Hey, mornin' came bright and early today. And we had enough beer in our fuckin' guts to keep us out for hours." He tucked his arm back behind his head. "Once that sun hits the water, we'll be awake. Shit, we'll be fuckin' wide awake!"

Vinnie lay in silence for several minutes. "Vuchie, we gotta talk." He turned on his side so he faced Vuch. His nose was just inches from Vuch's armpit; it smelled sweet.

"So talk," whispered Vuch.

Vinnie was quiet. He inhaled, taking in Vuch's natural body odor. He was beginning to recognize it. It was now the third night they had slept closely together. "I don't know where to begin. I don't know Vuchie... it's just that I want you to understand that it was okay what happened last night." His voice trailed off.

"Because we were drunk, you mean."

"No. No... I mean it was okay. I mean even without the beer. This ain't comin' out right." He inhaled deeply. Vuch's smell was so intoxicating. He brought his face in closer and let it press against Vuch's armpit. "I feel the same way you do, Vuchie."

"You don't know how I feel."

"Yeah, man... I do. I know. Cause I feel it too. It's just that... that, I don't know... I don't wanna be no queer."

Vuch pulled his arm back from behind his head. He tucked it into the sleeping bag, letting it come to rest against Vinnie's side. "We ain't no fags, Vinnie."

"No? You don't think so? Then you tell me, Vuchie... you tell me... what do you call it?" Vinnie closed his eyes, but let his face stay against Vuch's shoulder.

"I don't know."

"I don't wanna be no queer. And that's what this is, isn't it?"

Vuch was silent, then spoke very softly. "No. No it ain't. I don't know what it is." He turned his face and let his lips lay against Vinnie's hair. "I guess most everyone... all the guys... yeah, if they knew, they'd think what we did... what I feel anyways... is homo. But they know what Marino does... and they still look up to him. Christ, Vinnie, he's a great guy! No one judges him, they just like him for who he really is." His voice became a whisper. "I just wanna finally be who I really am. For once, ya know? Not worry about what other people think. Not my father, not the team... not even you, if you can't handle the real me. I wanna stop tryin' to put on this act of the great quarterback stud. That's not who I am. I'm just a kid who likes other guys, I guess. I know I like you. I like you a lot. I think about you... like when I sleep, you know. And when we play ball, and shit... well, I think about you then, too. I know it sounds fucked. I guess I'm fucked." He pushed his head deeper against Vinnie. "And it ain't cause I ain't got no girls lately. It has nothin' to do with that shit. I just don't want that no more, I guess."

"You don't gotta explain that to me, Vuchie... that's how I feel too. I think about you too. I can even nut over you... that happened to me last night. I blew my load."

"I know."

"You do?"

Vinnie tightened his eyes. He was very embarrassed.

"Yeah. That's why I left this mornin'. See Vinnie, up 'til now, I knew I fuckin' liked you and everything... but it was all safe, cause I knew that you couldn't possibly feel the same way. I mean what guy like you would? Shit, man, you appear so far away from this shit... so fuckin' huge... and tough. Well, anyways... when we both got into things last night... man, you... you..." He sighed deeply. "...you kissed me! Man, you fuckin' touched my lips with yours. Then you popped your wad. I could feel your whole body shake. Well, I was gonna try to say somethin'... I don't know, apologize or somethin'... but ya passed out. Cold, right then! Shit... come mornin' I just didn't wanna face you and have you blame me or somethin'. Or say you didn't like me anymore."

"Vuch, I wouldn't have said that."

"What would you have said?"

"I have no fuckin' idea. I'm not even sure what exactly I'm sayin' now." Vinnie moved his hand over and laid it on Vuch's stomach. He could feel the hard abdominal muscles; his fingers also detected stubble. "You gotta shave again, bro'."

"You sure you wanna do that? Put your hand against me?"

"Relax. Jesus... you make such a big deal about everything. I ain't doin' nothin'. Let's try to get some sleep, okay?"

"Yeah, sure, Vinnie." Vuch let his lips play softly in Vinnie's hair. "Hey, Vinnie?"

"Yeah?" Vuch pressed his lips against his hair. "Thanks for stayin' down here with me tonight."

"No problem. Let's go to sleep."

"Hey, Vinnie?"

Vinnie smiled. "Yeah?"

"We ain't no fags, Vinnie. We're just guys."

"Yeah... I know."

"Hey, Vinnie?"

Vinnie spread into a wide smile. "Yeah?"

"We gotta kick Revere butt tomorrow."

"Yeah. But how hard is it to kick ass against a team that hasn't got no footballs?" They both laughed.

"I'm gonna dream about the game tonight. Me and you poundin' on the football field. We'll be great, Vinnie! We're both gonna be fuckin' stars this year."

"Yeah, Vuchie... we are." Vinnie smiled again.

"Hey, Vinnie?"

"What."

"When we get on that bus tomorrow... well... that ain't gonna be it, is it? I mean, we still gonna be close? You know... see what happens?" Vuch moved his head, pressing it still harder into Vinnie.

"No, Vuchie... we ain't gonna just let this go. We'll just be home tomorrow, that's all. We'll still be us. We'll just have to see what happens."

"Okay." They lay in silence.

"Hey, Vuchie?"

Vuch grinned and bent his face down to meet Vinnie's. "Yeah?"

"What are ya doin' tomorrow night?"

Vuch flashed his white teeth. "Nothin'."

"Wanna go out an' do somethin'?"

"Sure. Anything with you, Manta. You really wanna do somethin'? Spend your first Saturday night home... with me?"

Vinnie hesitated. He sneered playfully, then raised his face up and let his lips very lightly brush against Vuch's. "Fuck yes! Jesus... try to give the prick a compliment!" he whispered.

They both smiled and closed their eyes. The football dreams were good that night.

If you enjoyed this book, you may like the following titles from our extensive fiction list:

Agustin Gomez-Arcos
THE CARNIVOROUS LAMB

The passionate story of two brothers growing up in post-civil war Spain, as soulmates and as lovers.

"A carnal poem, frank, provocative, triumphant"
— *Le Monde*

276pp   0 85449 019 1
UK £5.95   AUS $14.95   (not available in USA/Can)

Tony Duvert
WHEN JONATHAN DIED

This highly acclaimed French novel traces the relationship between an insecure artist and a young boy.

"One of the most intelligent, bold and subversive books of the year"
— *Le Monde*

176pp   0 85449 154 6
UK £7.95   US $12.95   AUS $17.95

Kenneth Martin
AUBADE

A summer romance for Northern Irish teenager Paul that will leave its mark for the rest of his life.

176pp   0 85449 097 3
UK £6.95   US $12.95   AUS $19.95

Andre Gould
A SUMMER'S EXILE

The American corn belt in its sultry midsummer heat is the setting for this poignant encounter of two young boys on the verge of adolescence. Steppin is beautiful, blond and wholesome — every mother's ideal son — while Mickey, the narrator, is deeply disturbed and has been expelled from school. Andre Gould evokes a microcosm in which the innocence of childhood is blighted by bigotry and suspicion.

144pp   0 85449 202 X
UK £6.95   US $10.95   AUS $14.95

Martin Foreman
THE BUTTERFLY'S WING

Andy and Tom are a well-matched couple in their thirties; Andy works for an international organisation, while Tom looks after their smallholding in Berkshire. Disaster strikes when Andy is kidnapped in Peru by the Shining Path guerrillas, and Tom has to work for his release.
Exploring the strengths and tensions of gay love in the 1990s, the story weaves in major issues of the contemporary world scene as it unravels towards a dramatic denouement.

256pp   0 85449 223 2
UK £8.95   US $14.95   AUS $19.95

Historical fiction from The Gay Men's Press:

Chris Hunt
THE BISLEY BOY

Queen Elizabeth I was fond of saying that she had "the heart and stomach of a king", but to her grave she took the secret that she really was a man. The astonishing story of the boy from a Cotswold village who became England's greatest queen has been rumoured down the centuries, and is now reconstructed in the first person by this acclaimed historical novelist.

336pp   0 85449 184 8
UK £8.95   US $14.95   AUS $19.95

STREET LAVENDER

In the foggy alleyways of Victorian London, sharp-mannered Willie Smith learns to use his youth and beauty as a means of realising fabulous wealth.

344pp   0 85449 035 3
UK £7.95   US $12.95   AUS $19.95

N FOR NARCISSUS

Set at the time of the Oscar Wilde trial, the story of Lord Algernon Winterton shows the dangers that beset the most respectable of English gentlemen when an old associate returns to stir up disquieting passions.

268pp   0 85449 136 8
UK £7.95   US $12.95   AUS $19.95

"Chris Hunt has carved out a comfortable niche as the author of highly readable historical epics set against a well-researched background" — *Gay Times*

Action-packed adventure from The Gay Men's Press:

Mel Keegan
DEATH'S HEAD

Space troopers Kevin Jarratt and Jerry Stone face annihilation and worse when they take on the corrupt Death's Head drugs syndicate, in this high-tech adventure from the 23rd century.
"Unputdownable. Keegan has taken the two-dimensional Marvel/ DC comic strip and made it flesh, and what flesh! — *HIM*

352pp   0 85449 162 7
UK £6.95 US $10.95 AUS $17.95

EQUINOX

Equinox Industries is a commercial monopoly mining the gas giant Zeus, challenged for its environmental record, and suspected of drugs trafficking. Enter Jarratt and Stone, joint captains in the paramilitary NARC force, and lovers whose minds have been bonded toether.

352pp   0 85449 200 3
UK £6.95 US $10.95 AUS $19.95

FORTUNES OF WAR

Mel Keegan returns from the 23rd century to the 16th with this rollicking yarn of gay pirates on the Spanish Main. A love story between an Irish mercenary and the son of an English earl, whocross swords with both Sir Francis Drake and some of their nastier fellow-pirates.
"With more historical detail than you would expect, *Fortunes of War* is a fine example of this genre" — *Gay Times*

344pp   0 85449 211 9
UK £7.95 US $10.95 AUS $17.95

Gay Men's Press books can be ordered from any bookshop in the UK, North America and Australia, and from specialised bookshops elsewhere.

If you prefer to order by mail, please send cheque or postal order payable to *Book Works* for the full retail price plus £2.00 postage and packing to:

Book Works (Dept. B), PO Box 3821, London N5 1UY
phone/fax: (0171) 609 3427

For payment by Access/Eurocard/Mastercard/American Express/Visa, please give number, expiry date and signature.

Name and address in block letters please:

Name
_____

Address
_____

_____

_____